CONSPIRACY NATION

EDITED BY PETER KNIGHT

CONSPIRACY NATION

The Politics of Paranoia in Postwar America

New York University Press • *New York and London*

NEW YORK UNIVERSITY PRESS
New York and London

Library of Congress Cataloging-in-Publication Data
Conspiracy nation : the politics of paranoia in postwar America /
edited by Peter Knight.
p.   cm.
ISBN 0-8147-4735-3 (cloth : alk. paper)
ISBN 0-8147-4736-1 (pbk. : alk. paper)
1. United States—Civilization—1945– 2. United States—Social
conditions—1945– 3. Popular culture—United States—History—
20th century. 4. Political culture—United States—History—20th
century. 5. Conspiracies—United States—History—20th century.
6. Paranoia—Social aspects—United States—History—20th century.
7. Cold War—Social aspects—United States. 8. American fiction—
20th century—History and criticism. 9. Conspiracies in literature.
10. Politics and literature—United States—History—20th century.
I. Knight, Peter, 1968–
E169.12 .P6216 2001
973.9—dc21   2001006231

New York University Press books are printed on acid-free paper,
and their binding materials are chosen for strength and durability.

Manufactured in the United States of America

10 9 8 7 6 5 4 3 2 1

Contents

Acknowledgments

This collection of essays has its origins in a conference on conspiracy cultures held at King Alfred's College, Winchester (UK) in 1998. The conference attracted interest and speakers from many academic disciplines, as well as journalists from outside the university: they came from film studies, from literature departments, from history, from sociology, from American studies, from religious studies, from social psychology, and from political science, as well as from left-leaning publications, UFO/paranormal magazines, local radio, and even *The Big Issue*, the UK's magazine sold by and for the homeless. Everyone had interesting case studies from their own area of expertise, and everyone seemed to have a different theory about what has been called the "culture of paranoia." But whether participants regarded conspiracy theories as a sign of the increasing gullibility of the masses or the mark of a healthy populist skepticism toward authority, nearly all agreed that the prominence of conspiracy culture tells an important story about contemporary culture in general, and American culture in particular. Unlike many other recent attacks on the discourse of conspiracy, the essays in this collection refuse instantly to dismiss it as the product of narrow-minded crackpot paranoia or the intellectual slumming of those who should know better. Instead they provide a wide-ranging analysis of the many different styles, meanings, and functions of conspiracy culture around the turn of the millennium.

The chief conspirator behind the conference at King Alfred's was Alasdair Spark, and much gratitude is due to him for plotting the event so successfully. We are also grateful to all the participants for making the occasion so enjoyable, and especially to Elaine Showalter and Patrick O'Donnell for providing provocative keynote addresses. Finally, thanks to Eric Zinner at New York University Press for sticking with the plot.

Lyrics from "Only God Can Judge Me" (Shakur/Forte/Rasheed/Fretty) © 1996 by kind permission of Universal Music Publishing Ltd.

Lyrics from "Hail Mary" (Shakur/Washington/Fula/Cox/Cooper/Wrice) © 1996 by kind permission of Universal Music Publishing Ltd.

Lyrics from "Death around the Corner" (Shakur/Jackson) © 1995 by kind permission of Universal Music Publishing Ltd.

Introduction

A Nation of Conspiracy Theorists

Peter Knight

pol. princ

THE HIDDEN AGENDA OF MANIFEST DESTINY

As a British American studies scholar working on the culture of conspiracy, I'm often asked why, compared with the rest of the world, the
United States is so obsessed with the rhetoric of plotting and paranoia.
A popular answer (though not usually one that I give) is that you can
hardly blame Americans for talking of conspiracy when they are surrounded by plots to deprive them of their freedom, and when the very
founding of the nation was the result of a far-reaching conspiracy. *so British!*

Just check out the dollar bill, the conspiracy-minded argument
goes. To the initiated, the great seal on the reverse tells the whole story:
the pyramid with the eye at its top is a Masonic symbol, not surprising
given that many of the Founding Fathers were Freemasons. The Ma- *Myth!*
sons, the story continues, were themselves under the control of the
Bavarian Illuminati, a secret society that orchestrated both the French
and American Revolutions, and has ever since been secretly leading us
to a New World Order of Satanic misrule. The date of 1776 in roman
numerals on the bill refers not to the Declaration of Independence, but
to the official founding of the Illuminati. Likewise, the portrait on the
front of the bill is in fact not of Washington but of Adam Weishaupt, the
leader of the Illuminati. The captions above and below the pyramid
("Annuit Coeptis" and "Novus Ordo Seclorum") announce the creation of a New World Order, the code word for the master conspiracy's
plan to bring about a one-world government that will wipe out the
sovereignty of free Americans. George Bush, Sr., a member of Yale's
Skull and Bones secret society, which has numerous historical links to
international banking dynasties, kept talking of a "new world order"

I

during the Gulf War. If you need proof of all this, we are told, just take a dollar bill:

> with a pen circle the first and last letters of "ANNUIT COEPTIS." The A and S. Then in NOVUS ORDO SECLORUM circle the N in NOVUS the last O in ORDO and the M in SECLORUM. Now connect the A and the S by drawing a line from one letter to the next extended under the base of the "capstone." Now connect those two letters to the O in ORDO that you circled to form an upside down triangle and then outline the pyramid.

The eye-in-the-pyramid first appeared on the dollar in 1933, commentators note, the same year that the Federal Reserve took over the issuing of notes. The Federal Reserve is, of course, a private bank linked to the cabal of European money men led by the Rothschilds, who in turn are part of the ongoing Illuminati plot for world domination:

> When the Scottish Rite Masons put the "great seal" on their confederate money with the pyramid and eye with the hidden hexgram the points of which point to letters that will form the word MASON they believed that this gave them power over all lower ranking MASONS and the "profain" or "vulgar" who are the non-masons. To some extent that is correct because it served as a reminder of their nefarious conspiratorial "master plan" and gave them the determination to see it through to the end while the common man would never suspect. So in fact the Scottish Rite MASONS put a "HEX" on all people of the USA and the people of the world so that they would have power, control and dominion over them.[1]

Given that the conspiracy's symbols and its influence are everywhere in the United States, the argument goes, Americans are quite right to feel paranoid. From the earliest days of the War of Independence to the triumphant return of the Masonic Bush dynasty to power, the destiny of the United States has been controlled by an all-seeing international conspiracy.

Tempting though these theories are in their own ways, however, it is not necessary to believe in a full-scale conspiracy theory of American history to recognize that conspiratorial ideas have been crucial in shaping the destiny of the new nation. For example, in his account of the

American Revolution, the historian Bernard Bailyn argues that (often quite justified) mutual suspicion of plots and hidden agendas between the American revolutionary leaders and the British played a significant role in dictating the course of events.[2] Indeed, it might plausibly be argued that the fear of alien influence, whether from foreign agents or from enemies within, has continued to be a vital force in the politics and culture of the United States from the Revolution to the present. "Is it possible," David Brion Davis asks, "that the circumstances of the Revolution conditioned Americans to think of resistance to a dark subversive force as the essential ingredient of their national identity?"[3] Confirming that suspicion, Richard Hofstadter's groundbreaking essay on "the paranoid style in American politics" and Davis's own copious collection of primary sources of "images of un-American subversion" document the repeated outbursts of demonological scare stories in U.S. history. From the anti-Masonism of the 1820s and 1830s to the anti-Catholicism of the 1830s and 1840s, and from the anti-Mormonism of the 1850s to the anticommunism of the 1950s, fears of invasion and infiltration by un-American influences have repeatedly dominated the national political scene. Looked at one way, the history of the United States is a history of conspiracy-minded countersubversion.[4]

Writing after the worst excesses of the McCarthy years were over but before conspiracy theories about the Kennedy assassination became widespread, Hofstadter was confident, however, that the "paranoid style" was no more than a blemish (albeit a persistent one) in the "normal political process of bargain and compromise" central to the ideal of consensus politics in America.[5] Hofstadter implies that there might be a long and infamous history of political demonology in the United States, but it is the product mainly of those discontented extremists and right-wing crackpots who fail to understand or participate in the properly American form of politics. Hofstadter offers the disclaimer that he is only focusing on American examples of this particular political pathology because he happens to be an Americanist: the implication is that Americans have no monopoly on the "paranoid style," even if they do furnish some of the more spectacular examples. He notes, for instance, that while Europeans were quick to see a conspiracy at work in the then very recent assassination of President Kennedy, Americans had on the whole wisely ignored such possibilities in the immediate aftermath of the event. More recently, several commentators on political paranoia have echoed Hofstadter's line, arguing that America does not have the worst historical record of populist paranoia (the prize goes to Hitler's and Stalin's regimes), nor is it currently the most avid or dangerous producer and consumer of conspiracy theories (here the award is given to the Middle East).[6]

In terms of sheer numbers or dire consequences, America may not be the most conspiracy-minded nation. Yet it might be argued that fears of un-American subversion—no matter how seemingly marginal or fanciful—have played a central role in defining who or what is to count as properly "American." It is not difficult to see that the imagination of imminent invasion has repeatedly helped to forge a sense of national identity.[7] As Davis explains, "movements of countersubversion have thus been a primary means of restoring collective self-confidence, of defining American identity by contrast with alien 'others,' and of achieving unity through opposition to a common enemy."[8] But the crucial question is *exactly what kind of* "American identity" these counter-subversive movements have defined. From the first encounters with the land and the people of the New World, the conspiratorial imagination of sinister forces has helped to constitute a sense of American national unity through a notion of *racial* identity. Early colonial scare stories of Indian cannibals conformed to classical moral cartographies that located the land of the primitive anthropophagi beyond the horizon. The typological radar of the Puritans likewise scanned their daily events and environment for clues to the deeper underlying plot of a Manichean struggle between savagery and civilization. Every discovery of a Satanic plot only served to confirm America's sense of a manifest destiny as God's chosen race.

Anti-Mormonism, anti-Catholicism, anti-Semitism, and other forms of nativism in the nineteenth century spoke of fears about the gradual dilution of WASP identity. The paranoid rhetoric of slave revolts, the specter of the black rapist, and the formation of the Ku Klux Klan as a racial counterconspiracy in turn worked to legitimate an emerging sense of national consciousness based on the ideology of white supremacy. (It is arguable that gothic fears of dark presences in the wilderness or below decks in the classic American romance novels of the eighteenth and nineteenth centuries have as much to do with these dramas of beset nationhood as they do with ultimate struggles between good and evil.)[9] In the twentieth century, for example, the conspiracy-minded rhetoric of the McCarthy witchhunts identified sexual and class "deviance" as distinctly "un-American." More recently, as we saw above, there are widespread claims to have uncovered a conspiratorial plan for global domination, hatched by the Masons in cahoots with (in Pat Buchanan's phrase) the "Manhattan money power," internationalist organizations such as the Bilderbergers and the United Nations, and possibly the devil himself. Although these fears hark back to well-worn demonological themes (the whiff of anti-Semitism hangs low over many of the accounts), these conspiracy theories can be read in part as panicked responses to the increasing multiculturalism and globalization of the present. This era brings with it—in the eyes of the proponents, if not in fact—an erosion of some of the traditional privileges of white, male middle America, and, since the oil crisis of 1973 and the coincident debacle of Vietnam, an erosion of America's sense of manifest economic and political destiny. Over the last half millennium, fears of "un-American" subversion and invasion have justified both domestic repression of scapegoated minorities and imperial expansion, from the Philippines to Nicaragua. In some of its more recent guises, however, the conspiratorial imagination now also betrays an edgy awareness that it is increasingly impossible to maintain a clear sense of what is truly American in the postnationalist new world order of the global economy. Where conspiracy-minded narratives of the individual and national immune system under threat might once have served to bolster a sense of (albeit restricted) communal identity, they now regularly register the far more scary anxiety that we can no longer tell the difference between Them and Us.

THE CULTURE OF CONSPIRACY

Until recently, then, conspiracy theories have helped historically to prescribe and preserve a sense of American national identity that is restrictive in terms of race, class, and gender. Despite exceptionalist claims, it is therefore arguable that there is a strong connection between notions of manifest national destiny and patterns of conspiratorial thought in the United States. Yet in addition to the role conspiracy theory has played in shaping ideas of national identity, there are other reasons to think that America is a nation of conspiracy theorists. You might be forgiven for thinking that paranoia is as American as apple pie because in recent decades it has become such a visible and widespread part of the cultural landscape. From the Kennedy assassination to

Hillary Clinton's accusation of a "vast right-wing conspiracy" against her husband, and from the novels of Thomas Pynchon to *The X-Files*, talk of conspiracy is everywhere. We're all conspiracy theorists now: you can hear it, read it, watch it, play it, and buy it everywhere—without necessarily having to buy into it. In short, a self-conscious and self-reflexive entertainment culture of conspiracy has become thoroughly mainstream. The United States is not necessarily the most "paranoid" nation on the planet (after all, *The X-Files* is broadcast in more than fifty countries), but there's much high-profile hand-wringing that it *might* be. Alarmist diatribes against the gullibility of the masses, not to mention cases such as the peculiarly literal-minded title of the 1997 blockbuster *Conspiracy Theory*, keep the idea of conspiracy *theory* (rather than merely the idea of conspiracy) in the public spotlight. The legion of published compendia of conspiracy theories and television magazine shows repackaging the same old "dark side" stories suggests that for every true believer there are many more casual spectators who are on the lookout for signs of an outbreak of popular paranoia, yet are happy to dabble with the camp aesthetics of conspiracy in the process. There seem to be, for example, almost as many spoof versions on the Web of the Masonic dollar bill story as there are serious ones. What's more, many of the straight-up accounts bear an uncomfortably close resemblance to the *Illuminatus!* trilogy, Robert Shea and Robert Anton Wilson's sprawling semi-spoof conspiracy novel from the mid-1970s. The serious and the entertainment versions of conspiracy theories are thus caught up in a spiraling mutual feedback loop, which, even if it doesn't produce more fully paid-up believers, certainly makes the culture of conspiracy theory more prominent.

Unlike previous eras of political demonology, conspiracy thinking is now so pervasive and persuasive because it is no longer confined to the dogmatic assertions of political extremists. Although traditional right-wing demonology has continued in some form or other (as the dollar bill example suggests), the last few decades have witnessed the emergence of a popular paranoia marked out by its half-serious, half-cynical suspicion toward the "official version" of events told by the authorities, whether scientific or governmental. Since the political assassinations of the 1960s, followed by the revelations about intelligence agencies that emerged in the 1970s, not forgetting the Watergate crisis itself, conspiracy theory has become the lingua franca of a countercultural opposition that encompasses a vast spectrum of political thinking, from the committed to the casual. In some cases, traditionally right-wing fears about the intrusion of "big government" into the lives of law-abiding, gun-wielding citizens have fused with typically left-wing conspiracy-minded concerns—in recent years most notably in the Iran-Contra affair—about the operation of an "invisible government."[10] If earlier outbursts of political demonology denounced occasional interruptions of the national destiny and the normal order of things by a conspiracy of "un-American" influences, then post-1960s conspiracy culture has often seen the American way of life as itself a permanent conspiracy against many of its citizens. But in addition to those prominent national scandals that have been narrated in the mode of conspiracy (Watergate, Iraqgate, Clintongate, and so on), there are countless other conspiracy-minded suspicions about current events. From African American rumors about crack in the ghetto to feminist suspicions that patriarchy itself amounts to a conspiracy, the rhetoric of paranoia has become a familiar part of the surrounding political terrain.[11]

Yet more important than any one particular political position or accusation is the pervading sense of uncontrollable forces taking over our lives, our minds, and even our bodies. The fear of being at the mercy of a complex conspiracy with vague but sinister intentions has become deeply ingrained in the popular imagination. In many ways conspiracy thinking has become not so much the sign of a crackpot delusion as part of an everyday struggle to make sense of a rapidly changing world. Given that the forces and institutions of globalization are affecting countless people across the planet, it is no surprise that a conspiratorial sense of being the victim of invisible and indefatigable forces is an everyday attitude in many countries. But the kind of low-level everyday paranoia that sees a hidden hand and a hidden agenda everywhere is more prominent in the United States than elsewhere because it taps into the traditional American obsession with ruggedly individual agency. In part, the United States is a nation of conspiracy theorists because the influence of larger social and economic forces in determining the lives of individuals is often regarded as a paranoia inducing encroachment on the self-reliance of individuals. So, for example, where other people might conceivably view the daily involvement of "big government" in the lives of its citizens as the caring embrace of the welfare state, many Americans see only surveillance, conspiratorial interference, and an erosion of individual autonomy. In the United States the fear of being influenced or controlled by external social forces is inseparable from the ideology of liberal individualism, and its concomitant refusal to entertain any notion of structural causation.

As many of the essays in this collection demonstrate, conspiracy thinking therefore has much in common with more orthodox ways of conceiving the relationship between individual and society in America. Conspiracy theory, as Fredric Jameson notes, is the "poor person's cognitive mapping" in the postmodern age; it is, in effect, a form of pop sociology cobbled together on the fly as people try to gain a handle on the complexities of social and economic causation in an era of rapid globalization. With the increasing overload of information from mutually competing sources, none of which seem entirely trustworthy, a hermeneutic of suspicion has become a routine operating procedure. Hence it makes little sense to dismiss talk of conspiracy wholesale as necessarily the product of individual or collective *paranoia*. In different ways, the following essays together challenge the usual knee-jerk dismissal of conspiratorial thought as a deluded and sometimes dangerous mindset. This is not to say, however, that these authors unquestioningly endorse every conspiracy theory or celebrate the transgressive power of alternative epistemologies in some fit of apocalyptic irresponsibility. On the contrary, these essays show that a glib rejection of conspiracy theory as merely a sign of the dumbing down of America fails to understand exactly what functions conspiracy thinking fulfils in each situation, why it appeals to new and different audiences, and even how certain popular explanations come to be labeled conspiracy theories in the first place.[12]

The first section explores different theoretical approaches to conspiracy theory. Skip Willman argues that as much as conspiracy theories are often dismissed as immature or inaccurate accounts of What Is Really Going On, those seemingly commonsense attacks hold an equally ideological view of social causation. The alternative to a conspiracy theory is usually taken to be the screw-up theory of history (a "contingency theory," in Willman's terms), which claims that events happen as much by chance as by malicious design. But in the haste to condemn conspiracy theory's fixation with hidden causes, contingency theory betrays an equally obsessive desire to deny that larger social forces might play a significant role in determining events. Following Žižek, Willman argues that this kind of false dilemma—seeing everything as the result of either conspiracy or coincidence—diverts attention from the far more important antagonisms in society. In effect, both conspiracy theories and contingency theories claim that anything that goes wrong in society is the result of a temporary interruption of normal service (whether through chance or conspiratorial choice), rather than the effect of deeper structural failings in social organization. Building on Jameson's notion that the postmodern paranoiacs are unable to make coherent sense of the totality of current social and economic events because they are totally immersed in that system, Willman goes on to argue that contingency theories demonstrate a similarly ideological inability to gain a clear overall picture of why bad things happen. To believe (as Homer Simpson puts it) that "stuff just happens"—whether good or bad—is to buy unthinkingly into the ideology of free market capitalism, which views life as a lottery. The "invisible hand" of classical economic theory in the long run might be no more sophisticated than the "hidden hand" of classical conspiracy theory, but, Willman concludes, at least the latter is sometimes prepared to countenance the possibility that there are deeper underlying causes to the unfolding of history.

Like Willman and many of the other contributors in this volume, Fran Mason takes up Jameson's provocative suggestion that conspiracy is the "poor person's cognitive mapping." For Jameson conspiracy theories are inevitable failures to map what's really happening: instead of providing a scientific account of the totality of social relations, they mistakenly create an ideological version featuring secret societies with totalitarian ambitions. Following Lyotard's notion of incommensurable "paralogical" ways of viewing the world, Mason takes issue with Jameson, arguing that, in their insistence that everything is connected, conspiracy theories provide rough-and-ready narratives that bring together past, present, and future into a coherent whole. In effect they offer substitute metanarratives for the ones whose loss has so often been identified with the crisis of postmodern knowledge and politics. Like other paralogical discourses, however, they are only legitimated within their own—often mutually exclusive—terms of reference, logic, and evidence. Jameson's patrician dismissal of conspiracy theories as the cognitive mapping of the "information poor" points to the reality that conspiracy theories are often a way for those disenfranchised from the centers of power and knowledge to imagine themselves heroically in the possession of secret information, even if what they find out is that the power belongs to a hidden elite. Conspiracy theorists in effect are both on the inside (because they are in the know) and on the outside (because they are not part of the conspiracy where the real power is believed to reside). But in this way conspiracy theory is not so much a "degraded" form of cognitive mapping (as Jameson suggests) but an uncanny echo of its inherent contradictions: to achieve an effective map of the bewildering complexities of the "new world order," you would need to be on the outside of history to have a global overview with some kind of critical distance, but you would also need to be on the inside of history to allow local involvement in the workings of the world.

Why have conspiracy theories become so popular since World War II across the entire social and political spectrum in the United States? Part of the answer, Timothy Melley suggests, is that they rely on a liberal individualist view of identity and agency that continues to underpin much American thought, both on the Right and the liberal Left, from the militias to African American communities. Conspiracy theories now tend to focus less on tight-knit cabals of cunning plotters than on more nebulous and convoluted activities of the interlocking vested interests of the so-called military-industrial complex. Talk of conspiracy has become so widespread not because it latches on to any particular event or enemy, but because it gives voice to a far more general anxiety about the loss of individuality and autonomy in the face of the increasingly vast and anonymous bureaucratic forces that seem to control our lives, and even our most intimate thoughts and bodily processes. It is this panicked sense of the erosion of individual agency that structures much contemporary conspiracy culture, Melley argues. But, in a process of what he terms "postmodern transference," the qualities of intention and will that are felt to be slowly siphoned away from individuals are found writ large in the seemingly all-powerful and all-knowing corporations and conspiracies. Like Willman, Melley reads conspiracy theory as a displaced (and often misplaced) attempt to come to terms with the possibility that underlying structural forces might well shape our destinies. Although conspiracy theories seem to take on board the idea of determinism, they paradoxically serve to reassure believers that the possibility of willful action remains alive—even if it is transferred onto the specter of a threatening global conspiracy. Conspiracy theorists in effect try to cope with a schizophrenic immersion in the information-saturated modern world (an immersion that tends to lead to the *dispersion* of a rooted sense of personal identity) by returning to the increasingly outdated notion of a thoroughly self-contained and self-reliant individuality in which we are all in control of our own minds and our own actions. In holding on to a faith in individual autonomy even as they confront the possibility of structural agency, conspiracy theories are very much in tune with many other contemporary sociological accounts.

The essays in the second section, "Alien Nation," deal with fears that the United States and its citizens are the victims of an alien conspiracy of cosmic proportions, with which the government is in cahoots. But the essays also draw attention to the increasingly widespread sense of alienation from any stable notion of truth or reality. Although accounts of abduction by aliens might look pretty weird, they are also, Jodi Dean suggests, in line with the wider crisis of epistemology in postmodern times. Whether we like it or not, all of us now live in a world in which there is a vast amount of information but none of it is ever complete: there is always one more theory to consider, one more expert opinion to consult, not helped by the possibility that the ultimate consequences of any event always threaten to mushroom outwards in a chain reaction of cause and effect. And with so many different, and often incommensurable, sources of information, there seems to be no higher authority to which we can appeal in order to get to the ultimate truth. This is not to say that conspiracy theories might be just as true as more orthodox accounts; rather, we have no way of guaranteeing in advance that conspiracy theories or other alternative accounts are mistaken, and no way of agreeing how to resolve the epistemological dispute. It is not only alien abductees, Dean warns, who feel a permanent uncertainty about any item of news or knowledge: this is a problem for all of us. In contrast to Jameson's account of conspiracy thinking as a failed attempt to grasp the totality, Dean argues that conspiracy theories now often express a sense of skepticism that there is a coherent Big Picture. This provisional and partial skepticism even doubts its own evidence and conclusions, endlessly deferring any final sense of conclusion. As with alien abduction narratives, conspiracy theory has now become an active, ongoing process of distrusting official accounts and finding new connections, rather than passively buying into a neatly packaged set of ready-made convictions.

Bridget Brown begins with the observation that the forced medical exam emerged as the principal alien abduction scenario in the 1960s and has become ubiquitous in the pop culture since the 1980s. In this way postwar atomic age fears of national invasion by alien forces have given way to anxieties about the mass manipulation of the intimate and seemingly sacrosanct realm of human fertility. To understand where these anxieties come from, Brown reads the abduction stories alongside contemporary discourses of technological medical management of the reproductive body. Lifestyle magazine articles from the 1960s about the new reproductive technologies viewed the female body as the new frontier of inner space. In these popular accounts of the technological pioneering spirit of (usually male) doctors, women's bodies are regarded as spacecraft carrying an alien cargo in the shape of a fetus, a situation that produces an alienation of self from self. It is no wonder, Brown notes, that in popular iconography the little gray alien with its huge eyes and tiny limbs resembles nothing so much as a fetus viewed with the new intrauterine imaging technologies. In both men's and women's accounts of close encounters, the abductees are presented as victims of coldly rational and cruelly detached alien scientific inquiry. These paranoia-inducing scenarios point to the rise of a technical-professional management class and the authority of scientific expertise in the postwar period. They express an often unspoken suspicion that technocratic disinterestedness can mask abuses of power. But, Brown warns, by displacing the blame for their feeling of disempowerment onto the aliens (and the abduction experts), the abductees renounce the possibility of collective political action that might help change the very abuses of expertise to which the stories imaginatively give voice.

The essays in the next section, "The Enemy Within," focus on the role of conspiracy thinking in shaping racial and sexual politics in the contemporary United States. Why is it, Jack Bratich asks, that some theories—about the origin of AIDS, for example—are deemed to be thinkable while others are dismissed out of hand as paranoid delusions? It is not the inner structure or content of any particular allegation that makes it a conspiracy theory, he suggests, but the social and institutional context in which such stories circulate. Bratich takes issue with both *psychological* theories of conspiracy culture, which dismiss it as paranoid, and *cultural* interpretations, which read conspiracy theories as imaginary attempts to get a handle on the real social problems. If there is no inherent pre-given meaning to a conspiracy theory, he argues, then it cannot be rejected in advance as either necessarily deluded or necessarily reactionary. A conspiratorial take on events might well become (in the terminology of Birmingham school cultural studies) articulated to any number of political projects, good or bad. It might turn out that many conspiracy-minded narratives—for example, rumors that AIDS was manufactured as a white supremacist biowarfare weapon against black Americans—are impossible to hook on to worthwhile political agendas, but that doesn't mean that their subjugated forms of knowledge can necessarily be disavowed in advance.

The next essay explores the flip side of racial paranoia, with an account of white fears of miscegenation and multiculturalism in the United States. In her analysis of William Pierce's two notorious white supremacist novels (the Oklahoma bomber is said to have been inspired by the second), Ingrid Walker Fields shows how the idea of conspiracy is used to legitimate a sense of American national identity as racially white. In calling for the eradication of an enemy within in order to preserve a purified form of national identity and destiny, the genocidal plot of *The Turner Diaries* employs a conspiratorial logic similar to that of the communist witchhunts of the 1950s—with the difference that in Pierce's version the true America is a white America. In contrast, Pierce's later novel, *Hunter*, appropriates the kind of populist antigovernment conspiratorial story line more familiar from the counterculture of the 1960s and 1970s. In this novel members of the general public are portrayed as victims of an establishment conspiracy led principally by the media. Unlike *The Turner Diaries'* classic conspiratorial call for the purging of a domestic enemy by the powers-that-be, *Hunter's* counterconspiratorial aim is merely to raise awareness among the masses in order to change those powers from within. Although in Pierce's career the outlook shifts from revolution to reform, and from calling for the top-down persecution of unwanted minorities to seeing WASPs as themselves a victimized minority, the white supremacist's overall strategy of using the language of conspiracy to naturalize nationality as race remains the same.

Eithne Quinn focuses on the contradictory meanings and functions of conspiracy thinking in African American culture through the lens of the rap star Tupac Shakur's inimitable "paranoid style." Although Tupac's death has been surrounded by conspiracy rumors, his artistic life was also articulated through a stylized rhetoric of paranoia. The essay locates Tupac's sophisticated aesthetic of conspiracy within the larger debate about black conspiracy culture: are African Americans justified in feeling "paranoid," given the structural racism of the United States, or are they just blaming other people for what should be their own responsibility? Quinn argues that Tupac's shifting and complex paranoid styles provide an astute (and at times conflicted) navigation between the opposing poles of institutional structure and individual agency. In the first phase of his career Tupac took on the role of a post–civil rights spokesman, becoming the "bad nigga" of white America's paranoid imagination, in a self-demonologizing maneuver that short-circuited the usual ideological connections of race in America. Tupac then began to develop an aesthetic of personal persecution, which was transformed, in circumstances not always under his own control, from a personal pathology into a highly eclectic (and highly commodified) form of conspiratorial commentary. Given the impossible situation he found himself in, Quinn concludes, Tupac used the language of paranoia to produce a meaningful way of thinking about the relationship between the individual and larger relations of power in America's racial cauldron.

The final section returns to the question of the ends or functions that conspiracy theory serves; it also considers whether there could or should be an end to the current proliferation of paranoia. The first two essays address *The X-Files*, which in many ways has taken the idea of conspiracy to its extreme. Unlike previous eras of the paranoid style, which ultimately affirmed U.S. institutions, Douglas Kellner argues, recent popular conspiracy culture betrays an understandable crisis of confidence in the secretive authority of government and big business. In the case of *The X-Files*, the parody of traditional film and TV generic formulas and the deconstruction of traditional epistemological certainties work to provide a critique of contemporary society, instead of merely being a symptom of it. According to Kellner, the show's seemingly modernist quest for ultimate truths is countered by its postmodern refusal to ever offer final confirmation or denial of the conspiracies it uncovers, or indeed a fixed perspective from which to make a judgment. But its critique of the authorities in the end remains ambivalent: on the one hand, it identifies the inner reaches of the government not as the solution to a cosmic conspiracy against the people but its very source; on the other, it glorifies a yuppie work ethic, and conjures up a conspiracy so vast and so slippery that opposing it can appear futile.

The next chapter considers what effect the current commodifying of conspiracy theory (from the cottage industry of "alternative" publications to the merchandising mania of *The X-Files* itself) has on the political function of paranoia. Conspiracy theorists, Clare Birchall notes, now often have not a dogmatic conviction but an ironic distance from their beliefs. Whereas some people have charged that the mass popularity of conspiracy culture dissolves its once potentially radical stance of alternative knowledge, Birchall argues that the very freedom to explore radical alternatives and question epistemological paradigms (in the safe zone of entertainment rather than in the trenches of political action) makes the pop culture of conspiracy a potentially—but not necessarily—productive outlet. What makes the kind of conspiracy culture typified by *The X-Files* so powerful, Birchall concludes, is that it subversively mimics more orthodox forms of knowledge.

In the final chapter John A. McClure considers what lies beyond contemporary conspiracy culture's potentially paralyzing insistence that "Their" omnipotent conspiracy reaches everywhere. In a rereading of Pynchon's and DeLillo's classic countercultural conspiracy novels, McClure notices that for these writers the solution to the claustrophobic and disempowering obsession with finding the ultimate conspiracy is to forget it. These novels feature lone detectives uncovering clues to a vast and endless conspiracy that in the end seems hardwired into the circuits of power in postwar society. In many ways this story line draws on the traditional ideological fantasy (outlined by Melley) of heroic individual agency. But in the works of Pynchon and DeLillo, McClure argues, the protagonists tend to find some form of hope and peace not through a paranoid re-entrenchment of the self, but the paradox of a willed disintegration of the self. The trick is to dissolve the ego rather than make it the center of attention—as is the case with a paranoid sense of persecution. This dispersal of personhood often takes on a spiritual dimension, inspired by Eastern forms of mysticism, but it is also in sympathy with posthumanist theory, which likewise seeks to understand the individual as immersed in a social flux. In the fictional worlds of these postmodern novels, the conspiracy is so powerful and so seductive that it ends up controlling your body and even your mind, with the result that you inevitably become "Their" double agent; or, in the terms of Foucauldian theory, even strategies of resistance end up being just another facet of the interlocking systems of oppression we're trying to combat. The solution to this impossible situation, however, is not necessarily more and better cognitive mapping (as Jameson counsels), but a deliberate stilling of the "engines of interpretation." The very success of a permanent conspiratorial hermeneutic of suspicion, in effect, might be its downfall. But, given that a radical disintegration of one's self, or even the quiet refusal to chase up one last clue, has failed to inspire popular appeal, then it seems that the United States is likely—for the time being—to remain a nation of conspiracy theorists.

NOTES

1. These extracts are taken from a long and remarkable posting by tamm@donet.com to parascope.com's message boards, "USA = United Satanic Alliance: Satanic Masonic Symbolism," <http://www.parascope.com/cgi-bin/psforum.pl/topic=matrix&disc=327&mmark=all>. The author goes on to integrate the symbolism of the dollar bill into a far-reaching numerological reading of a vast conspiracy that extends from ancient Egypt to Operation Desert Storm. For an example of a similarly eclectic account (and one that connects the Masonic symbolism with international banking cartels, the Federal Reserve, and even the prohibition of hemp), see "The Secret History of America: The Greatest Conspiracy on Earth," <http://users2.50megs.com/mysite/coverups/hiddenus1.html>, originally from the Web site of David Icke, the former UK sports commentator turned New Age guru and conspiracy theorist. The Masonic symbolism of the dollar bill is peremptorily dismissed in a historical article by a Mason that is cross-posted in many places on the Web; see, for example, <http://ncmason.org/book/eyepyr.htm>. For a roundup of conspiratorial theories about the dollar bill and the Federal Reserve (accompanied by a quirky dismissal of those theories for a Christian audience), see Gregory S. Camp, *Selling Fear: Conspiracy Theories and End-Times Paranoia* (Grand Rapids, MI: Baker Books, 1997).

2. Bernard Bailyn, *The Origins of American Politics* (New York: Knopf, 1968).

3. David Brion Davis, ed., *The Fear of Conspiracy: Images of Un-American Subversion from the Revolution to the Present* (Ithaca: Cornell University Press, 1971), 23.

4. For a more detailed consideration of ideas on countersubversion in American history and historiography, see Michael Rogin, "American Political Demonology: A Retrospective," in *Ronald Reagan, the Movie, and Other Episodes in Political Demonology* (Berkeley: University of California Press, 1987), 272–300.

5. Richard Hofstadter, *The Paranoid Style in American Politics and Other Essays* (London: Jonathan Cape, 1966), 39.

6. See Daniel Pipes, *Conspiracy: How the Paranoid Style Flourishes and Where It Comes From* (New York: Free Press, 1997); and Robert S. Robins and Jerrold M. Post, *Political Paranoia: The Psychopolitics of Hatred* (New Haven: Yale University Press, 1997).

7. For a wide-ranging account of such fears, see Eric Mottram, "Out of Sight but Never Out of Mind: Fears of Invasion in American Culture," in *Blood on the Nash Ambassador: Investigations in American Culture* (London: Hutchinson Radius, 1989), 138–80.

8. Davis, *The Fear of Conspiracy*, 362.

9. For a compelling presentation of this possibility, see Robert S. Levine, *Conspiracy and Romance: Studies in Brockden Brown, Cooper, Hawthorne and Melville* (Cambridge: Cambridge University Press, 1989).

10. The idea of a "fusion paranoia" is discussed by Michael Kelly in "The Road to Paranoia," *New Yorker*, 19 June 1995, 60–75. The outline of a shadow government of intelligence agencies was first sketched in David Wise and Thomas B. Ross, *Invisible Government* (New York: Random House, 1964).

11. For an extended discussion of the changing nature of conspiratorial rumors in the United States, see Peter Knight, *Conspiracy Culture: From the Kennedy Assassination to "The X-Files"* (London: Routledge, 2000).

12. Although the essays in this collection (including the present introduction) do not regard conspiracy theory as a manifestation of paranoia in any clinical sense, they nevertheless follow popular, nontechnical usage of the vocabulary of "paranoia" to mean little more than a broad sense of suspiciousness. Indeed, as Eithne Quinn demonstrates in the case of Tupac Shakur, the rhetoric of "paranoia" has been knowingly appropriated by those very people who once would have been diagnosed in its terms by experts in cultural symptomatology. Conspiracy theorists now often play on the paradoxical logic that you can't really be paranoid if you're aware that you are paranoid.

THEORIES OF CONSPIRACY THEORY

Spinning Paranoia

*The Ideologies of Conspiracy and Contingency in
Postmodern Culture*

Skip Willman

THE PROLIFERATION OF conspiracy theories in the 1990s has provided ample fodder for political commentators and cultural critics to
wax philosophic about the follies of paranoia as an ideology. For the
American media, the debunking of conspiracy theory has become a rit-
ualistic and virtually obligatory practice, elevating a figure like Gerald
Posner (who wrote the "definitive" book on the JFK assassination, *Case
Closed*, concluding that Oswald acted alone) into television's resident
conspiracy guru. While many of these critiques are quite savvy, the effort to debunk conspiracy theory and restore rationality to the public
sphere, as opposed to the irrationality and/or pathology (political, social, or psychological) of conspiracy theory, often relies on an equally
ideological vision of historical causality. The spinning of paranoia in
the American media represents a hegemonic struggle between the conspiratorial camp and the defenders of common sense over the status of
social reality. While each side contends that its perspective corresponds
to the way things really are, each side nevertheless constructs an ideologically coherent social reality rooted in social fantasy. Spinning paranoia, whether it be the construction or deconstruction of conspiratorial
narratives, is a symptomatic response to the social and spatial confusion Fredric Jameson identifies as intrinsic to postmodernity. Before exploring the relationship between conspiracy theory and multinational
capitalism outlined by Jameson, however, we need to examine the vision of historical causality shared by many of the critiques of conspiracy theory.

FROM CONSPIRACY THEORY TO CONTINGENCY THEORY

The debunkers of paranoia typically deride conspiracy theory as a compensatory fantasy that neatly orders the chaotic universe of the late twentieth century. For example, Jonathan Alter contends that conspiracy theory is "comforting" in his critique of *The X-Files* feature film for *Newsweek*: "Communism is dead; capitalism a given. That leaves conspiracism as the civic faith of the moment—a tidy, curiously comforting way to view the universe. At least someone's in control, even if he's evil."[1] In its ability, as Alter notes, to "explain anything" and to make "coincidences seem like they're not," conspiracy theory lends coherence to an often bewildering geopolitical landscape.[2] Refuting even the possibility of a government conspiracy like the one manipulating the world in *The X-Files*, Alter argues, "In fact, the history of secret government agencies, from botched coup attempts in the 1950s to botched monitoring of nuclear testing in the 1990s—is about screw-ups."[3] The attempt to downplay malevolent secret government agencies by pointing to their ineptitude flatters the public with the knowledge that the government is incapable of putting anything past the country: "You wanna talk conspiracies? Nowadays, the U.S. government can't cover up *anything*."[4] If there is any doubt, Alter squashes it with a sweeping generalization aimed to strike a chord of common sense with the magazine's cynical readership: "The biggest reason that conspiracism is a fallacious creed is that no American can keep a secret for long. If they could, reporters would have to find a new line of work."[5] Repression creeps into Alter's account; nowhere is mention made of successful coups, such as the CIA-run overthrow of Guatemala in the 1950s, or the "fact" that various failed government conspiracies have played a significant role in recent history, for instance, the Bay of Pigs invasion.

More important, Alter's attempt to debunk conspiracy theory posits its own vision of historical causality based on the idea that chance, accident, and "screw-ups," not conspiracy, largely determine history. Contingency theory, as I will henceforth refer to this conception of social reality, represents a new and widespread "strategy of containment" in the effort to dispel the "paranoid" fears raised by conspiracy theory.[6] In his editorial letter for the October 1998 issue of *George* examining "the enduring spell of mystery and conspiracy in American life," John Kennedy, Jr., offers a condescending explanation for the popularity of conspiracy theory that echoes Alter in its mobilization of contingency theory:

> The simpler explanation is that mystery is a necessary ingredient of fantasy and narrative, both of which have, on occasion, been employed by journalists and other storytellers. What better way to give meaning to random and confounding events than to bind them, through conjecture, as fruits of a shadow plot? It can be comforting, when one is blindsided by a pitiless "act of God," to assign responsibility to those made of flesh and blood.[7]

Kennedy adds yet another compensatory dimension to conspiracy theory by rehearsing Gordon S. Wood's argument that conspiracy theory desires and projects a distinctly moral universe, presuming "a world of autonomous, freely acting individuals who are capable of directly and deliberately bringing about events through their decisions and actions, and who thereby can be held morally responsible for what happens."[8] Kennedy aligns conspiracy theory with fantasy and storytelling, and posits a conception of historical causality driven by contingency, "random and confounding events" that defy the assessment of responsibility and resist the "comforting" conspiratorial narrative.[9]

Since the publication of Richard Hofstadter's influential essay "The Paranoid Style in American Politics," the most common strategy of debunking conspiracy theory has been to marginalize the purveyors of conspiracy theory as pathological.[10] Conservative political pundit George Will blends contingency theory with this more traditional approach in his denunciation of Oliver Stone's conspiratorial film of the Kennedy assassination, *JFK*. Lacking the liberal tolerance of Kennedy for this clearly deluded and juvenile paranoid style, Will begins his diatribe with a history lesson illustrating the impact of contingency on history with the assassination of Archduke Franz Ferdinand:

> On June 28, 1914, six young men were poised in Sarajevo, Bosnia, to throw bombs at the car of Archduke Franz Ferdinand. Five of them, intimidated by the crowds or unwilling to hurt the archduke's wife, did nothing. However, one asked a policeman which car was the archduke's, the policeman identified it and the boy threw his bomb, which bounced off the archduke's car and exploded under the following car.

One of the others, Gavrilo Princip, went off disconsolately for coffee at a corner café, where he loitered. Later, the Archduke, going to a museum, decided to visit the people injured by the bomb. His driver, confused about the route to the hospital, stopped in front of the café where the astonished Princip sat. Princip leapt up and shot the Archduke and his wife, thereby lighting Europe's fuse.[11]

In this anecdote, Will intends to undermine conspiracy theory by revealing the role chance plays in the triggering event of World War I. Without the accidental detour that delivers the archduke to his loitering assassin, the Great War would never have taken place: if only the driver knew the way to the hospital, or if only he hadn't stopped at this particular café, or if only the archduke wasn't so compassionate about the bomb victims. Since the assassination of Franz Ferdinand is anything but the flawless execution of a perfectly conceived conspiracy, Will rules out the conspiratorial explanation and its various compensations, and we are encouraged to believe that history is propelled on its erratic course by contingency.

Will also argues that the debunking of conspiracy theory does not deliver us from the fear and anxiety typically associated with the paranoid style. In his remarkably similar denunciation of Don DeLillo's novel of the Kennedy assassination, *Libra*, Will argues that a universe disrupted by the meaningless is scarier than one hijacked by conspiracy:

> DeLillo's lurid imaginings will soothe immature people who want to believe that behind large events there must be large ideas or impersonal forces or conspiracies. It takes a steady adult nerve to stare unblinkingly at the fact that history can be jarred sideways by an act that signifies nothing but an addled individual's inner turmoil.[12]

Against the backdrop of the often ludicrous claims of conspiracy theorists, Will's diagnosis seems like a welcome dose of reason and maturity. The desire of conspiracy theory for meaning, generally formulated as some immense Manichean struggle between the forces of good and evil, imposes a reductive interpretive framework on history. However, the rhetorical overkill of Will's condemnation of Stone and DeLillo, particularly in his equation of conspiracy theory with immaturity (as opposed to psychosis, as in Hofstadter's classic account of the "paranoid style") and "contemptible citizenship," demonstrates that the crucial

ideological stake of contingency theory is the assertion of the fundamental health of American society.[13] Contingency theory salvages the
American status quo by turning a blind eye to the social relations underlying "large events" and spinning these often traumatic moments as
the product of "addled individuals." As with Alter and Kennedy, in his
attempt to step outside the ideology of conspiracy theory, Will advances
an equally ideological view of the world by articulating a theory of historical causality determined by contingency.

We are thus trapped in an apparent antinomy over the status of our
postmodern social reality. Do we inhabit a conspiratorial universe in
which mysterious forces manipulate history, or one driven by contingency in the form of chance, accident, randomness, and chaos? These
two diametrically opposed conceptions of social reality point to a traumatic kernel or fundamental antagonism in American society, "an im-
balance in social relations that prevent[s] the community from stabiliz-
ing itself into a harmonious whole."[14] As Slavoj Žižek asserts, "the two
perceptions," in this case, conspiracy theory and contingency theory,
"are simply two mutually exclusive endeavors to cope with this traumatic antagonism, to heal its wound via the imposition of a balanced
symbolic circuit."[15] The goal of this essay is not to determine which of
these rival theories corresponds to reality, but rather to demonstrate
how conspiracy and contingency theories structure a coherent social reality through what Žižek calls the "foreclosure" or "primordial repression" of this traumatic social antagonism.[16] Žižek's post-Marxist explanation, however, fails to offer a convincing historical analysis of or reason for the popularity of conspiracy theory in the 1990s. In his
examination of conspiracy theory, Fredric Jameson restores the missing
historical dimension by articulating the conditions of possibility for its
reemergence in postmodern culture. As I shall attempt to demonstrate,
contingency theory develops out of these same conditions. In short, conspiracy and contingency theories may be rival ideologies depicting very
different social realities, but they represent two sides of the same coin.

CONSPIRACY AND CONTINGENCY THEORIES AS
SOCIAL FANTASY

Conspiracy and contingency theories succeed as ideologies, not as
forms of knowledge (although that is precisely what they purport to

be), but rather as forms of non-knowledge or nonrecognition of "the impossibility of society."[17] According to Žižek, the social field is structured around a constitutive social antagonism, a traumatic impossibility. Ideology intercedes in the guise of "social fantasy" to mask this antagonistic fissure and to construct "a vision of society which *does* exist, a society which is not split by an antagonistic division, a society in which the relation between its parts is organic, complementary."[18] Social fantasy serves as an imaginary support for the symbolic order that structures and regulates social relations, thereby lending ideological coherence and meaning to social reality.

Given this definition of the function of social fantasy, it may be difficult to conceive of conspiracy theory as a comforting ideological fantasy. The conspiratorial vision of social reality seems almost exclusively violent, antagonistic, and malevolent. Žižek supplies an answer to this conceptual dilemma by suggesting that social fantasy is "*a means for an ideology to take its own failure into account in advance.*"[19] The distance between the ideological representation of a harmonious society and the actual experience of an acrimonious society, the difference between what should be and what is, is attributed to "an external element, a foreign body introducing corruption into the sound social fabric."[20] However, this external agent of corruption represents merely the projection of the "antagonistic nature" of society itself onto what emerges as the "social symptom": "the point at which the immanent social antagonism assumes a positive form, erupts on the social surface, the point at which it becomes obvious that society 'doesn't work,' that the social mechanism 'creaks.'"[21] In other words, the social symptom is merely a fantasy construction enabling society to explain away its own impossibility. Žižek exemplifies this conception of the work of social fantasy with the figure of the "Jew" in fascist ideology. Fascism projects the responsibility for the antagonistic fissure preventing society from constituting itself as a harmonious whole onto the fantasy figure of the "Jew." Thus, fascist ideology believes that the elimination of the "Jew" from the social fabric will enable society to achieve this Utopian harmony.

Conspiracy theory, then, attributes the traumatic antagonisms of society to a hidden agency secretly pulling the strings behind historical events, a fantasy figure Žižek calls the "invisible Master."[22] Conspiracy theory thereby restores a comprehensible notion of historical causality to the social field, regardless of the valence of this "invisible Master." Žižek agrees with debunkers like Alter that conspiracy theory is "comforting," since it "provides a guarantee that the field of the big Other [the symbolic order that regulates social life] is not an inconsistent *brico-lage*: its basic premise is that, behind the public Master (who, of course, is an impostor), there is a hidden Master who effectively keeps everything under control."[23] Žižek concludes that conspiracy theory serves as the "ultimate support of power": "the myth of a secret parallel power . . . compensate[s] for the blatant inefficiency of the public, legal power and thus assure[s] the smooth operation of the social machine."[24] In its heyday, the CIA functioned as just such an "invisible Master" in the American imagination, though not necessarily in reality, operating behind the scenes during the Cold War to protect the nation's vital interests, while the leaders from each side of the Iron Curtain jousted ineffectually in the political arena.

Perhaps the most conspicuous example of the "invisible Master" in popular culture is the Cigarette-Smoking Man (William B. Davis) from *The X-Files*. While the "truth" of his role within the conspiracy of the series remains necessarily obscured, he pulls the strings of the "obscene, invisible, 'crazy' power structure" lurking behind the "public, legal power."[25] The parodic episode "Musings of a Cigarette-Smoking Man" traces the career of this mysterious figure from his recruitment into the JFK assassination plot through the other assassinations of the sixties into the secret corridors of power that effectively run what Fox Mulder (David Duchovny), the "paranoid" FBI protagonist, calls the "military–industrial–entertainment complex."[26] The Cigarette-Smoking Man determines even the outcome of the Oscars and the Super Bowl. While the Cigarette-Smoking Man assumes the role of the "invisible Master" responsible for many social woes, this figure also serves as the "ultimate support of power," guaranteeing "the smooth operation of the social machine."[27] In his role as a member of the Syndicate, the larger conspiratorial network of gentrified white men negotiating the "planned Armageddon" with the aliens, he maintains social order by controlling information about the aliens, squashing potentially damaging accidents (UFO crashes, black oil outbreaks, etc.), and supervising the secret operations (the harvesting of human ova through alien abductions, genetic testing, biological weapon testing, etc.) of the group. Despite the complicity of the Syndicate with the aliens and their colonization plans, the show hints that the Syndicate also holds the key for any possible resistance, primarily in the development of a vaccine for the black oil (the key pathogenic component of the aliens' colonization plans).

So much for conspiracy theory, but in what way is contingency theory an ideological fantasy? Žižek again provides the rationale for my contention that contingency theory constitutes an ideological fantasy. Contingency theory merely inverts what is commonly denigrated as the ideological component of conspiracy theory: that "the senseless contingency of the real is thus 'internalized', symbolized, provided with Meaning."[28] Žižek points out that "ideology is the exact opposite of internalization of the external contingency: it resides in externalization of the result of an inner necessity, and the task of the critique of ideology here is precisely to discern the hidden necessity in what appears as mere contingency."[29] Contingency theory maintains the existing capitalist system by attributing any deviations from the social equilibrium to chance and accident rather than immanent social antagonisms or contradictions. Anything that disrupts the flow of capitalism and the expansion of democracy is spun as a mere bump in the road. However, Žižek argues that these bumps in the road provide "the key offering us access to [society's] true functioning":

> all phenomena which appear to everyday bourgeois consciousness as simple deviations, contingent deformations and degenerations of the "normal" functioning of society (economic crises, wars, and so on), and as such abolishable through amelioration of the system, are necessary products of the system itself—the points at which the "truth," the immanent antagonistic character of the system, erupts.[30]

Contingency theory asserts that social symptoms, such as right-wing militia movements, lone gunmen, or violent teens on school rampages, are aberrations from an otherwise harmonious American society. Society is thereby delivered from responsibility for these isolated outbreaks of violence.

Conspiracy and contingency theories presuppose very different social circumstances. Conspiracy theories presuppose a fallen society, whose failure to constitute itself as a harmonious whole must be explained; the conspiratorial narrative resurrects the possibility of society even as it traces its demise through the agency of hidden forces. Not surprisingly, conspiracy theory often clings to a nostalgic conception of a bygone era of social harmony, such as Kennedy's Camelot. By contrast, contingency theories posit a smoothly functioning social system subject to random deviations and deformations introduced by external corrupting forces. Despite the differences in their ideological strategies, conspiracy and contingency theories share a common ideological purpose: the disavowal of the "impossibility of society." They accomplish this end in ways that are not altogether dissimilar. Conspiracy theory fantasizes an "invisible Master" responsible for social ills, while contingency theory produces a "positive cause of social negativity" that represses social antagonism.[31]

Žižek offers a convincing explanation of how conspiracy theory works as a "comforting" ideological fantasy, but he fails to address the historical conditions of possibility for the outbreak of conspiracy theory. This failure may be attributed in part to his theory of history, which emphasizes the "unhistorical." Following Walter Benjamin's critique of historicism, Žižek articulates a theory of history ("historical epochs") as repetition, a series of "failed attempts" to cope with an "unhistorical traumatic kernel which returns as the Same through all historical epochs."[32] In other words, the ideological narratives attempting to account for or repress this impossibility change, while this traumatic kernel persists throughout history. Depending on the context, Žižek defines this "unhistorical traumatic kernel" as social antagonism, class struggle, or "the impossibility of society," all of which he equates with the Lacanian Real:

> class struggle is "real" in the strict Lacanian sense: a "hitch," an impediment which gives rise to ever-new symbolizations by means of which one endeavors to integrate and domesticate it (the corporatist translation–displacement of class struggle into the organic articulation of the "members" of the "social body," for example), but which ultimately condemns these endeavors to ultimate failure. Class struggle is none other than the name for the unfathomable limit that cannot be objectivized, located within the social totality, since it is itself that limit which prevents us from conceiving society as a closed totality.[33]

Žižek's conception of historical repetition provides a rationale for the recurrent eruptions of conspiracy theory in American history; conspiracy theory repetitively and symptomatically marks the contested site of the "unhistorical traumatic kernel" of social antagonism. However, as Robert Miklitsch points out, "the accent in his work on the unhistoricality of the Real—whether as trauma or the Same, *jouissance* or antagonism—eventuates in just the sort of 'bad infinity' that he imputes to deconstruction: 'an endless variation . . . which does not *produce* any-thing new.'"[34] The evacuation of history from Žižek's analysis prob-lematizes the question of what triggers the reemergence of conspiracy theory at this particular historical juncture.

POSTMODERNISM AND THE CULTURAL LOGIC OF CONSPIRACY THEORY

To answer this question, we must turn to the seminal work of Jameson on postmodernism and multinational capitalism, in which the conspir-atorial narrative has emerged as something of a preoccupation. For Jameson, conspiracy theory represents a symptom of multinational capitalism and "must be seen as a degraded attempt—through the fig-uration of advanced technology—to think the impossible totality of the contemporary world system."[35] Jameson first establishes the link be-tween multinational capitalism and conspiracy theory in a mode of contemporary literature he dubs "high-tech paranoia."[36] He argues that the "technology of contemporary society is therefore mesmerizing and fascinating," particularly in cyberpunk, "because it seems to offer some privileged representational shorthand for grasping a network of power and control even more difficult for our minds and imaginations to grasp: the whole new decentered global network of the third stage of capital itself."[37] In a later essay, Jameson echoes his earlier diagnosis: "Conspiracy . . . is the poor person's cognitive mapping in the post-modern age; it is a degraded figure of the total logic of late capital, a desperate attempt to represent the latter's system, whose failure is marked by its slippage into sheer theme and content."[38] While Jame-son's description of conspiracy theory with its curious choice of adjec-tives ("degraded" and "desperate," the "poor person's cognitive map-ping") betrays a certain mandarin distaste for both the common and the overtly political (perhaps inherited from Adorno), this passage illus-trates his predilection for form, wherein the conspiratorial narrative represents an "imaginary or formal solution" to an "unresolvable social contradiction."[39]

In his full-fledged analysis of conspiracy films in *The Geopolitical Aesthetic*, Jameson discusses the conditions of possibility for this turn to the conspiratorial form:

In the widespread paralysis of the collective or social imaginary, to which "nothing occurs" (Karl Kraus) when confronted with the ambitious program of fantasizing an economic system on the scale of the globe itself, the older motif of conspiracy knows a fresh lease on life, as a narrative structure capable of reuniting the minimal basic components: a potentially infinite network, along with a plausible explanation of its invisibility; or in other words, the collective and the epistemological.[40]

Jameson laments the "widespread paralysis of the collective or social imaginary," which resurrects in conspiracy theory a residual form of historical causality or understanding, but elsewhere he accounts for this failure in terms of our "spatial and social confusion" in the wake of the transition into multinational capitalism: "this latest mutation in space—postmodern hyperspace—has finally succeeded in transcending the capacities of the individual human body to locate itself, to organize its immediate surroundings perceptually, and cognitively to map its position in a mappable external world."[41] Thus, Jameson describes the "figuration of conspiracy" as an unconscious attempt "to think a system so vast that it cannot be encompassed by the natural and historically developed categories of perception with which human beings normally orient themselves."[42]

Despite his disparaging remarks regarding conspiracy theory, Jameson locates, in true dialectical fashion, its Utopian kernel in what he dubs its "desire called cognitive mapping," its impulse to overcome the spatial and social confusion inherent to the postmodern condition.[43] Jameson defines "cognitive mapping" as the attempt "to span or coordinate, to map, by means of conscious and unconscious representations . . . the gap between the local positioning of the subject and the totality of class structures in which he or she is situated."[44] Jameson links the concept of "cognitive mapping" to an Althusserian conception of ideology as a "necessary function": "the Imaginary representation of the subject's relationship to his or her Real conditions of existence."[45] For Jameson, "cognitive mapping" designates the crucial task of any socialist political project, since "the incapacity to map socially is as crippling to political experience as the analogous incapacity to map spatially is for urban experience."[46] In this more positive light, Jameson describes conspiracy theory as an "unconscious, collective effort at trying to figure out where we are and what landscapes and forces confront us in a late twentieth century whose abominations are heightened by their concealment and their bureaucratic impersonality."[47]

While the impulse that gives rise to conspiracy theory may be Utopian, the failure of the various manifestations of conspiracy theory, in Jameson's eyes, involves the "slippage into sheer theme and content."[48] What precisely does he mean by this "slippage"? And why does he disparage "theme and content" in conspiracy theory? Jameson presumably criticizes conspiracy theories for their tendency to coalesce around traumatic events, the JFK assassination, for instance, or spurious objects, such as UFOs. For the committed Marxist, the real problem is, of course, the capitalist mode of production. The disappearance of class from the social equation designates the principal problem Jameson has with conspiracy theory (and American society in general). However, Jameson argues that the class content of the historical materials filters through the political unconscious in disguised form, necessitating a symptomatic and often allegorical reading of the conspiratorial text for this buried subtext.

Jameson's conception of conspiracy theory as a "degraded" form of cognitive mapping overlooks the way conspiracy theory has been absorbed by postmodern cynicism. To a certain extent, the suspicion of conspiracy theory has been universalized with the late capitalist subject who already knows and suspects too much; in other words, paranoia is not just for the right-wing lunatic fringe. This late capitalist subject is mired in a politically paralyzing "enlightened false consciousness": "they know very well what they are doing, but still, they are doing it."[49] For instance, the postmodern cynic is suspicious of the government and doesn't believe a word it says, and is, therefore, inclined to accept conspiratorial explanations for various traumatic events, such as the JFK assassination. By the same token, s/he rejects the conspiratorial explanation because such a plot generally involves a level of coordination and skill that the government or any other covert group clearly lacks; Watergate and Iran–Contra demonstrate the ineptitude on the part of would-be conspiratorial agents of the government. This paralysis leads to the opposite extreme of cognitive mapping, the absolute unwillingness to try to make sense of the social totality. The problem is not in the belief of most citizens; they already know, feel, or suspect that the big corporations pull the strings of the United States (i.e., Bill Gates and Microsoft run the computer age). The problem lies in their actions; they act as if the United States truly followed the tenets of economic and political liberalism. Jameson and Žižek approach this problem from different angles, but they both trace the cause of this political quietism to the belief in market ideology.

CONTINGENCY THEORY AND MARKET IDEOLOGY

The social and spatial confusion propelling the effort of conspiracy theory to integrate a disparate set of events into a coherent network of connections or master narrative also forms the condition of possibility for contingency theory. Contingency theory certainly reflects what Jameson calls the failure of imagination to fantasize "an economic system on the scale of the globe itself," but the emergence of contingency theory as a form of historical causality represents a renunciation of any attempt to grasp the operations of the social totality.[50] Resisting the totalizing impulse of conspiracy theory as reductive, contingency theory foregrounds the complexity of the social system. However, this emphasis on social complexity tends to produce an acceptance of the social and spatial confusion accompanying multinational capitalism. The ideological component of contingency theory does not necessarily lie in the recognition of the role of chance and randomness in our lives, but rather in the foreclosure of social relations from its vision of history. In its espousal of chance and randomness as the "natural" and final arbiters of historical events, contingency theory serves as the antithesis of conspiracy theory in postmodernity by articulating the impossibility of "cognitive mapping."

Forrest Gump reflects and popularizes contingency theory as a virtual "structure of feeling" in the now notorious salvo: "Life is like a box of chocolates, you never know what you're going to get."[51] While the film has prompted critics to object to the apotheosis of the simpleminded Gump on the grounds that his success is antithetical to the American meritocracy, *Forrest Gump* still celebrates the American market system. The message of such a film is that what separates the rich from the poor, the powerful from the weak, and the fortunate from the unfortunate is nothing but dumb luck, an apt message for a culture hooked on lotteries and Vegas. The popular slogan "Shit happens," which we learn in the film Gump inadvertently coins, represents something like the fundamental ideologeme of contingency theory. Gump's good fortune is celebratory of a free market that requires no skill, just luck; the market practically runs by itself. As ideological compensation, the trampled and exploited can attribute their lowly condition to chance and randomness, rather than their own inferiority. An existence presupposed to be governed by chance levels the playing field, since even success is achieved through merely being in the right place at the right time; Forrest Gump's "chance" expedition on the open seas during a hurricane, which subsequently decimates the fleet of Louisiana shrimping boats in the harbor, fortuitously bequeaths to him a virtual monopoly of the shrimp market since he owns the sole vessel capable of harvesting shrimp.

However, the apparent contingency governing the fate of the individual, symbolized in *Forrest Gump* by the feather blown in the wind that frames Gump's narrative, is a product of the free market. Theodor Adorno attributes the appearance of the governance of chance in the social field to market relations. When one is reduced to an equally replaceable cog within the social machinery and "alienated from the actual process of production in society," a certain "chaos" and arbitrariness creep into the different "fates" of individuals:

> Chaos defines the law according to which market-society blindly reproduces, with no consideration for the individual. It includes the continuing growth of power in the hands of those in command over all others. The world is chaotic in the eyes of the victims of the law of market value and industrial concentration. But the world is not chaotic "in itself." It is the individual—oppressed inexorably by the principles of this world—who considers it such. The forces which make the world chaotic in the eyes of the individual in the end assume responsibility for the reorganization of chaos because the world is at the mercy of these forces.[52]

The social atomization accompanying the development of capitalism lays the groundwork for this appearance of the chanciness of everyday existence by obfuscating the social relations between people.

Contingency theory functions as a support for market ideology. In order to illustrate this thesis, however, I will need to examine the rhetoric of the market. Against the various proponents of the "end of ideology" thesis following the fall of communism in the Soviet Union and the triumph of free market capitalism, Jameson asserts that the market exists "at one and the same time [as] an ideology and a set of institutional problems."[53] Refining this initial formulation, he argues that the "ideological dimension" of the market "is intrinsically embedded within the reality, which secretes it as a necessary feature of its own structure."[54] According to Jameson, the naturalization of the market constitutes the crucial ideological strategy of market capitalism, the proposition or "ideologeme" that, as he phrases it, "The market is in human nature."[55] Jameson argues that market ideology presents a "Utopian mechanism" invested in an "invisible hand" capable of resolving the social dilemmas imposed on humanity by the realm of necessity, primarily because the market is more in tune with human nature:

> For the exchange mechanisms of the market very precisely constitute an organization of necessity, a sum of purely mechanical requirements, which, at least according to the theory, is called upon to release freedoms . . . namely the fulfillment of private life along with the stabilities of representative or parliamentary democracy, law and order, a taming of the human beast, and the lineaments of justice itself.[56]

Jameson disputes this claim of market ideology as a misnomer on two counts. In an empirical vein, he first observes that "no free market exists today in the realm of oligopolies and multinationals," marking a relatively obvious discrepancy between rhetoric and reality.[57] Second, he refutes the claim that the market offers the consumer the widest variety of choices and freedoms of any system since the "market as a concept rarely has anything to do with choice or freedom, since those are all determined for us in advance."[58]

Jameson argues that "the force . . . of the concept of the market lies in its 'totalizing' structure, as they say nowadays; that is, in its capacity to afford a model of social totality."[59] Insofar as market ideology provides a model of the social totality, it also delivers us from the responsibility to decide or act as anything but consumers, thereby rescuing us from our own base human natures:

> Market ideology assures us that human beings make a mess of it when they try to control their destinies ("socialism is impossible") and that we are fortunate in possessing an interpersonal mechanism—the market—which can substitute for human hubris and planning and replace human decisions altogether. We only need to keep it

clean and well-oiled, and it now—like the monarch so many centuries ago—will see to us and keep us in line.[60]

As a "consoling replacement for the divinity," the market and its "invisible hand" constitute "the big Other."[61] Market ideology projects the motive force behind causality from the locus of the very visible social relations and activity of individuals into the realm of invisible forces and abstractions far beyond the comprehension of individuals. Market ideology, therefore, smuggles something very much like the "invisible Master" of conspiracy theory in the back door with its faith in the "invisible hand" of the market. However, the "invisible hand" regulates social life and guarantees the consistency of the big Other, whereas the "invisible Master" accounts for the inconsistency and deception of the symbolic order.

CONCLUSION

While conspiracy theories are accused of distorting history and are often interwoven with reprehensible racist beliefs, the erasure of history undertaken by contingency theory under the guise of a new recognition of the role of chance and accident in history is equally insidious. At the very least, the proliferation of conspiracy theory attests to the presence of an oppositional political culture in the shadow of the marketplace and its attendant consumerism. The work of Žižek and Jameson, therefore, serves as a necessary corrective to those cultural critics and political commentators who denigrate conspiracy theory and ostracize their proponents. In *Looking Awry*, Žižek reminds readers that the paranoid construction of reality is "an attempt to heal ourselves out of the real 'illness,' the 'end of the world,' the breakdown of the symbolic universe, by means of this substitute formation."[62] Jameson reaches a similar diagnosis with his equation of conspiracy theory and cognitive mapping. Multinational capitalism is constantly reshaping the social terrain, and conspiracy theory merely attempts to make sense of these changes. Both theorists would also agree that contingency theory partakes in the ideological maneuver Žižek calls an "over-rapid universalization"; contingency theory posits a universal history driven by chance and randomness "whose function is to make us blind to its historical, socio-symbolic determination."[63] The theoretical insight offered by Jameson and

Žižek enables us to see how conspiracy and contingency theories construct a vision of social reality and historical causality that resolves the social and spatial confusion encountered by the subject in a postmodernity driven by multinational capitalism.

NOTES

1. Jonathan Alter, "The Weird World of Secrets and Lies," *Newsweek*, 22 June 1998, 76.

2. Ibid.

3. Ibid.

4. Ibid.

5. Ibid.

This is a silly thing to cite

6. I have borrowed the term "strategy of containment" from the work of Fredric Jameson, specifically *The Political Unconscious: Narrative as a Socially Symbolic Act* (Ithaca: Cornell University Press, 1981). Jameson adopts the term from its usage in American foreign policy of the Cold War to designate the effort to confine the spread of communism. I have also adopted and developed the term "contingency theory" from Daniel O'Hara's essay "On Becoming Oneself in Frank Lentricchia," in *National Identities and Post-Americanist Narratives*, ed. Donald Pease (Durham: Duke University Press, 1994), 244.

7. John F. Kennedy, Jr., "Editor's Letter," *George*, October 1998, 18.

Equally silly.

8. Gordon S. Wood, "Conspiracy and the Paranoid Style: Causality and Deceit in the Eighteenth Century," *William and Mary Quarterly* 39 (1982): 409.

9. Kennedy, "Editor's Letter," 18.

10. Richard Hofstadter, "The Paranoid Style in American Politics," in *The Paranoid Style in American Politics and Other Essays* (Cambridge: Harvard University Press, 1965), 3–40.

11. George Will, "Giving Paranoia a Bad Name," in *The Leveling Wind: Politics, the Culture and Other News, 1990–1994* (New York: Penguin, 1994), 168–69.

12. George Will, "Shallow Look at the Mind of the Assassin," *Washington Post*, 22 September 1988, A25.

13. Will, "Giving Paranoia a Bad Name," 170.

14. Slavoj Žižek, "The Spectre of Ideology," in *Mapping Ideology*, ed. Slavoj Žižek (New York: Verso, 1994), 26.

15. Ibid.

16. Ibid., 21.

17. Slavoj Žižek, *The Sublime Object of Ideology* (New York: Verso, 1989), 126. Žižek adopts "the impossibility of society" from the anti-essentialist critique of Marxism undertaken by Ernesto Laclau and Chantal Mouffe in *Hegemony and Socialist Strategy: Towards a Radical Democratic Politics* (New York: Verso, 1985).

They reject the reductive economic determinism of vulgar Marxism, in particular, the base and superstructure model of society. Instead, they adopt a more flexible and discursive theory of the social field that necessitates a crucial revision of the conception of how ideology works. This reconceptualization of the function of ideology is most clearly articulated in Ernesto Laclau's essay "The Impossibility of Society," in *New Reflections on the Revolution of Our Time* (New York: Verso, 1990):

> The ideological would not consist of the misrecognition of a positive essence, but exactly the opposite: it would consist of the non-recognition of the precarious character of any positivity, of the impossibility of any ultimate suture. The ideological would consist of those discursive forms through which a society tries to institute itself as such on the basis of closure, of the fixation of meaning, of the non-recognition of the infinite play of differences. The ideological would be the will to "totality" of any totalizing discourse. And insofar as the social is impossible without some fixation of meaning, without the discourse of closure, the ideological must be seen as constitutive of the social. The social only exists as the vain attempt to institute that impossible object: society. (89)

18. Žižek, *Sublime Object of Ideology*, 126.

19. Ibid.

20. Ibid.

21. Ibid., 127–28.

22. Slavoj Žižek, "'I Hear You with My Eyes': or, The Invisible Master," in *Gaze and Voice as Love Objects*, ed. Renata Salecl and Slavoj Žižek (Durham: Duke University Press, 1996), 97.

23. Ibid., 96–97.

24. Ibid., 97.

25. Ibid., 96.

26. "Musings of a Cigarette-Smoking Man," from *The X-Files*, created by Chris Carter, written by Glen Morgan, directed by James Wong, Twentieth-Century Fox, WXIN, Indianapolis, 17 November 1996.

27. Žižek, "'I Hear You with My Eyes,'" 97.

28. Žižek, "Spectre of Ideology," 4.

29. Ibid.

30. Žižek, *Sublime Object of Ideology*, 128.

31. Ibid., 127.

32. Slavoj Žižek, *Enjoy Your Symptom! Jacques Lacan in Hollywood and Out* (New York: Routledge, 1992), 81.

33. Žižek, "Spectre of Ideology," 22.

34. Robert Miklitsch, "'Going through the Fantasy': Screening Slavoj Žižek," *South Atlantic Quarterly* 97 (1998): 490.

35. Fredric Jameson, *Postmodernism, or, The Cultural Logic of Late Capitalism* (Durham: Duke University Press, 1991), 38.

36. Ibid.

37. Ibid., 37–38.

38. Fredric Jameson, "Cognitive Mapping," in *Marxism and the Interpretation of Culture*, ed. Cary Nelson and Lawrence Grossberg (Urbana: University of Illinois Press, 1988), 356.

39. Jameson, *Political Unconscious*, 79.

40. Fredric Jameson, *The Geopolitical Aesthetic: Cinema and Space in the World System* (Bloomington: Indiana University Press, 1992), 9.

41. Jameson, *Postmodernism*, 54, 44.

42. Jameson, *Geopolitical Aesthetic*, 2.

43. Ibid., 3.

44. Jameson, "Cognitive Mapping," 353.

45. Ibid.

46. Ibid.

47. Jameson, *Geopolitical Aesthetic*, 3.

48. Jameson, "Cognitive Mapping," 356.

49. Žižek, *Sublime Object of Ideology*, 29.

50. Jameson, *Geopolitical Aesthetic*, 9.

51. *Forrest Gump*, dir. Robert Zemeckis (1994). Raymond Williams defines the term "structure of feeling" in *Marxism and Literature* (Oxford: Oxford University Press, 1977), 128–35.

52. Theodor Adorno, *Philosophy of Modern Music*, trans. Anne G. Mitchell and Wesley V. Blomster (New York: Continuum, 1973), 44–45.

53. Jameson, *Postmodernism*, 260.

54. Ibid., 262.

55. Ibid., 263.

56. Fredric Jameson, *The Seeds of Time* (New York: Columbia University Press, 1994), 59–60.

57. Jameson, *Postmodernism*, 266.

58. Ibid.

59. Ibid., 272.

60. Ibid., 273.

61. Ibid.

62. Slavoj Žižek, *Looking Awry: An Introduction to Jacques Lacan through Popular Culture* (Cambridge: MIT Press, 1991), 19.

63. Žižek, *Sublime Object of Ideology*, 50.

2

A Poor Person's Cognitive Mapping

Fran Mason

ACCORDING TO FREDRIC JAMESON at the end of his 1988 article "Cognitive Mapping," there are two existing ways to map postmodern multinational society. The first is the self-reflexive aesthetics of postmodernist art, an inferior way of mapping the global multinational space we inhabit, as Jameson sees it, because its interiorization of social representation resolves into an endless mapping and remapping of the world as a set of textual processes. Instead of providing a map of society, the postmodern text simply provides a map of itself. The second form of mapping, which is the more significant for this essay, stems from the "omnipresence of the theme of paranoia" in the contemporary world. According to Jameson, the "theme of paranoia" produces conspiracy theory, which, he argues, is "the poor person's cognitive mapping in the postmodern age; it is a degraded figure of the total logic of late capital, a desperate attempt to represent the latter's system."[1] "Cognitive mapping," in Jameson's view, provides a means to achieve an understanding of the complexities of the social relations that exist in what he terms the "multinational age"—and, indeed, is *necessary* for such understanding. Conspiracy theory is a degraded version of cognitive mapping because it cannot adequately represent these complexities. It either misrecognizes totality as totalitarianism or attempts to represent the unpresentable by analogy. In both cases there occurs a "misrecognition" that produces an illegitimate form of knowledge. Conspiracy theory does not represent ideology and system as they are (in the forms in which they actually occur in late capital), but as something else (conspiracy), as another system altogether. Conspiracy theory produces an analogy or approximation that is subsequently taken to be "real." It generates a map of the world that is actually a map of a different world entirely, a parallel or imaginary world of misrecognized social systems and power structures.[2]

Jameson, however, is actually fairly vague about what constitutes "cognitive mapping." He develops the term out of Kevin Lynch's work on the understanding of space and people's ability or lack of ability to map the city space that has exploded around them in contemporary culture.[3] With the addition of Althusserian politics, and particularly the notion of the "absent cause," Jameson proposes "cognitive mapping," a means by which the individual subject can locate and structure perception of social and class relations in a world where the local no longer drives social, political, and cultural structures or allows the individual subject to make sense of his or her environment. Deluged by a "perceptual barrage of immediacy," the subject is disconnected and fragmented in a more exaggerated form than ever before.[4] In the corporate multinational global economy of late capitalism, the multiple informational and sign systems that are made available cannot be synthesized by the individual subject or consciousness, a situation that also occurred in modernity, but which is exaggerated and magnified in late capital.[5] Jameson, therefore, calls for a new "cognitive mapping" of global society because "cognitive mapping" provides the ability to negotiate a relationship between the local and the global on the part of the individual subject so that he or she will be able to generate an informed and practical political response to the saturated sign-space of postmodernity in order "to enable," as Jameson puts it, "a situational representation on the part of the individual subject to that vaster and properly unrepresentable totality which is the ensemble of society's structures as a whole."[6]

What Jameson is calling for, in effect, is a way of presenting the unpresentable, making implicit reference to Lyotard's notion of the postmodern sublime. Jameson does not, however, directly invoke Lyotard's aesthetics of the postmodern sublime because it does not fulfill his political needs. Lyotard's argument that the postmodern sublime "puts forward the unpresentable in presentation itself" and that "it is our business not to supply reality but to invent allusions to the conceivable which cannot be presented" works principally in terms of aesthetics, analogy, and simulation, all of which are displacements away from the "real" that Jameson seeks to reveal through "cognitive mapping."[7] Conspiracy can be seen as a version of the postmodern sublime and offers a similar displacement away from the "real." A "true" conspiracy would be something that is absolutely unpresentable or absent, providing no signs or clues of its existence and would be a version of the sublime in the Romantic sense, because it is invisible and undetectable. As soon as it becomes represented it is no longer a conspiracy: a conspiracy cannot be visible (represented) because it derives its status as a conspiracy from its secrecy. In Lyotard's postmodern version of the sublime, conspiracy theory would provide an allusion to reality even though it isn't reality itself. The representation is not a representation of the conspiracy itself, just an approximation or an analogy. In this sense, conspiracy theory is a presentation of the unpresentable through signs and is a simulacrum in its fullest sense: a copy without an original.

For Jameson, on the other hand, conspiracy theory is not a presentation of the unpresentable "absent cause" but rather a metaphor or analogy, "a degraded figure of the total logic of late capital." Conspiracy is not a true presentation of either the "absent cause" of late capital's system and its power structures or its history. It is simply a narrative or story created through control and power and as such has ideological effects. Conspiracy theory, in Jameson's terms, can therefore be seen as a diversionary tactic directing attention away from the real causes of oppression in capitalism because it identifies secret societies or government agencies as the cause of oppression rather than the system itself.[8] Where the conspiracy groups are seen to be simply utilizing the current social system, they act as scapegoats for the system's failure and thereby focus disaffection on the abusers of the system rather than the system itself. If, on the other hand, they are seen as the creators of the current social system, they are effectively untouchable and transhistorical superagents who cannot be thwarted. In either case, conspiracy theory offers an ideologically produced response to oppression in Jameson's logic.

What is at issue, therefore, as far as Jameson is concerned, is the question of the legitimation of knowledge and how to produce knowledge that is real and not ideological. Jameson follows Habermas's position and desires an objectively legitimated knowledge that can be accepted as history or reality, a knowledge that incorporates the "absent cause" rather than referring to it by the analogy of narrative. Indeed, in his foreword to the English-language edition of *The Postmodern Condition* Jameson challenges Lyotard's argument that the master narratives of legitimation have disappeared to be replaced by small narratives of legitimation and suggests instead that they have simply passed underground.[9] Jameson, therefore, is offering "cognitive mapping" as a way of finding "real" knowledge rather than the analogies of narrative knowledge, or, as he puts it in *Postmodernism*, he is using "cognitive

mapping" as a way of overcoming the rift "between existential experience and scientific knowledge," where Lyotard would represent the former and Habermas the latter.[10] "Cognitive mapping" has three main
tasks: to revive the global truths and legitimating grand narratives that
have gone underground; to prevent the fragmentation that accompanies the move to Lyotard's small narrative units; and to bridge the gap
between the small narrative knowledges of existential experience and
the larger global or scientific narratives so that a properly legitimated
knowledge can be generated.

In opposition, Lyotard, in "A Missive on Universal History" in *The
Postmodern Explained to Children*, privileges the position of narrative;
first, because it holds together a multiplicity of heterogeneous discourses,[11] and second because

> legitimacy is secured by the strength of the narrative mechanism: it en-
> compasses the multiplicity of families of phrases and possible genres
> of discourse; it envelops every name; it is always actualizable and al-
> ways has been; both diachronic and parachronic, it secures mastery
> over time and therefore over life and death. Narrative is authority it-
> self. It authorizes an infrangible we, outside of which there is only *they.*
>
> This kind of organization is absolutely opposed to the organization
> of grand narratives of legitimation which characterize modernity in
> the West.[12]

Lyotard is describing what he termed "paralogy" in *The Postmodern Condition* (the creation of small performative narratives that challenge the
institutional and reified grand narratives of modernity).[13] Paralogy is itself a form of "cognitive mapping" and describes the positioning of the
subject within a community or society through the generation of new
knowledges and the rearrangement of existing knowledges. While it
would be wrong to conflate Lyotard's narratives of knowledge with either textual or historical narratives, there are nevertheless connections
between conspiracy and narrative production. Indeed, narrative or the
narrativization of events and facts is the main form of legitimating
knowledge in conspiracy theory. Every conspiracy theory provides a
narrative to legitimate its account of contemporary society, offering a
view of how things got to be as they are. Conspiracy theory provides archaeology in narrative form, locating causes and origins of the conspiracy, piecing together events, connecting random occurrences to organize

a chronology or sequence of sorts, and providing revelations and denouements by detailing the conspiracy's plans for the future. Narrative provides a form of mapping for conspiracy theory, offering not only an explanatory history but also a map of the future that is to come. This is the case whether it is a narrative of occultism and the Knights Templar, the Gnostics, and the Illuminati; a narrative of the New World Order; Alex Constantine's narrative of the founding of the Fourth Reich in America; or a narrative of mind control from Operation Paperclip to MK–ULTRA and Project Monarch.[14] These narratives also exist within a Lyotardian community of paralogy where members can add to the narratives, often by rearranging or combining narratives, so that the Illuminati narratives, for example, can also be combined with anti-Semitic Zionist narratives or with New World Order narratives—as is the case with Lyndon LaRouche's original spin on conspiracy in which the British monarchy is allied with other "cabals" and political groups such as Zionism, Freemasonry, the Rockefellers, and Muslim fundamentalists as it seeks to take control of the globe. Similarly, Texe Marrs's account of the New World Order takes in mind control conspiracies and state surveillance:

> A frightening behemoth is rising up from the depth of America's hidden establishment. Like a vast and monstrous silicon octopus, Project L.U.C.I.D. is stretching forth its ominous and high tech tentacles. Multitudes of unsuspecting helpless victims will very soon be encircled and crushed by Big Brother's new, Gestapo police state. Who among us can possibly escape from the electronic cages now being prepared for all mankind?[15]

The creators of these accounts, however, do not see them as narratives but as histories, and as such it might be better to term them "virtual histories" or "virtual chronologies." They are therefore both grand narratives and the small narratives of paralogy. Conspiracy theory can be seen in terms of the production of grand narratives in its impulse to totalize reality as a system of connections while it also arranges new events according to its existing thesis and thus has mapped reality in advance. On the other hand, conspiracy theory is not officially sanctioned knowledge because it offers alternative versions of reality and would therefore appear to be a matter of paralogy. A postmodernizing process occurs in which there is a proliferation of mutually exclusive knowledge systems each of which has a monocentric belief in its own truth but whose internal logic cannot be measured against any existing reality. The result is a proliferation of information systems all of which claim to be knowledge systems but which cannot legitimate themselves against the existing realities of multinational global culture. The post-modern phenomenon of contemporary conspiracy theory can thus be seen as a heterodoxy of orthodoxies, a set of paralogic narratives that claim to be legitimating grand narratives none of which can stand the existence of any other system.

The unlegitimated and "virtual" qualities of conspiracy narratives or histories lead Jameson to describe conspiracy as the "poor person's cognitive mapping." The term "poor person" is a rather strange one for a Marxist such as Jameson to use, however. Clearly, Jameson is suggesting that in opposition to conspiracy and other illegitimate cognitive mappings there is a legitimate cognitive mapping, but this doesn't detail what this legitimate "cognitive mapping" or "rich person's cognitive mapping" would look like. It would probably not look like the eclectic postmodernism that Lyotard describes, where "one listens to reggae, watches a western, eats McDonald's food for lunch and local cuisine for dinner, wears Paris perfume in Tokyo and 'retro' clothes in Hong Kong [and where] knowledge is a matter for TV games."[16] Lyotard intends this as his own "poor person's postmodernism," a matter of consumption rather than knowledge, though the jet-setting lifestyle it suggests at times implies something more than this. Nevertheless, although this doesn't provide any answers as to what a legitimate cognitive mapping would look like, it does raise the important question of access to information and knowledge. In some respects, quite surprisingly, Jameson suggests a utopian account of the availability of information in contemporary multinational society, which in its predominance of mediated signs allows the possibility for anyone to cognitively map their position in the global system.

The issue of asymmetrical access to information is nevertheless an important one if a legitimate "cognitive mapping" of global society (or reality) is to take place. The quality of perceived information and whether it has a "value" become crucial if unlegitimated information is to be transformed into legitimated knowledges through the alchemy of "cognitive mapping." Jameson's offhanded dismissal of conspiracy theory as a "poor person's cognitive mapping" suggests that the information that generates conspiracy theory has no "value," but he does not, at this point, take into account the possibility that the people who create conspiracy theories may not have access to "valuable" information. A theory that does consider levels of access to information is Charles Jencks's notion of the "cognitariat." Jencks argues that in a postindustrial information society a new class begins to appear, taking over from the proletariat of the industrial age, when manufacturing was the main force in economic production. He refers to this class as a "paraclass"—suggesting that it breaks down old class distinctions—and calls it the "cognitariat." He also argues that access to information will be uneven and that there will be "cognicrats" and "cogniproles" within this new category, those who are information-rich and those who are information-poor.[17] It would be into the category of "cogniprole" that, in Jameson's terms, the use of conspiracy as a form of "cognitive mapping" would fall. So, while cognicrats would have access to enough information to properly map global capital and its social alignments, the cogniproles would have to work with less information, creating degraded versions such as conspiracy theory and UFO narratives.

Jencks's idea of the cognicrats and cogniproles is not a new idea and has been a staple of conspiracy theory and paranoia for some time. It can also be seen as a conspiracy theorist's version of class relations, something that particularly finds its provenance in cyberpunk fiction's accounts of the relationship between information-rich corporations and their servants and the underclass that exists outside corporate enclaves.[18] Indeed, this account of information society can be found in a slightly different form in Philip K. Dick's novel *The Simulacra* (1964), which predates Jencks's *What Is Postmodernism?* (1986) by about twenty years. In this novel, Dick constructs a society polarized into the *Geheimnisträger* (the *Ges*), those who know secrets (particularly the secret that the president of the United States of Europe and America, a prototype perhaps of the New World Order, is a simulacrum or android) and the *Befehlträger* (the *Bes*), the carry-outers, as they are described; the obedient servants who follow orders in the hope that they will be rewarded with entry into the *Geheimnisträger* class.[19] As in many Philip K. Dick novels, government and social relations are constructed in terms of a conspiracy created by those who have knowledge in order to control an alienated underclass.[20] Indeed, in relation to conspiracy theory in the contemporary period it might be suggested that the generation of a conspiracy theory is as much about imagining yourself into the *Geheimnisträger* or "cognicrat" class as it is about describing or validating a sense of alienation or victimhood. Paranoia, for example, is not just an expression of marginalization and alienation in a seemingly hostile world, nor is it simply an attempt to find depth and meaning in the simulacra and multiple information systems of postmodernity. Paranoia also acts as a centering device for subjectivity by allowing all the world's random events to be explained in terms of the paranoid's version of conspiracy: paranoia provides coherence for subjectivity by providing coherence for society. This raises a paradox of identity in conspiracy theory, in that it functions to express a postmodern decentered subjectivity, but it can also be a way of expressing a meaningful and centered identity or subjectivity by apparently locating the self within the secret knowledges of the powerful. The paranoid is a figure who is both inside the secret operations of society (and therefore in a position of knowledge not shared by other marginalized subjects) and on the outside as one of the marginalized and powerless majority.

This is the ideal for "cognitive mapping," but it faces the same problems and offers the same contradictory subjectivity as paranoia. To negotiate a relationship between local and global or individual and system, cognitive mapping needs a subjectivity capable of the "critical distance" that Jameson has often argued is impossible in postmodernity.[21] Jameson's subject is one who has to distance him- or herself from the relationships he or she is trying to map and must therefore exist outside history and society. And yet the subject also has to be inside society and history in order to know what is relevant and legitimate. As a result, conspiracy, rather than being a "poor person's cognitive mapping," might actually be a paradigm of "cognitive mapping" and the difficulties it faces in creating a legitimate position of distance between the subject and the global society he or she inhabits. The postmodern subject does not have the stability that Jameson desires, placed within the morass of postmodern information systems and simulations in which signals suffer interference and thus intercut and merge like Baudrillard's FM radio band.[22] The postmodern or global subject is not the "subject-outside-history" that Jameson desires. The subject may be both local and global, but this is not the same as being inside and outside—with local knowledge providing inside information and global consciousness providing a wider overview. While cognitive mapping ideally provides the connections between local and global (or inside and outside), this depends on a stable self who can process the mass of information and simulacra made available in late capital. Similarly, Lyotard's narrative legitimation has a problematic position because his discourse, in its references to the Cashinahua tribe, is predicated on the subject having a stable position in a stable community, whereas conspiracy theory of course maps the subject's instability in an unstable society, which constantly inflates as external connections and systems are created.[23]

We can see the problematic of subjectivity that these discourses represent when we turn to conspiracy. Very often, conspiracy theories are constructed in order to create a subjectivity that is outside history and society so that, although the subject is threatened by the New World Order, the BATF, secret government agencies, or black helicopters, it is not complicit with the conspiracy itself. In conspiracy theory the subject is predicated as a perfect autonomous subject who, despite being one of the majority outside the conspiracy's elite, remains unaffected by the conspiracy's operations and untouched by its disinformation—unlike the rest of society. However, conspiracy theory also represents the independent autonomous subject under threat, struggling to maintain his or her identity in the face of an intrusive conspiracy. The representation of the body and the way it is probed by aliens, subjected to mind control, or implanted with electronic devices signifies this fear of the threat to "the rights of the individual" and the sanctity of the individual's mind. In UFO abduction narratives, anal probes and the insemination of women, for example, represent the ways the human body is turned into a thing, a soulless piece of meat. These claims are made, for instance, by Budd Hopkins when he writes that there are three possible functions for alien implants:

> They could function as "locators," in the mode of the small radio transmitters zoologists attach to the ears of hapless, tranquilized elk to trace their wanderings. Or they could be monitors of some sort, relaying the thoughts, emotions or even the visual and sensory impressions of the host. Or, and perhaps least palatable, they could have a controlling function as receivers, suggesting the possibility that abductees could be made to act as surrogates for their abductors.[24]

Such threats to the individual map a fear that individuality means nothing and that everyone is treated as a functional unit, a thing, or a commodity in contemporary society. And while such narratives may, by Jameson's criteria, offer a mapping that diverts attention away from the control of the total system of late capital, they nevertheless enact a cognitive mapping of real fears and anxieties in the age of corporations and multinational capital. Implant narratives map similar anxieties over cooptation and complicity in contemporary culture and the sense that there is no possibility for distantiation, as Jameson argues. Implants and mind control represent a discourse of making the "knowing" subject complicit without the subject being aware of their own complicity—a very postmodern concern—so that they are both knowing and unknowing at the same time. They are brought within the conspiracy while they still believe they are outside it and are both puppet and autonomous individual.

Militia groups and New World Order conspiracists, on the other hand, predicate themselves in terms of the notion of the subject as a "subject-outside-history." The fetishization of the Constitution and Bill of Rights represents an attempt to evade not only society as it exists but also history, something that can be seen in the desire to return to a mythical prehistory America—a "retro-topian" attempt to construct an alternative future by a nostalgic return to the past. Bo Gritz, indeed, is fond of stating on his lecture tours that the rights enshrined in the Constitution do not come from the Constitution itself. They are not given to the people of America in history (by the Founding Fathers) but, because they are *inalienable* rights, come from outside history—from God.[25] New World Order conspiracies can indeed be seen as a paradoxical cognitive mapping of global systems *and* a resistance to cognitive mapping. NWO conspiracies simultaneously map projected global systems in their imagined conspiracies and embody a desire to retreat from complex global systems to local communities. Again, Bo Gritz rails against the New World Order and global control systems while establishing his own community ("Almost Heaven") in Idaho, which he connects with a global system by setting it in opposition:

> Bill Clinton is more of a globalist than Bush. I think it means a loss of the United States as a separate nation, and our Constitution will eventually come under the UN charter. Maybe there are enough people in Idaho who think we ought to maintain our identity. If there aren't it doesn't make a difference. We'll have a Neighborhood Watch program if we have to. Meaning if there's only five of us we'll say, "Look, we're not going to hurt anybody, but don't you come in here and tread on us."[26]

Effectively, Gritz is offering a cognitive as well as a geographical map of the world here, in which "Almost Heaven" has isolated itself from the United States because it is a controllable and mappable unit. And because it exists outside larger systems, he is effectively arguing that a response to global control is to step outside global history even while his discourses still offer cognitive maps of global systems. Gritz has a literal Neighborhood Watch in his area of Idaho ("Almost Heaven") and a metaphorical Neighborhood Watch in his conspiracy theory map of global society.

The aim of "cognitive mapping," as has already been stated, is to form an interface between the immediate existential experience of, for example, Gritz's Idaho and larger global systems of knowledge, but without retreating from globalism into fragmented enclaves—whether these are geographical, cultural, cognitive, or epistemological enclaves. Nevertheless, Gritz's desire to be inside and outside society and history simultaneously is paradigmatic of "cognitive mapping" itself and represents the same desire to have a stable position from which global society can be controlled without the subject being controlled at the same time. Another way of putting it would be to say that conspiracy theory and "cognitive mapping" are attempts to map society without the subject being mapped him- or herself. By this logic, "knowledge" of the conspiracy seemingly gives the subject a position of independence and authenticity outside the domain of the conspiracy and its world of ignorance, control, and inauthenticity, while "cognitive mapping" seems to offer the same possibilities for living outside ideology. The conspiracist "subject-outside-history" sees him- or herself as free of the information systems controlled by the conspiracy, government, or secret society and sees subjects inside history and society as constructs of "alien" information systems in which thoughts, values, and beliefs do not originate with the subject. Conspiracy theory in this respect acts as a displaced substitute of ideology, a displacement that is itself ideological. The substitution of conspiracy for ideology can in many ways be seen as a rightist or libertarian attempt to understand control and power in contemporary society and marks an interesting intersection between Marxist theories of ideology popularized by Herbert Marcuse in the 1960s—in the notion of "the System"—with rightist or libertarian paranoia. In this interface, control is moved from a class to the individual and responses to control entail individual knowledge or empowerment rather than social transformation. Conspiracy theory can be seen, in these terms, as an ideological response to ideological control and, as such, a "poor person's cognitive mapping." Yet it is also a paradigm for "cognitive mapping" as a whole because conspiracy theory enacts the difficulties of mapping society without the subject being mapped in the process. Or, more properly, conspiracy theory represents the difficulties of generating a map that is not itself a product of the subject having already been mapped or interpellated by ideology.

Implant and mind control discourses represent exactly this problematic. They present a version of society in which subjectivity has already been generated by the group or agency that is being mapped: the conspiracy that the subject claims has introduced the implant or mind control information in the first place. Conspiracy theory and conspiracy fictions are full of stories of people whose actions have been determined for them through mind control or implanted technology. Alex Constantine claims that Sirhan Sirhan, like Lee Harvey Oswald, was a "hypno-patsy";[27] Timothy McVeigh apparently had an implant placed in his buttocks by the army; and Cathy O'Brien tells of her "experience" as a CIA-controlled prostitute and drug courier in *Trance: Formation of America*.[28] In UFO stories the picture is the same: abductees are implanted, monitored, and controlled by aliens or have "actual" aliens implanted into their cerebral cortex (both of which have become a staple of other kinds of popular fiction, as seen in Scully's neck implant in *The X-Files* and aliens as implants in *Dark Skies*). These conspiracy fantasies represent several things. They are a way of explaining a feeling of disempowerment in contemporary society, but they also allow people to avoid taking responsibility for their own actions. Equally, these narratives hypothesize the entry of the conspiracy into the subject. The conspiracy is internalized and does not just exist as a threatening but recognizable external agency. It is both inside and outside, with the implant or mind control trigger acting as an on-off button. The conspiracy is outside until the implant or mind control trigger is activated, at which point the subject becomes part of the conspiracy. The claims that the CIA has developed "remote viewing" technology (whereby the implanted victim becomes the eyes of a distant receiver) are the clearest example of this type of conspiracy fiction.[29] In this instance, the "victim" apparently sees the world through the eyes of the conspiracy agency and becomes a stooge or puppet during the period they are under control—what Ron Patton, a mind control believer, calls the Marionette Syndrome.[30]

Stephen Bury's *Interface* provides a more self-aware example of the contradictions of implant conspiracies and the problematic subjectivity that results.[31] The novel tells the story of a conspiracy behind the presidential campaign of William Cozzano, a wealthy politician who has suffered a stroke, but who is seen by a secret conspiracy of the wealthy (called "The Network") as necessary to their control of America. He is given an implant that mends the neural networks, but that also allows him to be controlled, without his knowledge. At the same time as this, his campaign staff come upon a new device (the PIPER 100) that straps on to the wrist and will allow people's emotions and responses to stimuli to be accurately observed. Cozzano is not given one of these, but one hundred selected volunteers are, and their responses to Cozzano's political opinions and rhetoric are measured. Among the group being monitored is Floyd Wayne Vishniak, part of the social category the research campaigners call "economic roadkill": an unemployed, alienated white male prone to conspiracy fantasies.[32] It is no surprise, therefore, that wearing the PIPER 100 on his wrist causes Floyd Wayne to fantasize a conspiracy in which wealthy William Cozzano is a front man for a secret network of the super-rich who want to take over America and who are using the PIPER 100 Floyd Wayne wears to monitor and control the minds of Americans. The conspiracy is mapped by Floyd Wayne because he believes he is being mapped and controlled by the conspiracy. Yet Floyd Wayne's construction of a conspiracy is accidental: the device he wears is not an implant (although it transmits, the messages are not subliminal), but Floyd Wayne maps the world as if it were an implant and as if he were being mapped and controlled by it. His belief that he is being controlled leads him to both resist the messages he believes are coming from the transmitter (which are actually in his own mind) and thwart "The Network." He kills Cozzano and helps to end "The Network's" conspiratorial threat, the result of which is the election of one of the marginalized, who has plans to transform the United States.

Interface offers an account of mind control that questions the basis of conspiracy versions of control, but it also gestures to the difficulties of "legitimately" mapping society. It suggests, through Floyd Wayne's fantasy of conspiracy, that everything is an implant in postmodern global society even if the implants are not material objects, but simulations, discourses, ideologies, and knowledges. The subject is already pervaded by the social processes he or she wishes to map. *Interface* simply extends the process by imagining the technologization (or cyborgization) of the mapping process to enact the simultaneous internalization of society and externalization of the self. Similarly, while mind control narratives assume an autonomous independent subject existing before the mind control experiments, they also unconsciously represent uncertainties about the autonomy of the subject because of mind control's claimed ability to alter personality structures and identity. Floyd Wayne believes he has a new subjectivity constructed for him by the conspiracy, but it is actually his own creation. Floyd Wayne, like the "victims" of mind control experiments, fantasizes a conspiracy and a controlled subjectivity for himself. Likewise, accounts of mind control (in the form, for example, of the hypnotic suggestion, electroshock, and LSD experiments of MK-ULTRA and Project Monarch) and implants (whether at a general level in the form of tracking devices, remote-control chips, and human telemetry devices or more specifically in the neurophone or stimoceiver) unwittingly focus on the permeability of the human brain and on the continued effects of the control even once the subject has realized what has happened. As is the case with conspiracy disinformation narratives, it becomes unclear whether the information about the conspiracy is truly experienced or planted in the subject's mind despite the fact that all "victims" of mind control and implants claim to be "subjects-outside-conspiracy" once they become aware of the implant device or mind control techniques that have been used against them. Mind control and implant conspiracies imply an interface between the subject and the "conspiracy," the result of which is a circular self-reflexive mapping. The subject is mapped by conspiracy only because he or she maps a conspiracy, effectively meaning that subjectivity and conspiracy are conjured into existence at the same moment— a fabulation Jorge Luis Borges would be proud of. The production of conspiracy knowledge becomes self-fulfilling and conspiracy theory begins to look rather like Jameson's postmodern text, which produces not a map of society but a map of itself: conspiracy theory maps neither conspiracy nor society but provides a map of itself and the subjectivity that created it.

In many ways, conspiracy theory offers not a "poor person's cognitive mapping" but a "cyborg's cognitive mapping"—but this may be the only form of "cognitive mapping" available in a multinational global society pervaded by technologies and simulacra. As such, the conspiratorial subject is not a product of conspiracy but a product of the postmodern global society he or she is trying to map through the medium of conspiracy. The conspiratorial subject represents a postmodern self incapable of critical distance, the result of which is a self-reflexive subjectivity that is itself a reproduction of postmodern culture. Subjectivity is exteriorized and made as fluid as the discourses, simulations, and ideologies it tries to map, unsure of whether knowledge is perceived or implanted and unclear where subjectivity ends and where global society begins. Conspiratorial subjectivity is a paradigm of a scattered postmodern and global subjectivity and, as such, conspiracy theory is less a "poor person's cognitive mapping" than a paradigm of "everyone's cognitive mapping" in its attempt to make sense of the confusions of subjectivity in a multinational global society.

NOTES

1. Fredric Jameson, "Cognitive Mapping," in *Marxism and the Interpretation of Culture*, ed. Cary Nelson and Lawrence Grossberg (London: Macmillan, 1988), 356.

2. Jameson's antipathy to conspiracy theory as a form of cognitive mapping also stems from his Marxist insistence on the primacy of economic forces in the creation of social, political, and cultural relations. In *Postmodernism, or, The Cultural Logic of Late Capitalism* (London: Verso, 1991) he states that conspiracy has as its generating principle an overstated view of technology that produces "high-tech paranoia" (38) and a view that forces other than economics produce social relations. Thus, in conspiracy theory, economic forces are either created by a conspiracy or a secret society (as in anti-Semitic Zionist conspiracy theory) or used by the conspiracy for its own ends (as in New World Order conspiracies).

3. Jameson, "Cognitive Mapping," 353.

4. Ibid., 351.

5. Jameson notes that not even apparently omniscient or omnipotent figures such as Hegel, Queen Victoria, or Cecil Rhodes could hold imperialist global realities together. Ibid., 350.

6. Jameson, *Postmodernism*, 51.

7. Jean-François Lyotard, *The Postmodern Condition: A Report on Knowledge*, trans. Geoff Bennington and Brian Massumi (Manchester: Manchester University Press, 1984), 81.

8. Daniel Pipes, for example, writes of the way conspiracist views in post–World War I Germany attributed the loss of the war to "Jews, Freemasons,

socialists, Bolsheviks and others—anyone but the actual leaders of Germany."
Pipes, *Conspiracy: How the Paranoid Style Flourishes and Where It Comes From*
(New York: Free Press, 1997), 136.

9. Fredric Jameson, foreword to Lyotard, *The Postmodern Condition*, xi–xii.

10. Jameson, *Postmodernism*, 53.

11. Jean-François Lyotard, *The Postmodern Explained to Children: Correspondence, 1982–1985*, trans. Julian Pefanis and Morgan Thomas (London: Turnaround, 1992), 42.

12. Ibid., 44.

13. Lyotard, *The Postmodern Condition*, 60–61.

14. For an example of the Knights Templar narrative, which also takes in early Christianity and the Merovingian dynasty, see Michael Baigent, Richard Leigh, and Henry Lincoln, *The Holy Blood and the Holy Grail* (London: Arrow, 1996); for a New World Order narrative, see Texe Marrs, *Project L.U.C.I.D.* (Austin: Living Truth, 1996); for the Fourth Reich in America, see Alex Constantine, *Virtual Government: Mind Control Operations in America* (Portland, OR: Feral House, 1997); and for mind control narratives, see Ron Patton, "Project Monarch: Nazi Mind Control," *Paranoia: The Conspiracy Reader* 4, no. 3 (1996): 2–11.

15. Marrs, frontispiece, *Project L.U.C.I.D.*

16. Lyotard, *The Postmodern Condition*, 76.

17. Charles Jencks, *What Is Post-Modernism?* 3d ed. (New York: St. Martin's, 1989), 44.

18. This is a dominant theme throughout cyberpunk, but notable examples include William Gibson, *Neuromancer* (London: Grafton, 1986); Richard Kadrey, *Metrophage* (New York: Ace, 1988); and Pat Cadigan, *Synners* (London: Grafton, 1991).

19. Philip K. Dick, *The Simulacra* (New York: Ace, 1964), 36–37.

20. Perhaps the best example of this is Dick's novel *The Penultimate Truth* (Harmondsworth: Penguin, 1970), which describes a postapocalyptic world in which an elite class lives a life of luxury on a verdant renewed Earth while the majority of the world's population lives an austere existence underground, believing that World War III is still being fought.

21. According to Jameson

> What the burden of our preceding demonstration suggests, however, is that distance in general (including "critical distance" in particular) has very precisely been abolished in the new space of postmodernism. We are submerged in its henceforth filled and suffused volumes to the point where our new postmodern bodies are bereft of spatial coordinates and practically (let alone theoretically) incapable of distantiation. (*Postmodernism*, 48–49)

22.

This is the result: a space, that of the FM band, is found to be saturated, the stations overlap and mix together (to the point that it no longer communicates at all). Something that was free by virtue of space is no longer. Speech is free perhaps, but I am less free than before: I no longer succeed in knowing what I want, the space is so saturated, the pressure so great from all who want to make themselves heard.

Jean Baudrillard, "The Ecstasy of Communication," in *Postmodern Culture*, ed. Hal Foster (London: Verso, 1985), 131–32.

23. Lyotard, *The Postmodern Condition*, 20–21.

24. Budd Hopkins, *Intruders: The Incredible Visitations at Copley Woods* (New York: Random House, 1987), 70.

25. Adam Parfrey, "Guns, Gold, Groceries, Guts 'n' Gritz," *Cult Rapture* (Portland, OR: Feral House, 1995), 249.

26. Bo Gritz, quoted in Parfrey, *Cult Rapture*, 265.

27. Alex Constantine, *Psychic Dictatorship in the U.S.A.* (Portland, OR: Feral House, 1995), 11. See also Jim Keith, *Mind Control, World Control: The Encyclopedia of Mind Control* (Kempton, IL: Adventures Unlimited, 1997), 151–54 for similar claims about Sirhan Sirhan.

28. Cathy O'Brien and Mark Phillips, *Trance: Formation of America—The True Life Story of a CIA Mind Control Slave* (Nashville: Reality Marketing, 1995).

29. See Constantine, *Psychic Dictatorship*, xii–xiii, 43, for an account of "remote viewing" ideas and for the astonishing claim that it is linked to SDI research and the production of orbiting masers, which will control the minds of the Earth's population.

30. Patton, "Project Monarch," 5.

31. Stephen Bury is the pseudonym for authorial collaborations between Neal Stephenson (whose solo works include *Snow Crash* and *Cryptonomicon*) and J. Frederick George.

32. Stephen Bury, *Interface* (London: Signet, 1997), 340.

3

Agency Panic and the Culture of Conspiracy

Timothy Melley

IMAGINING SOCIAL CONTROL

Conspiracy theory has animated the political culture of the United States from the early Republican period to the present, at times deeply influencing popular opinion. But its influence has never been greater than now. "This is the age of conspiracy," says a character in Don DeLillo's *Running Dog* (1978), "the age of connections, links, secret relationships."[1] By all accounts, this view has become increasingly common in the postwar period. For several decades, cultural critics have observed that "a kind of paranoia has settled over many communities" and that many social groups seem to depend on conspiracy theory for their survival. More recently, major news magazines have described the United States as a nation in the grip of "conspiracy mania" and have pronounced the arrival of a "new paranoid style in the American arts"—although such a style has clearly been flourishing for decades. "The rhythm of conspiracy," notes another, "once background noise, is now a dominant theme of everyday life."[2] Whether the postwar era is really an "age of conspiracy" seems uncertain at best; the important fact is that many people believe it is such an age. Americans now account for all sorts of events—political conflicts, police investigations, juridical proceedings, corporate maneuvers, government activities, and a wide range of other phenomena—through conspiracy theory. Conspiratorial explanations have become a central feature of American political discourse, a way of understanding power that appeals to both marginalized groups and the power elite.

Perhaps not surprisingly, conspiracy theory has also been a fundamental organizing principle in American film, television, and fiction since World War II. Numerous postwar narratives concern characters who are nervous about the ways large, and often vague, organizations might be controlling their lives, influencing their actions, or even constructing their desires. Film and television, from Cold War alien flicks to the highly popular *X-Files*, have so frequently depicted corporate, political, and otherworldly conspiracies that Richard Donner's 1997 film *Conspiracy Theory* seems at once historically emblematic and utterly redundant. Writers such as Kathy Acker, Margaret Atwood, William S. Burroughs, Don DeLillo, Philip K. Dick, Joan Didion, Ralph Ellison, William Gibson, Joseph Heller, Diane Johnson, Ken Kesey, Joseph McElroy, Norman Mailer, Thomas Pynchon, Ishmael Reed, Leslie Marmon Silko, Kurt Vonnegut, and Sol Yurick have all produced narratives in which large governmental, corporate, or social systems appear uncannily to control individual behavior, and in which characters seem paranoid, either to themselves or to other characters in the novel. As Tony Tanner remarked in 1971, "The possible nightmare of being totally controlled by unseen agencies and powers is never far away in contemporary American fiction."[3]

Of course, this nightmare was never absent in earlier moments and may be traced to colonial traditions. But the postwar years have witnessed a dramatic intensification of interest in this view of the world, and an increasing popular acceptance of its central premises. Indeed, concerns about social control have also been the subject of numerous other discourses, from social theory to self-help literature to addiction discourse. A large and influential body of popular sociological writing, for instance—from David Riesman's *Lonely Crowd* (1950) and William Whyte's *Organization Man* (1956) through the Unabomber "Manifesto" (1996)—has lamented both the "decline" of individual self-control and the increasing autonomy of large social structures, especially government and corporate bureaucracies, control technologies, and the media.[4]

One implication of this diverse body of materials is that the seemingly marginal forms of paranoia and conspiracy theory must be understood as symptoms of a larger and more mainstream set of anxieties about human agency. But why has the peculiar form of conspiracy theory become such a popular vehicle for such concerns? As others have noted, the idea of conspiracy offers an odd sort of comfort in an uncertain age: it makes sense of the inexplicable, accounting for complex events in a clear, if frightening, way. By offering a highly adaptable vision of causality, conspiracy theory acts as a "master narrative," a grand scheme capable of explaining complex social events. Most conspiracy theories are virtually impossible to confirm, yet this built-in impediment to certainty is precisely why they have flourished in an age supposedly marked by the disappearance of grand explanatory schemes and master narratives. They require a form of quasi-religious conviction, a sense that the conspiracy in question is an entity with almost supernatural powers. In fact, the term "conspiracy" rarely signifies a small, secret plot any more. Instead, it frequently refers to the workings of a large *organization, technology, or system,* a powerful and obscure entity so dispersed that it is the very antithesis of the traditional conspiracy. "Conspiracy," in other words, has come to signify a broad array of social controls.

The increasing appeal of conspiracy theory is directly linked to this newly expanded definition, which accords the conspiracy broad explanatory power and enormous political utility. In its new form, "conspiracy" can be used to label political enemies who are doing nothing more devious or sinister than their accusers. In the midst of the Korean War, for instance, President Truman could declare that "[t]he Communists in the Kremlin are engaged in a monstrous conspiracy to stamp out freedom all over the world" without also observing that, by such a definition, he was also involved in a "conspiracy" to promote capitalism.[5] At virtually the same moment, the Supreme Court could dramatically toughen its three-decade-old "clear and present danger" test on the grounds that a conspiracy to teach dangerous ideas must not be permitted, even though the "conspiracy" in question was an informal gathering of socialist educators who had neither taken nor advocated any action whatsoever against the state. In its ruling, the Court rejected "the contention that a conspiracy to advocate, as distinguished from the advocacy itself, cannot be constitutionally restrained, because it comprises only the preparation. *It is the existence of the conspiracy which creates the danger.*"[6] In short, the panic-stricken rhetoric of conspiracy has often been sufficient to mobilize support for serious state action, even the significant abridgment of individual freedoms.

But the state has not had a monopoly on the rhetoric of conspiracy. In the United States, that rhetoric has been widely deployed by both disempowered and comparatively privileged groups to imagine the controlling power of private enterprise, of regulatory discourses and systems, of the state itself, or of some complex and bewildering combination of these things. As Fredric Jameson has observed, postwar narratives deploying conspiracy theory and "high-tech paranoia" have provided important representations of global capitalist networks. Conspiracy theory, Jameson remarks, is "a degraded attempt—through the figuration of advanced technology—to think the impossible totality of the contemporary world system," to map networks of power too vast to be adequately represented.[7] In this account, conspiracy theory's oversimplifications stem partly from the sublime objects it attempts to make visible. Instead of being merely a comforting form of misrepresentation, conspiracy theory is a reductive (or "degraded"), but still useful, form of political representation. Jameson's view thus allows room for a defense of some conspiracy theories. Yet it leaves open a number of crucial questions about the conspiracy form itself. Why represent a massive economic system as a conspiracy? Why conserve a sense of *intentionality* when explaining the manipulation of individuals by huge social and economic networks, labyrinthine webs of power?

Some general observations about postwar conspiracy culture point toward a fuller answer to these questions. First, in many conspiracy narratives, conspiracies are understood to be hermetically sealed, marvelously efficient, and virtually undetectable. Second, as Jameson's comments imply, conspiracies allow characters or authors to conceptualize the relation between individuals and larger social bodies. Third, and most important, the conspiracy is often understood as a structure that curtails individuality, or that is antithetical to individualism itself. As the narrator of Don DeLillo's *Running Dog* puts it, "All conspiracies begin with individual self-repression."[8] According to this view, the members of a conspiracy "repress" their own desires and aims for a set of communal goals, a small social compact.

This assumption has a vital, though often ignored, corollary: if conspiracy begins with self-repression, then conspiracy *theory*—the apprehension of conspiracy by those *not* involved in it—begins with individual self-protection, with an attempt to defend the integrity of the self against the social order. To understand one's relation to the social order through conspiracy theory, in other words, is to see oneself in opposition to "society." It is to endorse an all-or-nothing conception of agency, a view in which agency is a property, parceled out *either* to individuals like oneself *or* to "the system," a vague structure often construed to be massive, powerful, and malevolent. This way of thinking is rooted in long-standing Western conceptions of selfhood, particularly those that emphasize the corrupting power of social relations on human uniqueness. As Ralph Waldo Emerson warned some 150 years ago in the classic American account of self *versus* society, "Society everywhere is in conspiracy against the manhood of every one of its members."[9] This familiar sense of individual struggle against a collectivity is essential to contemporary conspiracy theory. One of its problematic effects is to hide the specific political features of the struggle it attempts to represent. Its monolithic conception of "society" (or "system," or "organization") obviates the need to conceptualize particular interests within that collectivity, interests that might be based on class, gender, race, or other factors. Hence the political malleability of conspiracy theory, and the apparent contradictions of figures like the Unabomber, whose professed "ambition" was not only "to kill a scientist, big businessman, government official or the like" but also "to kill a Communist."[10] These facts offer a crucial lesson: by making diverse social and technological systems enemies of "the self," the conspiratorial views function less as a defense of some *clear* political position than as a defense of individualism, abstractly conceived.

It is not surprising that extremely self-defensive postures of this sort are often understood as "paranoid." Clinically paranoid individuals, after all, frequently express a general fear and distrust of their environment. Yet the highly popular conception of self I have just outlined cannot simply be read as a sign of pathology. Indeed, conspiracy narratives would not be on the rise if that self-concept were not broadly popular. Only the continuing appeal of liberalism, and its vision of an autonomous self beleaguered by society, can explain why the controlling "agencies and powers" in postwar narratives are so often "unseen" or elusive, why they so rarely consist of specific conspirators, why they vary from text to text, and why they often look nothing like conspiracies in the traditional sense of the word. The appeal of liberalism also explains why conspiracy narratives have displayed such extraordinary political flexibility—why they have registered concern about such a diversity of social organizations and why they are as appealing to African Americans who wish to explain racial discrimination as they are to white racist groups who believe the United States is under the control of "Zionist Occupied Government" (ZOG) or some other coalition of foreigners and minorities.[11]

The recent surge in conspiracy narratives, in other words, cannot be explained as a response to some *particular* political issue, social organization, or historical event, such as Watergate, or the Kennedy assassination, or even the Cold War. It is better understood as a response to the sense that, to quote one cultural critic, "our specialness—our humanness—has been taking it on the chin a lot lately."[12] It stems largely from a sense of *diminished human agency*, a feeling that individuals cannot effect meaningful social action and, in extreme cases, may not be able to control their own behavior. "At this moment in history," wrote R. D. Laing in 1967, "we are all caught in the hell of frenetic passivity."[13] For Charles Reich, "The American crisis . . . seems clearly to be related to an inability to act."[14] And for Donna Haraway, "Our machines are disturbingly lively, and we ourselves frighteningly inert"—a view, she admits, that once would have seemed "paranoid" though "now we are not so sure."[15] Sentiments like these are related to a widely circulated postwar narrative, a story about how the new "postindustrial" economy has made Americans more generic and less autonomous than their rugged forebears, and how social structures—especially government and corporate bureaucracies, control technologies, and "the media"—have become autonomous agents in their own right.

Despite their widespread appearance in diverse postwar narratives, these anxieties take a remarkably consistent form, which I will refer to as *agency panic*.[16] By agency panic, I mean intense anxiety about an apparent loss of autonomy or self-control—the conviction that one's actions are being controlled by someone else, that one has been "constructed" by powerful external agents. This anxiety is expressed most dramatically in fiction and film, though its underlying view of the world is central to many nonfiction texts as well. In most cases, agency panic has two features. The first is a nervousness or uncertainty about the causes of individual action. This fear sometimes manifests itself in a belief that the world is full of "programmed" or "brainwashed" subjects, addicts, automatons, or "mass-produced" persons, as is the case in Heller's *Catch-22*, Reed's *Mumbo Jumbo*, Kesey's *One Flew over the Cuckoo's Nest*, virtually all of Burroughs's work, much science fiction, and many of the nonfiction texts I have already mentioned. Just as often, the anxiety consists of a character's fear that he or she has been personally manipulated by powerful external controls. Many postwar narratives depict characters who feel they are acting out parts in a script written by someone else, or who believe that their most individuating traits have been somehow produced from without. Margaret Atwood's characters, for example, are forever enacting classically feminine behavior, even though they know it is harmful and undesirable. Some of Pynchon's characters suspect that their sexual responses, among other things, have been determined by a massive espionage program. DeLillo's Lee Harvey Oswald feels that his participation in Kennedy's murder has been planned by powerful forces beyond his control. And in the junked-up world of Burroughs, sadistic government and corporate technologies continually regulate all kinds of human behavior.

In addition to these primary anxieties about individual autonomy, agency panic usually involves a secondary sense that controlling organizations are themselves agents—rational, motivated entities with the will and the means to carry out complex plans. These organizations are sometimes concrete agencies, like DeLillo's CIA or Heller's corporatized Army, but they are just as often more diffuse structures—Pynchon's "Them," Burroughs's "junk virus," Atwood's "men," Reed's "Atonist" culture industry, cyberpunk's autonomous corporations, or even the general "world system" invoked by Jameson and much postwar political rhetoric. In moments of agency panic, individuals tend to attribute to these systems the qualities of motive, agency, and individuality they suspect have been depleted from themselves or others around them. Thus, agency panic not only dramatizes doubt about the efficacy of individual human action; it also induces a *postmodern transference* in which social regulation seems to be the intentional product of a single consciousness or monolithic "will."

Because the convictions I have been describing usually arise without much tangible evidence, they often seem to be the product of paranoia. Yet they are difficult to dismiss as paranoid in the clinical sense of pathologically deluded. As Leo Bersani points out, the self-described "paranoids" of Thomas Pynchon's fiction are "probably justified, and therefore—at least in the traditional sense of the word—really not paranoid at all."[17] Theorists of schizophrenia working against traditional psychological models, from Laing and Gregory Bateson to Gilles Deleuze and Félix Guattari, have shown that pathologizing judgments of such abnormal modes of experience may be products of overidentification with normalizing clinical assumptions. In fact, Laing goes so far as to suggest that schizophrenia can be "a conspiracy" perpetrated *against the schizophrenic* by family and health care workers, who wish to reduce the patient's "full existential and legal status as human agent."[18]

Nonetheless, there is now a wealth of scholarship, following Richard Hofstadter's classic analysis of "the paranoid style in American politics," that continues to view "political" paranoia as an easily diagnosed ailment, something that can be readily dismissed by appeal to a universal authority.[19] What many such accounts refuse to recognize is that conspiracy theory arises out of radical doubt about how knowledge is produced and about the authority of those who produce it. Ironically, by uncritically labeling certain claims "paranoid" and therefore dangerous to society (in general), such accounts miss the most important meaning of conspiracy theory: that it develops from the refusal to accept someone else's definition of a universal social good or an officially sanctioned truth. This is not to say we must open our arms to all manner of conspiracy theories. It is merely to assert that diagnoses of political paranoia are themselves political statements reflecting particular interests. Until we discover some magically unmediated access to reality, conspiracy theory cannot simply be pathologized in one sweeping gesture. Indeed, while many conspiracy theories seem far-fetched, insane, or even dangerous, others seem to be logical responses to technological and social change, to the radical insights of poststructuralism and systems theory, and even to the breathless sociologies of "future shock," "global village," and "postindustrial society."[20]

For these reasons, my intention here is not to assess the validity of particular conspiracy theories, but rather to sketch the cultural significance of such theories and the anxieties from which they stem. Above all, those anxieties indicate a crisis in recent conceptions of personhood and human agency. The importance of agency panic lies in the way it attempts to conserve a long-standing model of personhood—a view of the individual as a rational, motivated agent with a protected interior core of beliefs, desires, and memories. This concept of the liberal individual, which C. B. Macpherson termed "possessive individualism," derives from the liberal political philosophy of Hobbes and Locke, and has long been celebrated in American political culture, particularly in the guise of "rugged individualism" and atomistic "self-reliance."[21] That these forms of individualism have masculine associations helps to explain why so many postwar texts understand social communications as a feminizing force and why narratives of dwindling human autonomy are so often connected, in our culture, to masculinist outbursts of "regeneration through violence" (from John Birch tactics to the work of the Unabomber and contemporary "patriot" groups).[22]

Indeed, the culture of paranoia and conspiracy may be understood as a result of liberal individualism's continuing popularity despite its inability to account for social regulation. Agency panic dramatizes precisely this paradox. It begins in a discovery of social controls that cannot be reconciled with the liberal view of individuals as wholly autonomous and rational entities. For one who refuses to relinquish the assumptions of liberal individualism, such newly revealed forms of regulation frequently seem so unacceptable or unbelievable that they can only be met with anxiety, melodrama, or panic. Agency panic thus reveals the way social communications affect individual identity and agency, but it also *disavows* this revelation. It begins with a radical insight, yet it is a fundamentally conservative response—"conservative" in the sense that it conserves a traditional model of the self in spite of the obvious challenges that postwar technologies of communication and social organization pose to that model. Its widespread appearance on the postwar landscape indicates a broad cultural refusal to modify a concept of self that is no longer wholly accurate or useful, but that still underpins a long-standing cultural fantasy of subjectivity.

This concept of self stands in sharp contrast to poststructural and postmodern theoretical reconceptions of subjectivity, which have exploded the assumptions of liberal individualism, arguing that identity is constructed from without, repeatedly reshaped through performance, and (in extreme accounts) best understood as a schizophrenic and anchorless array of separate components. "Instead of mourning the loss of the self," Gabriele Schwab remarks, poststructural theory "celebrates its end."[23] In the wake of such theories, many cultural critics have emphasized the relation between postmodern narrative and these newly "fragmented" or "decentered" concepts of subjectivity—frequently associating modernism with paranoia and postmodernism with schizophrenia, respectively.[24] But when understood as stark oppositions, such associations are misleading. Texts that are the very emblems of postmodernism invest heavily in paranoia, and rarely seem to *celebrate* the fragmentation of the self. Even the fluid and uncertain subjects of William Burroughs, which have been used to illustrate postmodern "schizophrenia," are products of a fraught attempt to conserve traditional liberal humanist assumptions about the self.[25] Agency panic, then, may be understood as a nervous acknowledgment, and rejection, of postmodern subjectivity. Its appearance in writing commonly considered postmodern is an index of liberalism's continuing appeal in the face of serious theoretical challenges.

Despite the significant problems with some panic-stricken defenses of liberal individualism—which include the encouragement of individual, rather than collective, forms of resistance to social control—I want to stress that agency panic is not simply a misguided or irrational response. In fact, it bears an important likeness to sociological thinking, often illuminating the obscure and powerful sources of social regulation. Yet, paradoxically, it produces quasi-sociological insights by attributing intentionality to the level of the social order. Those possessed by it find hidden communiqués inside generic social messages; they view mass social controls as forms of individual persecution; and they see social and economic patterns as the result of *willful* malevolence. In other words, they unearth forms of human intentionality where a strictly sociological analysis would find only institutions, mores, economic structures, and discourses. Their attempts to trace social effects to an intending subject depends on a form of misrecognition, but one that is difficult to avoid and often quite fruitful. My refusal to make sweeping assessments of conspiracy theory in general, then, stems from the intelligence and political usefulness of some such narratives. But it also stems from theoretical considerations, to which I now turn.

INTERPRETIVE DISORDERS

Because they attempt to unearth hidden forms of control and communication, theories of conspiracy and mass manipulation depend heavily on the interpretation of half-hidden clues, telltale signs, and secret messages. In postwar literature, such procedures are frequently intertwined with explorations of paranoia, which figures prominently in a stunning array of texts. This is not surprising, because paranoia is an interpretive disorder that revolves around questions of control and manipulation. It is often defined as a condition in which one has delusions of grandeur or an unfounded feeling of persecution, or both. Understood less judgmentally, it is a condition in which one's interpretations seem unfounded or abnormal *to an interpretive community*. These descriptions highlight a problem inherent in the definition of paranoia: despite the seemingly obvious marks of extreme (or pathological) paranoia, it is remarkably difficult to separate paranoid interpretation from "normal" interpretive practices. Freud himself repeatedly noted that paranoid interpretations are akin to the very philosophical and psychoanalytic schemes necessary to define and diagnose the disorder. "The delusions of patients," he writes, "appear to me to be the equivalents of the constructions which we build up in the course of analytic treatment."[26] Because of this similarity, cases of paranoia take the form of *interpretive contests* between analyst and patient, each of whom claims to have unearthed the hidden truth about the patient's (apparent) persecution. Consider, for instance, Freud's remarks on the purported homoerotic foundation of paranoia:

> Paranoia is precisely a disorder in which a sexual aetiology is by *no means obvious*; far from this, the strikingly *prominent* features in the causation of paranoia, especially among males, are social humiliations and slights. But *if we go into the matter only a little more deeply*, we shall be able to see that the *really* operative factor . . .[27]

I could have cited many other passages from Freud's work, because going "more deeply" into the "obvious" would serve as a crude definition of psychoanalysis in general. But what is significant in this passage is how much Freud's description of paranoia has in common with paranoia itself. First, both psychoanalysis and paranoia depend on interpretations that move beyond "prominent" or "obvious" factors. Second and consequently, both appeal to the category of the real—to the "really operative factor," foundation, or causal agent for certain events. (As the popular slogan insists, "It's not paranoia if they're *really* out to get you.")

It is this second move that has made the fictional representation of conspiracy and paranoia increasingly popular in a period marked by skepticism about unmediated access to reality. Because diagnoses of paranoia depend on a strong concept of reality—a conviction that the patient's claims do not correspond to events transpiring in a measurable reality—the postmodern tendency to put "the real" in quotation marks has undermined the pathologization of paranoia. As a result, if what is real seems more and more to be a construct, and if the procedures for pathologizing insane interpretations seem increasingly indistinguishable from the procedures of the insane, then paranoia (or "paranoia") becomes an obvious vehicle for writers to use in illustrating the politics of interpretation, normalization, and knowledge production (this despite theories that continue to associate paranoia with modernism and not postmodernism). This problem has underwritten virtually the entire corpus of Philip K. Dick's science fiction, which obsessively depicts characters attempting to assess their own sanity in situations of radical ontological uncertainty. It has also encouraged many postwar writers to represent paranoia as a positive state of mind, an intelligent and fruitful form of suspicion, rather than a psychosis. Pynchon's characters, for instance, often believe that "operational paranoia" and "creative paranoia" can serve as effective forms of resistance to social or political control.[28] Heller's "paranoid" bombardier Yossarian stays alive in part because he believes "everyone" is trying to kill him, a view that seems increasingly sound as *Catch-22* unfolds. The same strategy pays off for many of Margaret Atwood's characters, who learn that their fears of being watched or stalked are a reasonable response to heterosexual relationships. The postwar literature of conspiracy and paranoia, in other words, is driven by a sense that knowledge and power are inextricably linked and that to be "paranoid" may only be to reject the normalizing ideology of the powerful.

Yet, given the political stakes of conspiracy theories, and the violence associated with some forms of political "paranoia," it may seem especially important to be able to say for certain who is paranoid and who is not. One might thus object to my association of psychoanalysis and paranoia because it seems to undermine the grounds for making such decisions. After all, do not severe cases of paranoia, such as Dr. Daniel Paul Schreber's famous "nervous illness," the subject of Freud's major study of paranoia, go well beyond a mere tendency to draw meanings from what is not clearly "prominent" or "obvious" to others? Schreber's apparent *conviction* that certain evils are being perpetrated against him, it might be argued, is quite different from more recent instances of "operational paranoia," which are marked by a self-critical *suspicion* of the world. We might then distinguish between cases where an individual develops a highly rigid and socially unacceptable interpretive scheme (Schreber's complex system of "nerves" and "rays," for instance) and cases where an individual merely feels uncertainty about the agency of apparently meaningful events (as is the case in most of the texts I examine here). This distinction would be of use in isolating cases of the sort that arise frequently in postwar narrative: cases where individuals not only *suspect* an array of invisible determinants to be at work, but also *suspect their own suspicions*. The secondary suspicion seems to indicate the process of a rational, self-effacing, skeptical mind—precisely the opposite of irrational or delusional self-inflation.

This distinction, however, is not as easy to make as it first might seem, because a self-effacing uncertainty is not always absent from more serious or "pathological" cases of paranoia. Louis Sass has convincingly argued that extreme cases of paranoid schizophrenia often result from hypercognitivity and excessive self-reflection. Furthermore, interpretive certainty cannot by itself be a sign of insanity, because even Schreber, who was highly committed to a rigid and unorthodox interpretive scheme, is no more certain of his views than Freud is of his own. In fact, Sass's extraordinary analysis of Schreber's *Memoirs of My Nervous Illness* (1903) demonstrates that the apparently rigid claims of a pathological paranoiac may be, in part, the products of overly rigid interpretation on the part of the analyst (or reader of the *Memoirs*). A more self-effacing reader might begin to wonder, as Sass does, if Schreber's apparently insane claims are not actually the work of a brilliant and complex mind:

> One may be tempted to think that the delusions and near-hallucinations it describes are little more than the almost random products of a state of pure irrationality, perhaps of some kind of near-dementia, or of a delirium in which virtually any random fancy passing before the mind can be extracted and treated as real. Yet . . . one cannot help but wonder whether it is possible to discover a coherent system lying behind it all.[29]

Here, the interpretive drive of the analyst—the desire to find some kind of "coherent system lying behind" what initially seems to be "random fancy"—is structurally analogous to the interpretive drive of the paranoiac, whose disorder is characterized by the tendency to locate coherent motives in what others believe to be "random" or "chance" events. As Sass remarks earlier in his study, "paranoid thinking can be viewed as, in some sense, an almost obvious, logical development—in a world . . . where all events feel interpretable, so that nothing can seem accidental and everything therefore appears to be somehow consciously intended" (61).

If the sense that there are no accidents—that everything is connected, intended, and meaningful—is a hallmark of paranoia, then the difference between a paranoid theory and a brilliant theory may only be a matter of how much explanatory power the theory has for a given interpretive community. And if this is so, then the work of sorting out paranoid claims from justifiable claims—the work of diagnosing, pathologizing, and normalizing—will require a vision at least as penetrating as the one to be judged. Indeed, Sass's desire to match Schreber's own perspicuity seems to be part of what compels him to look for a "coherent system" in Schreber's account, where other analysts have found only "pure irrationality" and "random fancy" (244). Sass even goes on to suggest that Schreber's paranoid system bears a powerful resemblance to sophisticated social theories, such as Foucault's account of panoptic surveillance. Given such resemblances, we might say that the interpretive differences between Freud's account of Schreber and Schreber's account of himself amount to something like a contest between psychoanalysis and sociology—a disciplinary dispute about whether the "really operative factors" in a series of events are best located through study of individuals or analysis of social institutions. Even in the spectacularly delusional case of Schreber, then, serious and intelligent readers disagree about whether Schreber's vision is a profound perception of the social realm or a pure projection of internal material outward. To put the matter in the terms Kathy Acker uses in *Empire of the Senseless* (1988), "Dr. Schreber was paranoid, schizophrenic, hallucinated, deluded, disassociated, autistic, and ambivalent. In these qualities he resembled the current United States President, Ronald Reagan."[30]

This sort of challenge to traditional conceptions of paranoia is a central preoccupation of much postwar writing. One of the reasons stories of paranoia and conspiracy have become so popular recently is that they stage a contest over the reality, or social basis, of a potentially paranoid individual's perceptions. These conflicts have become preoccupations of recent social and cultural theory, because they reveal that "knowledge and power are simply two sides of the same question: who decides what knowledge is, and who knows what needs to be decided?"[31] What is often overlooked in such debates is the degree to which they revolve around issues of agency—questions about *who* or *what* is producing the meaning in a set of signs. Paranoid interpretation, in fact, may be understood as a complex, and often self-defeating, attempt to think sociologically about agency while *simultaneously* retaining a concept of individual action that is at odds with sociological work. It sometimes amounts, then, not only to a self-defensive posture in the face of external controls, but to a fraught and paradoxical defense of liberal individualism itself.

Consider, for instance, Freud's early encounter with the problem we have just been examining, an encounter that occurred in his 1901 study of motive and accident and became pressing as he attempted to make the critical distinction between psychoanalytic and irrational forms of interpretation. When explaining potentially meaningful coincidences, Freud claims that "superstitious" persons behave "just like paranoics," while he, on the other hand, explains coincidence rationally:

> The differences between myself and the superstitious person are two: first, he projects outwards a motivation which I look for within; secondly, he interprets chance as due to an event, while I trace it back to a thought. But what is hidden from him corresponds to what is unconscious for me, and the compulsion not to let chance count as chance but to interpret it is common to both of us.[32]

A strict definition of the boundary between self and world here grounds Freud's distinction between rational and irrational interpretation. While "irrational" interpretations find motive in *external* determinants, psychoanalytic interpretation locates motive and agency *within* the individual.

This would seem to separate psychoanalytic and paranoid approaches rather nicely. Yet it must be noted that the deepest "inside," the unconscious, is in some ways only another kind of "outside"—a region outside conscious control. Locating motive there, in other words, is not *radically* different from locating it in the suprapersonal agencies (or gods) of the superstitious, or in the collective networks (or conspiracies) of the paranoid. Indeed, we might even say that psychoanalysis solves the problem of whether interpretation is overzealous, or paranoid, by relocating motive from the unitary consciousness of an *intending* subject to a shadowy agent (the unconscious) whose deliberations are veiled and not easily subject to interrogation. This "solution" bears a striking resemblance to conspiracy theory. After all, the unconscious, as Freud later theorized it, is not an affective state, but a mental agency or "system."[33] Freud's "discovery of unconscious processes," writes Paul Ricoeur, "invites us to form the idea of 'belonging to a system'"— precisely the idea so terrifying to the conspiracy theorist.[34] The "systems" in both cases, we might add, govern many of our actions, thoughts, and desires, and are frequently described in a rhetoric according them motive, unity, and efficacy. Lest my comparison of these mental and social systems seem far-fetched, it is worth adding that the very same analogy allowed Freud to develop social and historical theories on the basis of his mental model.

The real difference between "irrational" and "rational" interpretation, then, lies not so much in *whether* one believes in uncontrollable determinants or agents as in *where* one locates those determinants—and, thus, in how one conceptualizes the agency of persons. For Freud, human action is governed by a complex of mental systems. Freudian theory, to borrow Ricoeur's words, results in a "wounded Cogito . . . a Cogito that posits itself but *does not possess* itself" (439; my emphasis). This conception of the self reverses the basic presumption of possessive individualism, which identifies self-possession and "freedom from the wills of others" as "the human essence."[35] Freud's model also dispenses with the voluntarist aspects of the liberal self—the idea that rational will is the primary determinant of human action—even as he rejects the paranoid compulsion to interpret "chance" as the work of willful actors. We can in fact hypothesize that paranoia is a defense of—perhaps even a component of—liberal individualism. The paranoid, like the superstitious, cannot dispense with the notion that *intentions* are the supreme cause of events in the world, that coincidences are never simply "accidents." In the words of William S. Burroughs, an open enemy of psychoanalysis and postwar America's high priest of agency panic, "there is no such thing as a coincidence. . . . Nothing happens in this universe . . . unless some entity *wills* it to happen."[36]

Whether such a view is "paranoid" in the sense of "wrong" is hard to say. More clear is its implicit view of the self as an atomistic, rational agent beleaguered by other (often immense) rational agents—a view that the writing of Burroughs, among others, articulates with great frequency. Rather than accepting a view of self-control as divided and *less-than-absolute*, the so-called paranoid stance retains an all-or-nothing concept of agency. And unlike Freud, the paranoiac finds the idea of being dispersed into an ineffable system of control (even if it is only his or her own unconscious) wholly intolerable. Paranoia is therefore not merely an interpretive stance, but part of a discourse about agency. Within that discourse, it often produces compelling insights about social control, yet it also tends to promote forms of hyperindividualism, extraordinary desires to keep free of social controls by seeing the self as its *truest* self when standing in stark opposition to a hostile social order. I now want to offer two distinct, yet equally popular, examples of this sort of thinking from the early Cold War. I offer these texts, in place of more extreme examples, in order to illustrate the popularity and cultural centrality of postwar conspiracy theory's central premises.

THE DEPTH BOYS

In 1957 Vance Packard described a postwar phenomenon he found deeply troubling. "Large-scale efforts," he claimed, are "being made, often with impressive success, to channel our unthinking habits, our purchasing decisions, and our thought processes by the use of insights gleaned from psychiatry and the social sciences."[37] According to Packard, a vast array of "subterranean operations," designed to manipulate the behavior of individuals, had been established by public relations firms, advertisers, "social engineers," and political operatives (8). "Typically," he wrote, "these efforts take place beneath our level of awareness; so that the appeals which move us are often, in a sense, 'hidden.' The result is that many of us are being influenced and manipulated, far more than we realize, in the patterns of our everyday lives" (3).

The notion that a network of agents might be operating "beneath the surface of American life" (9–10) was certainly not original. Nervousness about the supposedly extraordinary powers and dangerous motives of large organizations has long been a feature of U.S. political culture. In Hofstadter's account of it, this paranoid "style" insists that important events are controlled by "a vast and sinister conspiracy, a gigantic and yet subtle machinery of influence set in motion to undermine and destroy a way of life."[38] Of course, Hofstadter associated this "paranoid style" not with the sort of cultural criticism practiced by Packard, but with traditionally "political" texts—that is, documents having to do rather directly with the control of government bodies.

For a more conventional example of the paranoid style from the same period as *The Hidden Persuaders* we might consider J. Edgar Hoover's *Masters of Deceit* (1958), a popular account of communist infiltration. "The communist," Hoover warns, "is in the market places of America: in organizations, on street corners, even at your front door. He is trying to influence and control your thoughts."[39] Like Senator Joseph McCarthy and other practitioners of "paranoid" Cold War politics,

Hoover regards communism as a veiled "plot" (81), a revolutionary "conspiracy" (53) with extraordinary powers.[40] It is "virtually invisible to the non-communist eye, unhampered by time, distance and legality" (81). Significantly, these extraordinary powers seem to lie less in the conspirators themselves than in their massive and half-hidden "thought-control net" (93). Despite the rhetoric of conspiracy, in other words, the real threat is not so much a specific agent or group as *a system of communications*, an organized array of ideas, discourses, and techniques.

In all of these regards, Hoover's account is remarkably similar to Packard's, which also posits a large and powerful program designed to manipulate unwitting Americans. Yet there is a striking political difference between the two texts, and this difference makes their structural resemblance all the more odd: Packard's book exposes a dangerous facet of corporate *capitalism*, while Hoover's hopes to foil *communist* activity. The question, then, is why these accounts of national crisis look so similar when they seem to be at ideological cross-purposes.[41] One possible answer, a familiar one, is that they are part of a "paranoid" tradition transcending particular ideologies and historical conditions. But the notion of a transhistorical paranoid style does not by itself explain why such politically different projects might find a strategic advantage in the notion of conspiracy. Nor does it account for the specific historical conditions that may have shaped these postwar accounts. Even Hofstadter, who traces political paranoia back to colonial America, notes that the nature of paranoid politics is different after World War II, focused on domestic rather than foreign threats and especially concerned about "the effects of the mass media."[42]

These are significant changes, plainly visible in the texts at hand and striking in their consequences. In the first place, they crack open the notion of the paranoid style, making room for texts like Packard's, which is not a traditional "political" document but which nonetheless detects a "gigantic yet subtle machinery of influence" at work in American mass culture. More important, changes in postwar "paranoid politics" indicate an important shift in popular conceptions of political power. After all, to suggest that *conspiracies* are perpetrated through the mass media is to rethink the very nature of conspiracy, which would no longer depend wholly on private messages, but rather on mass communications, messages to which anyone might be privy. This new model of "conspiracy" no longer simply suggests that dangerous agents are *secretly* plotting against us from some remote location. On the contrary, it implies, rather dramatically, that whole populations are being *openly* manipulated without their knowledge. For mass control to be exercised in this manner, persons must be significantly less autonomous than popular American notions of individualism would suggest. The postwar model of conspiracy, in other words, is dependent on a notion of diminished human agency. And it is *this* concept that makes *The Hidden Persuaders* and *Masters of Deceit* so much alike, despite their distinct ideological underpinnings. Like so many other postwar narratives, both are deeply invested in a traditional concept of individual autonomy and uniqueness, and both reveal this investment through expressions of nervousness about its viability.

One index of this shared anxiety is that Hoover and Packard each posit a secret effort whose real goal is the mass re-engineering of persons. Hoover, for instance, insists that the Communist Party is "a vast workshop where the member is polished and shined, his impurities melted out" (159). The rhetoric of such passages connects communist indoctrination to deindividuation, simultaneously implying that capitalism guarantees human freedom and uniqueness. What is most frightening about communist training, in Hoover's view, is that it seeks to remove *all* "undigested lumps of independence" (163). The "communist thought-control machine" (188) is designed to refashion "renegades" and "deviationists" (185) through a program of "ruthless uniformity" (172). The hypocrisy of this view is rather stunning, since Hoover devotes his book (and devoted his career) to rooting out deviants in order to conserve the ruthless uniformity of *American* politics.[43]

My intention here, however, is not to critique the familiar illogic of Cold War anticommunism. It is rather to show how that illogic governs the impulse toward conspiracy theory. Hoover's unwillingness to consider anything like *capitalist* "thought control"—that is, his failure to portray both communism and capitalism as ideologies—is central to his conspiratorial view of communist training. Because he refuses to see capitalist training as training, he views communist training as a *secret* and *total* means of social control. How else can we account for the fact that, when Hoover reveals the deep secret of communist thought control, it turns out to be nothing more sinister than education? The Communist Party, Hoover explains, is "an educational institution. . . . One of the first things a new member does is to go to a school" (160). Of course, for Hoover, this is no ordinary school; through its diabolical curriculum, the originally autonomous individual "is made into *communist man*" (159). What allows Hoover to present this little tale of education in the form of a horror story is his assumption that education in a capitalist society, by contrast, is not ideologically shaped and does not construct individuals by its own mechanisms of "thought control." The ironic corollary to this view is not simply that it borrows (and hugely simplifies) an account of ideology from Marxism, but that it undercuts its own premises. If Americans are defined by their extraordinary individual autonomy, then why do they need powerful government protections from communism? The answer can only be that autonomy is precisely what they *lack*, since they are easily turned into "brainwashed" communist dupes. It turns out that for all their putative individuality, Hoover's Americans are deeply susceptible to ideological controls.

The same problem of agency haunts *The Hidden Persuaders*, which asserts that scientists have discovered secret new ways to manipulate human desire. According to Packard, these motivational researchers—"known in the trade as 'the depth boys'" (8)—exploit a model of personhood derived from psychoanalysis, employing special "triggers of action" and "conditioned reflexes" (24) to control components "deep" inside persons. They use packaging and display techniques to induce a "hypnoidal trance" in shoppers, causing them to "[pluck] things off the selves at random" and buy more than they can afford (107); they use "subthreshold effects" (subliminal messages) that might someday make "political indoctrination . . . possible without the subject being conscious of any influence being brought to bear on him" (43); and, in the words of one public relations expert, they are involved in "the most important social engineering role of them all—the gradual reorganization of human society, piece by piece and structure by structure" (217). While Packard suggests that most of these depth experts only "want to control us just a little bit" (240), he speculates that their work may lead to practices like "biocontrol," in which "a surgeon would equip each child with a socket mounted under the scalp" so that "subjects would never be permitted to think as individuals" (239–40).

For Packard, this lurid fantasy—in which "electronics could take over the control of unruly humans" (239)—reveals the real threat of motivational research: it is a technology for the radical reconstruction of persons. Even motivational researchers themselves, in Packard's view, are "custom-built men," barely separable from the "sample humans" on whom they perform manipulation experiments: each trade school "socially engineers" them to be more compatible with corporate needs (5-6). Such assumptions generate a problem of control much like the one implicit in Hoover's argument. If even the agents of persuasion have been constructed, then who governs the system of depth manipulation? Indeed, if we carry Packard's view to its logical extreme, the very idea of manipulation, in the sense of a *willful* attempt to control others, becomes obsolete, since attempts at manipulation are themselves only products of previous manipulation. In Packard's world, the system of depth manipulation is self-regulating. Control has been transferred from human agents to larger agencies, institutions, or corporate structures.

This way of understanding social control is certainly not new. Social theory has frequently relied on the notion of structural agency, often linking it to the problem of ideology. We might even say that Packard and Hoover have begun to formulate crude theories of ideology—crude not because they are wholly mistaken (advertisers *do* try to manipulate us and communists *do* train new recruits), but because they view social control as a mysterious and magical process, activated instantaneously and capable of utterly disabling rational self-control. The concepts of thought control and depth manipulation provide theories of social conditioning not by accounting for the complex effects of numerous institutions, discourses, rules, and agents, but rather by reducing those effects into a simple mechanism, a "trigger of action" that almost instantaneously converts people into automatons. In other words, Packard and Hoover both attempt to describe a *structural* form of causality while simultaneously retaining the idea of a malevolent, centralized, and *intentional* program of mass control.

This odd conjunction of the intentional and the structural is the essence of agency panic, the motive force of postwar conspiracy culture. It stems from a paradoxical desire to conserve one of the central fantasies of liberalism—the notion that Eve Sedgwick has called "pure voluntarity," an absolute freedom from social control.[44] But in the postwar period this fantasy has come under considerable stress, and the postwar rhetoric of diminished individual agency has often registered this stress with a sense of shock or surprise. Texts from the last half of the twentieth century are replete with the frightening "discovery" that human behavior can be regulated by social messages and communications. What is striking about such texts is their concomitant assumption that, once revealed, social controls should be so ubiquitous, so effective, so *total*. It is this all-or-nothing conception of agency that in turn feeds the imaginative projection of the liberal self—with all its rationality, autonomy, and self-enclosure—onto the level of the social order, onto the very bureaucracies, information-processing systems, communication networks, and institutions that seemed so threatening in the first place. The most significant cultural function of these texts has been to sustain an increasingly embattled notion of individualism. Conspiracy theory, paranoia, and anxiety about human agency, in other words, are all part of the paradox in which a supposedly individualist culture conserves its individualism by continually imagining it to be in imminent peril.[45]

NOTES

Adapted by permission of Cornell University Press from *Empire of Conspiracy: The Culture of Paranoia in Postwar America* by Timothy Melley. Copyright © 2000 by Cornell University.

1. Don DeLillo, *Running Dog* (New York: Knopf, 1978), 111.

2. Alvin Toffler, *The Third Wave* (New York: William Morrow, 1980), 347; Rick Marin and T. Trent Gegax, "Conspiracy Mania Feeds Our Growing National Paranoia," *Newsweek*, 30 December 1996, 64–71; Michiko Kakutani, "Bound by Suspicion," *New York Times Magazine*, 19 January 1997, 16; Bob Hoover, "Conspiracy Theories Are Sign of the Times," *Toledo Magazine*, 24 March 1996, A1.

3. Tony Tanner, *City of Words* (London: Jonathan Cape, 1971), 15. See also Patrick O'Donnell, *Latent Destinies: Cultural Paranoia in Contemporary U.S. Narrative* (Durham: Duke University Press, 2000); and Mark Fenster, *Conspiracy Theories: Secrecy and Power in American Culture* (Minneapolis: University of Minnesota Press, 1999). The tendency I am commenting on is obviously not exclusive to the United States. Yet the nation's historic embrace of liberal individualism, its relatively uniform political culture, and its lack of feudal and revolutionary traditions have created an especially fertile climate for conspiracy theory.

4. For a more thorough discussion of this range of fiction, film, and nonfiction, see Timothy Melley, *Empire of Conspiracy: The Culture of Paranoia in Postwar America* (Ithaca: Cornell University Press, 2000).

5. Harry Truman, "The Recall of General Douglas MacArthur (Department of State Bulletin, 16 April 1951)," in *Documents of American History*, ed. Henry Steele Commager, 8th ed., vol. 2 (New York: Appleton-Century-Crofts, 1968), 568.

6. *Dennis v. United States*, 341 US 494 (1951), 564; my emphasis.

7. Fredric Jameson, *Postmodernism, or, The Cultural Logic of Late Capitalism* (Durham: Duke University Press, 1991), 38.

8. DeLillo, *Running Dog*, 183.

9. Ralph Waldo Emerson, "Self-Reliance" (1841), in *Essays and Lectures*, ed. Joel Porte (New York: Library of America, 1983), 261.

10. Theodore Kaczynski quoted in David Johnston, "In Unabomber's Own Words, a Chilling Account of Murder," *New York Times*, 29 April 1998, A16. In May 1998 Theodore Kaczynski was sentenced for what the FBI dubbed the "Unabom" crimes, a series of mail bombings against industrialists and scientists.

11. In *I Heard It through the Grapevine: Rumor in African-American Culture* (Berkeley: University of California Press, 1993), Patricia Turner has documented the importance of conspiracy discourse in African American communities. Comparable tales circulate in a range of communities. See Robert Singh, *The Farrakhan Phenomenon: Race, Reaction, and the Paranoid Style in American Politics* (Washington, DC: Georgetown University Press, 1997); and Daniel Pipes, *Conspiracy: How the Paranoid Style Flourishes and Where It Comes From* (New York: Free Press, 1997). For a prominent example of white supremacist conspiracy fiction, see Andrew Macdonald [William Pierce], *The Turner Diaries*, 2d ed. (Hillsborough, WV: National Vanguard Books, 1980).

12. Charles Siebert in "Forum: Our Machines, Ourselves," moderated by Jack Hitt, *Harper's*, May 1997, 45–54.

13. R. D. Laing, *The Politics of Experience* (New York: Ballantine, 1967), 51.

14. Charles Reich, *The Greening of America* (New York: Bantam, 1970), 10.

15. Donna Haraway, "A Cyborg Manifesto: Science, Technology, and Socialist-Feminism in the Late Twentieth Century," in *Simians, Cyborgs, and Women: The Reinvention of Nature* (New York: Routledge, 1991), 152.

16. My explanation of this response is indebted to Mark Seltzer's *Bodies and Machines* (New York: Routledge, 1992), esp. 17–21, 84, 155–56.

17. Leo Bersani, "Pynchon, Paranoia, and Literature," *Representations* 25 (1989): 101.

18. Laing, *Politics of Experience*, 84.

19. Richard Hofstadter, *The Paranoid Style in American Politics and Other Essays* (New York: Knopf, 1965). For Pipes, "*conspiracy theory* is the fear of a nonexistent conspiracy. *Conspiracy* refers to an act, *conspiracy theory* to a perception" (21). By this absurd definition, conspiracy theories are always wrong and thus no actual conspiracy could ever be theorized—except by a paranoiac. While Robert Robins and Jerrold Post note the "contextual nature of what is paranoid," they never pursue their occasional observations about the difficulty of diagnosing paranoia, instead presuming they have unmediated access to the truth. *Political Paranoia: The Psychopolitics of Hatred* (New Haven: Yale University Press, 1997). Tellingly, their example of incorrectly

diagnosed paranoids is a group of Soviet dissidents wrongly jailed for anti-communist views.

20. Alvin Toffler, *Future Shock* (New York: Random House, 1970); Marshall McLuhan, *Understanding Media: The Extensions of Man* (New York: McGraw-Hill, 1964); Daniel Bell, *The Coming of Post-Industrial Society: A Venture in Social Forecasting* (New York: Basic Books, 1973).

21. C. B. Macpherson, *The Political Theory of Possessive Individualism: Hobbes to Locke* (Oxford: Oxford University Press, 1962).

22. See Richard Slotkin, *Regeneration through Violence: The Mythology of the American Frontier, 1600–1860* (Middletown, CT: Wesleyan University Press, 1973). For an account of contemporary patriot groups, see Kenneth Stern, *A Force upon the Plain* (New York: Simon and Schuster, 1997).

23. Gabriele Schwab, *Subjects without Selves: Transitional Texts in Modern Fiction* (Cambridge: Harvard University Press, 1994), 5.

24. In his early list of schematic differences between modernism and postmodernism, Ihab Hassan associates paranoia with modernism and schizophrenia with postmodernism. "The Culture of Postmodernism," *Theory, Culture, and Society* 2 (1985): 123–24. Jameson and David Harvey have also accepted such associations without an explanation of why paranoia has been so dramatically present in postmodern narratives. See Jameson, *Postmodernism*, 26–34, 345, 375; and Harvey, *The Condition of Postmodernity: An Enquiry into the Origins of Cultural Change* (Oxford: Basil Blackwell, 1989), 43, 53. If I were to situate my argument in these psychoanalytic terms, I would say that the threat of "schizophrenic" dissolution provokes "paranoid" attempts to defend the integrity of the self in postmodern narrative.

25. For a detailed defense of this assertion, see Melley, *Empire of Conspiracy*, 161–84.

26. Sigmund Freud, "Constructions in Analysis" (1937), in *The Standard Edition of the Complete Psychological Works of Sigmund Freud*, ed. and trans. James Strachey (London: Hogarth, 1953–74), 23: 268. See also "Psycho-Analytic Notes on an Autobiographical Account of a Case of Paranoia (Dementia Paranoides)," *Standard Edition*, 12: 79; "Preface to Reik's 'Ritual: Psycho-Analytic Studies,'" *Standard Edition*, 17: 261; and "On Narcissism: An Introduction," *Standard Edition*, 14: 96.

27. Freud, "Psycho-Analytic Notes," 60; emphases added.

28. Thomas Pynchon, *Gravity's Rainbow* (New York: Viking, 1973), 25, 638.

29. Louis A. Sass, *Madness and Modernism: Insanity in the Light of Modern Art, Literature, and Thought* (New York: Basic Books, 1992), 244. Further references cited in the body of the text.

30. Kathy Acker, *Empire of the Senseless* (New York: Grove, 1988), 45.

31. Jean-François Lyotard, *The Postmodern Condition: A Report on Knowledge*, trans. Geoff Bennington and Brian Massumi (Minneapolis: University of Minnesota Press, 1984), 8–9.

32. Sigmund Freud, *The Psychopathology of Everyday Life* (1904), *Standard Edition*, 6: 259, 257–58.

33. Sigmund Freud, "The Unconscious" (1915), *Standard Edition*, 14: 172.

34. Paul Ricoeur, *Freud and Philosophy: An Essay on Interpretation*, trans. Dennis Savage (New Haven: Yale University Press, 1970), 119. Further references are cited in the body of the text.

35. Macpherson, *Political Theory of Possessive Individualism*, 3.

36. William S. Burroughs, "On Coincidence," in *The Adding Machine: Selected Essays* (New York: Arcade, 1985), 99, 101.

37. Vance Packard, *The Hidden Persuaders* (New York: David McKay, 1957), 3. Further references are cited in the body of the text.

38. Hofstadter, *Paranoid Style*, 29.

39. J. Edgar Hoover, *Masters of Deceit: The Story of Communism in America and How to Fight It* (New York: Henry Holt, 1958), 191. Further references are cited in the body of the text.

40. For McCarthy, communism is "a conspiracy on a scale so immense as to dwarf any previous such venture in the history of man." *America's Retreat from Victory: The Story of George Catlett Marshall* (New York: Devin-Adair, 1951), 169. For other postwar instances, see Hofstadter, *Paranoid Style*.

41. I am not suggesting that Packard is offering a radical leftist critique. Indeed, he embraces the same liberal values that drive anticommunist thought. Nonetheless, the political implications of Packard's account are strikingly different from those of Hoover's.

42. Hofstadter, *Paranoid Style*, 24. Hofstadter underestimates the importance of these historical changes because, like many other analysts, he views it as a transhistorical phenomenon.

43. Hoover knows that "communists quickly accuse anybody who disagrees with them of being guilty of thought control" (81–82), but he is unconscious of the way his own actions mirror or double those of his enemies. While he critiques communists for promulgating instructions, for inculcating loyalty, and for operating in secret, he does all of these things himself, even offering "spy-hunting" instructions.

44. Eve Kosofsky Sedgwick, "Epidemics of the Will," in *Incorporations*, ed. Jonathan Crary and Sanford Kwinter (New York: Zone, 1992), 582–95.

45. See Louis Hartz, *The Liberal Tradition in America: An Interpretation of American Political Thought since the Revolution* (New York: Harcourt, Brace and World, 1955). By "supposedly individualist," I refer to what Hartz called the United States' "irrational Lockianism" (11)—its paradoxically conformist stance to individualism (63) and its "aversion to systematic social thought" (307).

ALIEN NATION

4

If Anything Is Possible

Jodi Dean

STRESSING DOUBTS

Leah Haley first used hypnosis to explore the possibility that she had been abducted by aliens in March 1991. By the summer of 1996 she had gone public, attending the annual meeting of the Mutual UFO Network (MUFON) and autographing a book recounting her abductions and the conspiracy to keep her quiet. At the meeting, I overheard some conference participants whispering that Haley was in a saucer when the government shot it down.

Haley describes the alien and governmental interventions in her life in *Lost Was the Key*.[1] Her world "started to crumble" in July 1990, when her brother told her about a book by UFO researcher Budd Hopkins. During their conversation, Haley tells her brother about dreaming of being in a spaceship surrounded by little creatures with large black eyes. Her brother mentions that a woman in Hopkins's book, *Intruders*, had a place in her yard where the grass wouldn't grow. Haley says that the yard of her previous home had a similar spot. Drawing from Hopkins, Haley's brother asks her if she'd ever had any strange illnesses. She answers that around the time of the spaceship dream she went to the hospital for tests because of pain and burning in her kidneys, bladder, and urinary tract. Haley explains, "The doctor couldn't find anything wrong, so he told me my problem must be caused by stress. Several months later, I concluded by trial and error that spicy food was causing the problem."[2] She also mentions pain in her ear. She attributes it to an allergy to copy-machine ink. When her brother asks whether the doctor agreed, Haley replies that he didn't, adding, "The doctor couldn't find anything at all wrong with me, so he said it must be stress. Doctors are such jerks. Why can't they admit they don't know what the problem is instead of telling people it's just stress?"[3] Haley and her brother talk about seeing a UFO as children.

After this weekend, Haley considers writing to Budd Hopkins in New York. Unsatisfied by the doctor's diagnosis, unsettled by the nagging sense that something remains to be explained, she's tempted to look elsewhere, beyond the answers of science. But she puts it off, not yet ready to venture outside the comforting fantasy of reality. Her explanation for waiting contributes to the impression that she finds, or wants to find, the whole thing "nonsense." She insists her dream was just a dream, although she isn't completely sure. What is available to her as a real explanation, as an explanation of the real, is less and less comforting. Still, she covers over her doubt, at the same time inviting a nod of recognition from readers who have heard this story before, readers who know where doubt might lead.

For most abductees, acknowledging alien interference in their lives is painful and time-consuming. They are plagued by uncertainty. Their books are offered as testimonies to their experience. In painstaking detail, they document the fleeting, ambiguous evidence of abduction, the process of becoming abductees, of coming to think about their lives, experiences, and memories in ways most of them would have dismissed or laughed at had it not happened to them. Abductee Anna Jamerson writes,

> I accept and reject their existence daily. I can believe in them when I know I have been abducted the night before, but that only lasts for a few weeks. When they become inactive for a month or so, I'm sure I made all this stuff up. I go back to denying that they are really abducting me. . . . Beth calls it my denial phase. I go through it continuously it seems.[4]

For most abductees the struggle over the real is interminable, ceaseless, an entangled process of tracing and retracing signs and events, all the while knowing that certainty will hover just out of reach.

At the same time, certain pleasures accompany abductees' break with conventional reality. Not only do they find themselves in the thick of conspiracies of global political significance, not only are they now important, historical figures, personages of worth and impact, but they are no longer duped by "the system." The trauma of their break with consensus reality, in other words, is accompanied by the pleasures of knowing that things are not as they seem. Their enjoyment arises out of this alien knowledge's uncertainty and fragility; they know something the rest of us do not. They know that the reality that the rest of us take for granted is virtual, a screen for more complex processes and machinations, the comprehension of which remains just beyond our reach. Like most of the conspiratorially minded, abductees don't know exactly how these processes work, who is behind them, and what it all means. And they can't do much to stop their abductions (or those of the rest of us), besides work on attitude, awareness, and possibly acceptance. So they navigate the entangled paths between knowledge and doubt, enjoying the excesses of evidence, significance, interpretation, and meaning possible in conspiracy's networks.

Haley eventually contacts Hopkins, who recommends that she consult with John Carpenter, a licensed clinical social worker from Springfield, Missouri. Carpenter has hypnotized or counseled over a hundred people who suspect that they've been abducted. At first, Haley talks and Carpenter listens. Haley describes the time she and her brother saw the UFO. She relates the dream about being in a spaceship and the allergy to copy-machine ink. She mentions problems with the security system in her home, anxieties stemming from headlights reflected in her rearview mirror, and noises seemingly coming from her game room. Haley documents the inexplicable unsettling her everyday life. She recalls an uneasy time when she saw two men in a restaurant, men she thought were watching her. She tells of a strange young man in her office who she feared would rape her.

In the first hypnosis session, Haley recovers the details of her childhood sighting. Searching in the woods for the UFO, which appeared to have landed, she comes across a hairless, chalky-colored creature with large black eyes. A beam of bright light approaches her. She sees a round, silver object hovering in the clearing. Lying on a platform aboard the craft, she discovers that she is naked, that additional creatures surround her, that they are poking her arms and legs with a needle-like instrument. During her second session, Haley remembers a night when her teenage daughters were toddlers. Having felt an urge to go outside, she finds herself standing in the middle of the yard, looking at a spaceship and a beam of light. On the spaceship creatures perform "gynecological procedures" on her and "lab tests." She feels a piercing sensation as if something were being inserted behind and inside her right ear.

Later she watches videotapes of two women who retrieve abduction experiences through hypnosis. Haley explains, "I sensed that John wanted me to see the videotapes so I would accept the reality of the abduction experiences and admit that I had indeed been hypnotized."[5] Her doubt thus pervades the procedures as well as the content of her recollections. Uncertain about the reality of spaceships and lab tests, she understands that the videos are meant as independent verification, that sameness is supposed to guarantee reality. At that same time she acknowledges her sense of Carpenter's desire, that he wanted her to admit that she had been hypnotized, she forestalls questions about her own: why would she want to act as if she had been hypnotized?

COLLIDING CERTAINTIES

The overwhelming, undermining, all-pervasive uncertainty that Haley recounts expresses a suspicion many share as the global networks of the information age become increasingly vivid, entangled, and ever-present. George Marcus emphasizes two components of contemporary life that ready it for the installation of conspiracy: the mentality of the Cold War and the crisis of representation often denoted as the postmodern.[6] I agree, but with a different emphasis. Thinking conspiratorially is compelling, attractive, and unavoidable because of the networked possibilities of technoculture, possibilities that provoke collisions between the modern and the postmodern or that inaugurate confrontations between drives to fundamentalization and drives to pluralization within the postmodern.[7] Like conspiracy theorists, we're imbricated in evidence and suspicion. We're entangled in a world of uncertainties, a world where more information is available, and hence, a world where we face daily the fact that our truths, diagnoses, and understandings are incomplete—click on one more link, check out one more newscast, get just one more expert opinion (and then, perhaps, venture into the fringe; after all, some HMOs cover alternative remedies). Without reliable portals, trustworthy authorities, the gigabytes of information flow into streams of doubts and details that we quantify without comprehending. I think of this vast terrain of interfacial media, doubt, information, and possibility as cyberia.[8]

Cyberia's uncertainties offer more than anxiety and doubt. They have a variety of pleasures all their own. Excessive information and its merchandising make us feel part of things, in the know. We can be up-to-the-minute, bleeding edge, members of the inner circle, the now-crowd. We have the sense that we can know what happens, when it happens. Embedded in infotainment, we're in the thick of, if not history, then at least the event: we enjoy criticizing the hype *and* buying the T-shirt. A prominent refrain: "I'm not a conspiracy theorist, but . . ." More-over, suspicion lets us imagine that we haven't been co-opted: we know that commercials make us want things, that politicians lie, that corpo-rations pay for scientific studies. Drawing from Lacan, Slavoj Žižek de-scribes this sense as that of the fool who "publicly displays the lie of the existing order, but in a way which suspends the performative efficiency of his speech."[9] The suspicion that gives us that feeling of being in the know, in other words, may well supplement the ideological hold of the existing order. I know that politicians lie, but what's the alternative? I know that George Lucas heavily orchestrated all the publicity around *The Phantom Menace*, but I still purchase the Darth Maul action figure, Anakin Skywalker backpack, pod-racer Micro-machines.

In addition to the anxieties and pleasures of cyberia's perpetually incomplete information, we also confront the convictions and beliefs of those who strike us as so unfathomably *wrong* that it's really too much to bear. To be sure, the mistaken and the different have always been there. But because of the interconnections made possible through global media and networked communications technologies, ignoring them and the strangeness of their ways of thinking is harder than it was be-fore. Transnational communication, configured through American con-sumer entertainment media, forces multiple linkages and previously unimaginable connections.[10] What happens when those initiated into the mysteries of faith healing, cabala, and quantum mechanics become imbricated into a cell-phoned, surveilled, and digitalized suburbia?[11] The sense that anything might be possible haunts the interface of na-tional and global, modern and postmodern power formations. It is an uneasy sense of the links that have not yet been made, a sense expressed as conspiracy theory.

Abductees' reports, their experiences, the contradictory, paranoid, fantastic, fragmented, overlapping, interconnecting, alien content they provide, enact modes of being human in a technological, televisual, vir-tual earth. Indeed, alien abduction is a thematic that brings into sharp relief the tensions at the national/global interface. If a key issue for the nation is the certain establishment of who "we" are, then this question is virtually unanswerable in global technoculture. The alien presence evokes not a unified planet or global human species, but an amalgam of conspiracy, accusation, fear, violence, and doubt. An abductee told me that he had good reason to suspect that Harry Truman, when faced with the alien invasion, had divided up the American people into the protected and productive straight white middle class and the abductable racial and sexual minorities. That "we" are simply "all of us" is belied by the suspicious uncertainties connoting that extraterrestrial perspective capable of grasping, clutching, the global. The strange familiarities of everyday life tell us that interconnection doesn't guarantee a "we." "We" may all be connected, but such connections are fraught with dangers. How can we imagine the global other than through the webs of anxiety that carry destructive viruses, voracious creditors, and unredeemable claims?

Abduction narratives suggest a subject position more of us more frequently are forced to occupy, a position not quite that of the paranoid, a position more akin to that of the conspiracy theorist, the thinker who looks for secrets, making links and sifting through evidence.[12] That abduction accesses cyberia's stresses and excesses doesn't get to the truth of abduction (as if getting to the truth were still a possibility). But it does suggest why the alien icon of conspiratorial secrets hovers in the pathways and on the screens of American popular culture. Aliens are icons for the dilemma of truth in the information age, the age of networked doubts and possibilities. Clicking on this icon, indeed, most any icon, positions us as subjects of conspiracy. We want to find the truth, discover the secret. The link makes—and withholds—the promise that all will be revealed. As I've argued elsewhere, abduction reports, alien stories fabricated in the context of a postwar American articulation of NASA space, communications technology, and invasive, image-preoccupied government, express contemporary tensions around truth and trust.[13] That their eerie uncertainties half-resemble the doubts haunting global technoculture, that their insatiable drive for evidence links to the dynamics of the information economy suggests that conspiracy theory, despite efforts to push it to the margins, may well be the dominant mode of thinking today.[14]

Reality is at issue in cyberia. "Events and phenomena call to us as haunting specters lodged somewhere within the endless proliferation of images and reports," Kathleen Stewart writes: "the more you know, the less you know."[15] We don't know who to trust, what to believe. "We" can't even serve comfortably as a grammatical subject. Movie stills reappear as illustrations in magazine articles that purport to be factual. A graphic produced for a Web site becomes evidence in print media for the reality of that which it depicts. A prop for a film becomes an exhibit in a museum and subject to autopsy. That a person has appeared on television is evidence of sincerity and importance. In Stewart's words, "The Internet was made for conspiracy theory: it *is* a conspiracy theory: one thing leads to another, always another link leading you deeper into no thing and no place . . ."[16] Information circulates through and interconnects nearly all commercially available media— books, magazines, television, video, movies, newspapers, tabloids, tapes, and the Internet—and each cross-references and legitimizes the other, resisting integration into a whole, rejecting the delusion of totality. That cultural practices intersect and reinforce each other isn't itself new—but cyberia's degree of saturation is.[17]

Conspiracy theory is a mutating, morphing informational assemblage. Its vectors, valences, and valuations are inconstant; they signify differently at specific times, in specific places. At the interface of the postindustrial and information ages, conspiracy's articulation of lines of power and possibilities for agency via the publicity/secrecy portal is routed through doubt, detail, and the presumption of interconnection. These, then, are the themes I take up in the remainder of this essay.

MANAGING EVERYTHING

Some theorists of conspiracy thinking suspect that it promulgates totalizing, absolutist theories. Richard Hofstadter, whose essay on paranoid style has influenced interpretations of conspiracy since the 1960s, criticizes conspiracy theory for its overwhelming coherence: "it leaves no room for mistakes, failures, or ambiguities. . . . it believes that it is up against an enemy who is as infallibly rational as he is totally evil, and it seeks to match his imputed total competence with its own, leaving nothing unexplained and comprehending all of reality in one overreaching consistent theory."[18] Mark Fenster, although critical of Hofstadter, nonetheless agrees that a primary characteristic of conspiracy theory is its "desire to find, understand, and represent the totality of social relations."[19] Fenster sees conspiracy theory as "one of the few socially symbolic attempts in contemporary culture to confront and represent totality."[20] Žižek concurs that today "the only way to achieve a kind of global 'cognitive mapping' is through the paranoiac narrative of a 'conspiracy theory.'"[21] Even Stewart can't let go of the notion that thinking conspiratorially is premised on a conviction that the Big Picture is available: "Who can tell the truth from the mistake, the inaccuracy, the flight of fancy, the lie, the cover-up, the manipulation, the disinformation? The paranoid can—that's the point of conspiracy theory."[22]

I read conspiracy theory differently, especially in the context of the networked media of the information age. For even if once upon a time conspiracy theorists offered totalizing systems mapping the hidden machinations of Illuminati, Freemasons, Bilderburgers, and Trilateralists (and, in fact, I don't think they ever did but won't argue the point here), the defining feature of the conspiratorial haunting of the present is doubt, uncertainty, and the sense that if anything is possible, then reality itself is virtual (or at least as variable as neurotransmitters and computer effects). So although conspiracy theory, like other Enlightenment theories with claims to truth and reason, posits a relation to facticity, causality, coherence, and rationality, this relation isn't what distinguishes conspiracy from "legitimate" theory. In fact, in the information age, at the interface of modernity and postmodernity, the defining characteristic of conspiracy theory is suspicion. It emphasizes that *something* has been withheld, that all the facts aren't known, that what we see isn't all there is. Conspiracy theory demands more information. Too humble to offer a totalizing account, its accumulated assertions *remind us that we don't know.*

For example, most of us know that there are conspiratorial explanations for the JFK assassination, the origins of the AIDS virus, the crash at Roswell, the eye and pyramid images on American currency. But we don't know what these explanations are, what sorts of plots and shadowy figures are involved. All we know are bits and pieces without a plot. This is the way conspiracy theories work. Most fail to delineate any conspiracy at all. They simply counter conventional narratives with suspicions and allegations that, more often than not, resist coherent emplotment. The possibilities of malevolent, elite plays of power link facts, speculations, and questions. Was the mass suicide in Jonestown, Guyana, part of a CIA mind control experiment?[23] What explains the fact that the CIA was the first to report the massacre and the presence of

CIA agent Richard Dwyer? Was it a plot to kill hundreds of African Americans? Rather than mapping totality, conspiracy's insinuations disrupt the presumption that there is a coherent, knowable reality that could be mapped.

Leah Haley's sense of an abducted life was stimulated by "odd noises on the telephone." Describing the noises as "sometimes clicking sounds, sometimes other phones ringing in the background, sometimes music," she also perceived "a faint sound like a cassette tape winding slowly around a reel."[24] Her computer disks, moreover, were somehow rearranged and left out of order. She reports, "I was frustrated over my inability to exercise control over these strange incidents that left me baffled as to their purpose."[25] Uncertainty manifests itself on her body as well. At one point Haley writes, "I could not understand how I had acquired this flu-like illness. To my knowledge, I had not been near anyone who was ill. . . . As I thought about my condition, I realized how easy it would be to eliminate someone merely by injecting germs or drugs."[26] Haley presents herself as becoming an abductee, as reluctantly coming to grips with a horrible reality of governmental and extraterrestrial conspiracy. She doesn't first present the conspiracy and then read herself into it.

This style, this presentation of becoming, is prominent in UFO and conspiracy writing. Rather than relying on what Fenster understands as a "totalizing conversion," whereby everything in a person's world is reinterpreted once and for all, conspiracy thinking involves creeping doubt, uncanny displacements, the pleasures of desiring and supplying reassuring information.[27] As an example of this totalizing conversion, Fenster uses a scene from *The X-Files*: in the final episode of the first season, "The Erlenmeyer Flask," agent Dana Scully obtains laboratory evidence of alien DNA. She tells her partner, agent Fox Mulder, "I've always held science as sacred. I've always put my trust in accepted facts. . . . For the first time in my life, I don't know what to believe."[28] Fenster interprets this scene in terms of conversion, claiming that Scully "now believes."[29] But this is not what she says. Fenster substitutes clarity for uncertainty. Scully isn't convinced that aliens are real; all she knows is that her scientific training is starting to collapse in on itself, that it is telling her something that it, science, has long denied. Fenster's emphasis on totalizing conversion is thus misplaced: conspiracy thinking is so uncertain that one is rarely fully convinced; instead, one becomes involved in a reiterative back-and-forth that mobilizes doubt and reassurance into a never-ending, never-reconciled account of possibility.

Fenster may interpret conspiracy as a mapping of totality because he collapses into his notion of the "classical conspiracy narrative" three positions that need to remain distinct: that of the author, the protagonist, and the reader or audience.[30] Consequently, for Fenster a specific act of conversion, "the narrative pivot" or point where the protagonist of a story uncovers convincing evidence of conspiracy, danger, and the ultimate truth, establishes the defining relationship of conspiracy theory, that of the individual to history. The individual protagonist, through his or her investigations, discovers totality, the truth of history.[31] Moreover, via this discovery, the protagonist can "save" history by bringing to light the hidden truth.

While Fenster may be right about film and fiction, conspiracy theory presenting itself as nonfiction, that is, conspiracy theories like those around UFOs, JFK, Jonestown, CIA mind control, the death of Princess Diana, and the shootings in Littleton, Colorado, don't work this way. First, the perspective of the author is separate from that of the reader. Working within a framework of objectivity and fairness, conspiracy authors go to great efforts to present their evidence with the intent of convincing their readers. Rarely does the author assume that the audience agrees with everything presented; members of the audience are presumed to be skeptical, even hostile. We might say that conspiracy theory posits a "split audience" of believers and unbelievers.[32] Believers will recognize the accumulated facts as evidence. Unbelievers will consider these same facts as potential challenges to the status quo, as questions that may not be answered, as indications that there are people who think something is going on. Readers are confronted with a choice, instructed that they will have to make their own decision after confronting the "facts." Budd Hopkins, for example, ends the preface to his 1996 book on alien abduction with "The final judgment is yours to make."[33] Numerous authors call for "open minds" and serious consideration of the evidence. Indeed, they often write new books, with new information, trying to convince people anew. The matter of truth is never certain or closed.

Second, the perspective of the author is not that of the narrator or protagonist, even in first-person accounts. For the protagonist, belief causes, sets in motion, the drive to interpret the facts. Fenster, as I've mentioned, emphasizes the particular instance when nonbelief is converted to belief. For the conspiracy author, however, belief is an effect of the very practices of searching, finding, and interpreting. Making links, searching for knowledge, produces belief. Precisely because this knowledge is unstable, because it is imbricated in constitutive uncertainties, it depends on the generation of ever more evidence, ever more interpretations, for sustenance. Ufologists report more sightings, more missing fetuses. Assassination theorists find new witnesses. Even after Scully and Mulder get clear evidence of the alien conspiracy, in the next episode they remain searching, skeptical, uncertain.

Žižek describes the external customs supporting belief in terms of a precarious "believing without knowing it," a paradoxical *"belief before belief."* He writes, "by following a custom a subject believes without knowing it, so that the final conversion is merely a formal act by means of which we recognize what we already believe."[34] My claim is that conspiracy thinking operates prior to a final conversion; indeed, it is an anxious sort of pre-belief, a thinking that is a longing that one suspects, fears, and even desires will never be fulfilled. Ever suspicious, it disavows the closure of a final explanation, theory, or political and moral order. To read conspiracy theory in terms of a final conversion, then, misses its distinctive feature of suspicious longing and thereby mistakes the practices of the belief before belief as the excesses that result from its failure to map totality. Once we recognize that conspiracy is marked by doubt, however, its preoccupation with searching and finding appears as a nervous enactment to produce belief—but not yet.

SPECIFYING DETAILS

Like cyberia's networked information streams, conspiracy theory's irreconcilable doubt generates massive amounts of evidence. Forgoing the comfort of closure for the pleasure of the search, it privileges the specific fact. Information is everything. And, as in the networked world of bits and bytes, everything is information, capable of being sorted, categorized, and analyzed from a multiplicity of perspectives. Action, agency, involves finding and knowing, surveilling, observing, and bringing to light.

Abductee writing, for example, relies on unceasing waves of minute detail. Katharina Wilson provides a "researcher's supplement" to her book *The Alien Jigsaw*. In this supplement she correlates her abductions with specific points in her menstrual cycle. She concludes that her abductions most often took place in the week immediately following ovulation. She analyzes further the memories and dreams recorded in her journal, and published in *The Alien Jigsaw*, in order to provide quantifiable data on the physiological and emotional effects of her abduction. During or after 3 percent of her abduction experiences (she recalls or has reasons to believe that she was abducted 119 times), Wilson felt full or bloated; during or after 2 percent of her experiences she felt pain in her nostril.[35] She details the presence of military personnel in abductions, the various locales visited during an abduction, and the different sorts of aliens involved. Wilson does not conclude that her evidence actually proves anything. Rather, she provides it as a supplement to the evidence offered by other researchers and abductees.

Karla Turner, Beth Collings, and Anna Jamerson all describe daily rituals of combing their bodies for evidence. They discover small cuts, scars, and bruises. They find needle-like puncture marks, bumps, and sometimes blood. Jamerson says that even when new marks turn up, she isn't convinced they are necessarily new.[36] Turner observes, "As evidence of alien contact, they are useless if there is no memory of an event to go with them."[37] Still, as they search for evidence, these abductees become ever more preoccupied with the minutiae of the everyday, observing and recording details that would have remained unnoticed. What cannot be explained, understood, remembered, suggests the alien even if it doesn't prove it.

For over a week, Turner records the sounds of her house at night. The tape from the third night played back a series of eighty-five sounds not unlike "the noise a six-foot-tall can of hair spray might make: short, breathy aspirations that were more mechanical-sounding than organic."[38] Her efforts to document abductions are as ultimately unsuccessful as Collings and Jamerson's. At the Abduction Study Conference at MIT, Richard Boylan, a psychologist who is also an experiencer, dismissed attempts to "capture an event on electromagnetic recording equipment, or to use stealth technology." Boylan argued, "You're dealing with people who can read your minds, what do you mean stealth technology? If they don't want to be captured, they'll catch it while you're forming the plot. They can also sense you coming through technologies better than we'll evolve for awhile."[39]

The vast compilations of data, of information, are confounded by an inability to determine not just what it all might mean or where it all might fit, but whether it is real or staged data. Many studying and experiencing abduction think that the telepathic and technologic superiority of aliens enables them to produce experiences and memories. What is not clear is whether these productions can be thought of as real and what real means in this case. All abductees report screen memories. Haley mentions a light show seemingly put on just for her to photograph. The pictures don't turn out. Wilson views theatrics as a central part of the aliens' study of human behavior. She considers whether some of the variety of alien forms might be due to masks or disguises, "since the only thing we *are* sure of is that the aliens are extremely good at deceiving us."[40] Budd Hopkins explains the multiply witnessed abduction of Linda Cortile in New York City in 1989 as an event deliberately staged for an important political leader.[41] Hopkins includes the text of a letter sent to him by this "third man," a witness Hopkins suggests is a highly placed official in the United Nations although he refers to him as "Poppy."

The drive for evidence is thus complicated by the troubling possibility that the evidence isn't real. Put somewhat differently, conspiratorial doubt goes so far that it can't trust the very evidence it tries to accumulate. It doesn't know what the evidence is for, what exactly it proves. Ever suspicious, it undermines the authority of coherent narratives before it closes doors or eliminates possibilities. Any information could be misinformation or disinformation. Any information could be factual, reliable, well-supported, and helpful. Without a stable structure of interpretation, then, evidence breaks down into doubts and detail, the key elements of conspiracy, the motivating attributes of cyberia.

CONNECTING VIRTUALLY

What links doubt and detail is a presumption of interconnectivity. Conspiracy theory, in other words, relies on the notion that everything is or can be connected. So it isn't a question of knowing the whole versus knowing only parts. Rather, it's the possibility of multiple networks of meaning. And this sense of associative links, of what Steven Johnson describes as hints of filiation and haunting, half-glimpsed resemblances, is what makes conspiracy so compelling in the information age.[42]

Abductees link every odd or uncomfortable occurrence in their lives. They connect their computers' missing files with missing fetuses.

They connect gazes from strangers sitting across a room with phones that ring once and then stop. They connect the emotions they feel when seeing a picture of a big-headed Gray with enormous black eyes with their inability to remember details from their pasts. Beth Collings finds that none of the conventional explanations offered for abduction, "coincidence," "lucid dreams," or "faulty human memory," can "justify the whole."[43] "Until something better came along, something that could explain *all* the connecting events, we had no choice but to continue as we had been," she writes, "examining each unexplained event, comparing notes on shared memories, talking candidly with family and friends, and keeping an open mind." Collings takes the interconnections among discrete events as a given. She knows that they are linked, although she's uncertain as to how or why they are linked. The fact of linkage is the only thing about which she's certain.

Katharina Wilson finds evidence of an affiliation between the government (or covert groups within the government) and the aliens. She urges the UFO community to look into the matter:

> Do not discount what I and other abductees are reporting simply because your mind will not allow you to believe there is a connection between some members of our government and some of the aliens. Do not discount what I am reporting because you automatically lump all such information into your government conspiracy category. I am not a government agent disseminating disinformation. . . . I have to remain open to the idea, although it is extremely difficult for me, that our government may in fact be trading alien technology for genetic material.[44]

Similarly, abductee Karla Turner notes connections between mass media, government, and the aliens. She considers the rumor that the American government was at one point allied with the aliens, but that this alliance has since crumbled, bringing on the imminent possibility of a mass confrontation.[45] Turner notes, "the aliens who are here now are just the forerunners for a much larger group, and that group's arrival is expected within the next four years. The government hopes to avoid worldwide panic by preparing us through advertising and entertainment media for our encounter with alien beings."[46] Turner and her family carry out investigations designed to establish whether there is any truth to the rumor. They find that, just as predicted, during the period of alliance, *E.T.* and other alien-friendly movies appeared, part of an effort to get Americans to feel affection for aliens. After relations between the aliens and the U.S. government soured, so did the media's treatment of aliens. Turner writes,

> When the rift took place—a shoot out of sorts at an underground base, in which the humans got the worst of it all—the government attitude changed, and we were presented with malevolent reptilian aliens in the miniseries "V." And now we had a new series, "War of the Worlds," which we watched anxiously each week. In every episode, we saw some fact or detail which we recognized from actual cases, mixed in with the more creative aspects of the show, and as we watched we did feel as if a deliberate effort were being made to acquaint the public with at least part of the truth.[47]

The government, she thinks, told Hollywood what kinds of images to depict. Together they told Americans what to desire or fear. For Turner and her family, governmental alliances, made-for-television movies, and alien abductions are all connected, linked to one another as signs, messages, plans, and possibilities. It sounds like she's been cruising the Net, clicking on icon after icon, finding and making unimaginable and barely repeatable links.

Of course, Turner doesn't think that all this is necessarily true. She doesn't know what to believe. Not knowing, she allows for possibilities she would have previously ridiculed—"the government's deal with aliens, the underground installations with vats of human body parts and prenatal nurseries of stolen fetuses."[48] As she researches the stories for herself, she becomes ever more confused, discovering that the various truths and rumors conflict, contradicting each other and themselves. She tries to fight off "feelings of anger and fear and disorientation," telling herself that "Humans can lie, and so can aliens." But this doesn't really help, since she still doesn't know who to believe, who to trust, and when.

Those UFO researchers trying to make sense of what they understand as the human-alien breeding project motivating abduction also presume a fundamental interconnectedness. They assume a chromosomal genetic compatibility between humans and aliens. How such interstellar hybridity is possible isn't baffling—we're all connected, linked to such an extent that reproduction can occur. UFO researchers also assume that abductions are interconnected with each other. Abductions affect families, occurring in successive generations. "It's very much like an assembly line," says researcher David Jacobs.[49] Budd Hopkins adds that aliens bring people together deliberately, associating them through an intricate "cosmic micro-management" that he calls "controlled pairing."[50] Each abduction has a link to another one; they are all part of something larger, something that links humans and aliens, earth and outer space. Connection in abduction reenacts connection in cyberia: like so many tied-in and prominently placed products, humans too are multiply, excessively, virtually integrated. As the network extends and the plot thickens, we are revamped into something else, something alien.

Although I've been talking about alien abduction, making connections dominates conspiracy theory more generally. After the high school shootings in Littleton, Colorado, some folks linked the teenage killers with symbols in the Denver airport, the Lockheed-Martin corporation, CIA mind control, antidepressants, and the death of child beauty queen JonBenet Ramsey. Conspiracy theorists emphasize what links people, associations, interests, and events; they try to discover—or produce—the relevant associations. Did people go to the same schools, join the same clubs, serve in the same branches of government or military? Who are the overlapping members on corporate boards? Which scientific projects receive governmental funding? Noting the interconnections between large banks and corporations, as well as the fraternity among business leaders and officials in the Federal Reserve System, Jim Marrs complains that "the mainstream media consistently fails to mention the connections between America's leaders and the organizations to which they belong."[51]

Conspiracy theory's focus on connection, the sense that there is a connection or that one can be made, is compelling in networked technoculture.[52] Nearly every computer commercial relies on fast cuts to link the manufacturer's product to multi-aged, -hued, and -cultured people, to awe-inspiring images of nature, to moonwalks, and to change in Eastern Europe and South Africa. For well over a year, most every news story in mainstream media found a way to link itself to Monica Lewinsky. During the summer of 1999, the same held true for *The Phantom Menace,* and this only extended the by now common marketing strategy that links a "major movie event" with toys, clothes, posters, fast food, candy, sheets, paper, pens, pencils, backpacks, cups, and so forth. They are all connected, linked through the *Star Wars* image/icon. Like conspiracy theorists and George Lucas, consumer-users of computer-mediated communication link everything too. We can't avoid it. Interconnectivity is the mantra, buzzword, slogan of the global information economy.

When we search, find, and link, when we make a connection and ask what it means, we think like conspiracy theorists. Indeed, because what's interconnected is interactive, because links generate new pages and possibilities, we'll never see it all. We'll only be able to suspect.

INFORMING DESIRE

What happens in cyberia is an unending disruption of settled beliefs and ideas, be they about TWA Flight 800, the best mulch for azaleas, or the meaning of abduction. Focusing on any one site or network of links is thus a mistake. The disruptions are produced by the possibility of available alternatives, by the endless buttons to click and windows to open, by the amassing of information to which we have fragmented and unclear relations.

These disruptions are also fun. Even with the anxieties and uncertainties they bring, or better, precisely because of the anxieties and uncertainties they bring, the challenges to presumptions of authority and expertise have pleasures all their own. Indeed, critics of cyberia and conspiracy alike seem most resentful of the enjoyment that accompanies linked speculations. Most of the derision heaped on the Internet has focused on pornography and cybersex, although numerous commentators scorn the drivel and trivialities of chat rooms, fan sites, and UFO Web rings. Critics of conspiracy warn against its "seductions." For example, Daniel Pipes asserts that "conspiracist writings constitute a quite literal form of pornography (though political rather than sexual)." "Recreational conspiracism titillates sophisticates much as does recreational sex," he writes; "artists explore conspiracist fantasies in a spirit akin to sexual ones."[53]

Criticism of conspiracy theory oscillates between two extremes: the theory is either irrational or hyper-rational; it has no evidence or it has too much; it renders individuals too passive or too powerful.[54] According to Žižek, "such an oscillation is an unmistakable sign that we are dealing with *jouissance.*"[55] The point, then, is not whether conspiracy thinking is irrational or not; it's rather the enjoyment that accompanies it. A focus on conspiracy's relation to totality, to a logical, coherent, all-encompassing plot, or even to the powerful, controlling enemies who may lurk behind the scenes, is thus mistaken. It relies on a (resentful) assessment of conspiracy's excesses, failing to attend to the very elements conspiracy thinkers themselves emphasize—doubt, detail, and interconnection.

The same is true for Net-critics. Their laments over technoculture focus on its excesses.[56] Either too many are on the Net, or too few. There is either too little or too much information. Computer-mediated interaction is too fast or too slow. Denizens of cyberia are either work-obsessed geek entrepreneurs making uncountable millions or lazy click-potatoes masturbating all day long as they type on sticky keyboards. The oscillating disparagements demonstrate a resentment of cyberian pleasures, a spiteful annoyance at what appears to be an obscene enjoyment of searching, linking, connecting, and doubting.

Žižek's account of the pleasures accompanying the symbolic articulation of loss, of "pleasure in pain," is helpful for understanding the attractions of conspiracy thinking in the information age. "The surplus of enjoyment over mere pleasure is generated by the presence of the very opposite of pleasure, that is, pain," Žižek writes. "Pain generates surplus-enjoyment via the magic reversal-into-itself by means of which the very material texture of our expression of pain . . . gives rise to enjoyment."[57] Conspiracy theory is necessarily an expression of pain, of the violation of a body politic (be it configured territorially, ideationally, or ethnically) or a body that stands in for the body politic (as with celebrity death conspiracy theories such as those around Marilyn Monroe, Jim Morrison, and, of course, Elvis). Abductees' personal suffering marks a specific inscription of larger efforts to rewrite *homo sapiens'* genetic code. Many suspect, after all, that their eggs or sperm are extracted from them as part of a plan to create a hybrid human-alien species.[58] Conspiracy writing, especially in the exuberance of its interpretations and associations, seizes a pleasure from the pain caused by the conspiracies it documents. That it is prevalent today suggests another pleasure in pain, an enjoyment at the site of a perceived diminishment of political and economic efficacy that substitutes a different sort of agency, one configured around linked screens, around watching and knowing. "Being informed" stands in for "being engaged," reformatting political agency in terms of the consumption- and celebrity-driven appetites of cyberia. We click because we want to know. We make the links to discover the secrets.

The pleasures of conspiracy fit well at the technocultural interface of the national and the global. Typing, pointing, clicking, and dragging incessantly, we know that we don't know everything, but believe nevertheless that we're informed, in the know. Fenster criticizes conspiracy theorists for a failure of agency, for producing accounts of power so pervasive that action becomes pointless if not impossible.[59] My argument is that conspiracy theory in cyberia functions differently. Configuring agency through links, doubts, and information, it provides a window to the ideological supports of networked technoculture. The pleasures of the wired world are pleasures of knowing, of no longer being duped by the system. In cyberia, action—like the action of the conspiracy theorist—is reconfigured as watching, surveilling, exposing, interpreting, linking, knowing. And it's a reconfiguration driven by suspicion.

NOTES

I want to thank Van Zimmerman, Lee Quinby, and Paul Passavant for providing helpful comments on an earlier draft of this essay.

1. Leah Haley, *Lost Was the Key* (Tuscaloosa, AL: Greenleaf Publications, 1993).

2. Ibid., 14.

3. Ibid., 15.

4. Anna Jamerson and Beth Collings, *Connections: Solving Our Alien Abduction Mystery* (Newberg, OR: Wildflower Press, 1996), xx.

5. Haley, *Lost Was the Key*, 46.

6. George Marcus, ed., *Paranoia within Reason* (Chicago: University of Chicago Press, 1999), 2–5.

7. I'm drawing here from William Connolly's argument in *The Ethos of Pluralization* (Minneapolis: University of Minnesota Press, 1995).

8. Ziauddin Sardar and Jerome R. Ravetz distinguish between cyberspace, "the ether that lies inside and occupies the in-betweens of all the computers," and cyberia, "the new civilization emerging through our human–computer interface and mediation." See their introduction to their edited volume, *Cyberfutures* (New York: New York University Press, 1996), 1.

9. Slavoj Žižek, *The Plague of Fantasies* (London: Verso, 1997), 45. See also Žižek, *The Ticklish Subject* (London: Verso, 1999), 206.

10. My thinking here is informed by Joseba Gabilondo, "Postcolonial Cyborgs," in *The Cyborg Handbook*, ed. Chris Hables Gray (New York: Routledge, 1995), 423–32.

11. See Lee Quinby, *Millennial Seduction: A Skeptic Confronts Apocalyptic*

Culture (Ithaca: Cornell University Press, 1999), esp. chap. 7. I develop this point with respect to *The X-Files* in Jodi Dean, "Uncertainty Conspiracy Abduction," in *Reality Squared: Televisual Discourse on the Real*, ed. James Friedman (New Brunswick: Rutgers University Press, forthcoming).

12. Lee Quinby presents three subject positions producing and produced by millennial technoculture: terminal cynicism, conspiracy mania, and avatarism. I agree that technoculture's rapid changes are impacting subjectivity and, indeed, contributing to the pleasures of conspiracy thinking, but I disagree with her claims that conspiracy theory necessarily entails a commitment to moral and epistemological absolutism. See Quinby, "Millennial Civilization and Its Discontents," *Psychohistory Review*, Winter 1999, 1–16.

13. This is my argument in Jodi Dean, *Aliens in America: Conspiracy Cultures from Outerspace to Cyberspace* (Ithaca: Cornell University Press, 1998).

14. I discuss mainstream pluralism's exclusion of radical views via the labeling and trashing of a view as "conspiracy theory" in Jodi Dean, "Declarations of Independence," in *Cultural Studies and Political Theory*, ed. Jodi Dean (Ithaca: Cornell University Press, 2000).

15. Kathleen Stewart, "Conspiracy Theory's Worlds," in Marcus, *Paranoia within Reason*, 13.

16. Ibid., 18.

17. I'm indebted to Van Zimmerman for this point.

18. Richard Hofstadter, *The Paranoid Style in American Politics and Other Essays* (Cambridge: Harvard University Press, 1996), 36.

19. Mark Fenster, *Conspiracy Theories: Secrecy and Power in American Culture* (Minneapolis: University of Minnesota Press, 1999), 93.

20. Ibid., 116.

21. Žižek, *The Ticklish Subject*, 362.

22. Stewart, "Conspiracy Theory's Worlds," 14.

23. Jonathan Vankin and John Whalen, *The Sixty Greatest Conspiracies of All Time* (Secaucus, NJ: Citadel Press, 1997), 288–94.

24. Haley, *Lost Was the Key*, 26.

25. Ibid., 132.

26. Ibid., 90.

27. Fenster, *Conspiracy Theories*, 112.

28. Ibid., 137.

29. Ibid.

30. Fenster's conflation of protagonist and author appears in the following passage:

> Having glimpsed this essential truth, the protagonist begins the long and arduous task of successfully effecting change on the increasingly vulnerable larger historical structures that finally are visible to him.

This is equally true for fictional narratives and the narratives embedded in "factual" accounts of conspiracy; in the latter, the metanarrative pivot, the point in the writer's life in which the conspiracy reveals itself to him/her . . . serves a similar purpose in enabling the narrating act contained in the text. (*Conspiracy Theories*, 112)

Fenster's conflation of protagonist and audience appears on p. 113, when he foregrounds "the cognitive act of interpretation as performed by both protagonist and audience," and on p. 131, where he observes that finding conspiracy "is an act of reconstruction performed by both protagonist and audience alike."

31. Ibid., 112.

32. Van Zimmerman suggested this formulation to me.

33. Budd Hopkins, *Witnessed* (New York: Pocket Books, 1996), xiv.

34. Slavoj Žižek, *The Sublime Object of Ideology* (London: Verso, 1989), 40.

35. Katharina Wilson, *The Alien Jigsaw Researcher's Supplement* (Portland, OR: Puzzle Publishing, 1993), 42.

36. Jamerson and Collings, *Connections*, 115.

37. Karla Turner, *Into the Fringe: A True Story of Alien Abduction* (New York: Berkley Books, 1992), 97.

38. Ibid., 119.

39. Andrea Pritchard et al., eds., *Alien Discussions: Proceedings of the Abduction Study Conference* (Cambridge: North Cambridge Press, 1994), 542.

40. Wilson, *Alien Jigsaw*, 121.

41. Hopkins, *Witnessed*.

42. Steven Johnson, *Interface Culture* (New York: HarperCollins, 1997), 112–13.

43. Jamerson and Collings, *Connections*, 228.

44. Wilson, *Alien Jigsaw*, 284.

45. Turner, *Into the Fringe*, 91.

46. Ibid., 92.

47. Ibid., 92–93.

48. Ibid., 106.

49. As quoted by Patrick Huyghe, "The Secret Invasion: Does It Add Up?" *Omni* 17, no. 9 (winter 1995): 60.

50. Hopkins, *Witnessed*, 3–21.

51. Jim Marrs, *Alien Agenda* (New York: HarperCollins, 1997), 392.

52. See also Nigel Clark, "Earthing the Ether," in Sardar and Ravetz, *Cyberfutures*, 90–110.

53. Daniel Pipes, *Conspiracy: How the Paranoid Style Flourishes and Where It Comes From* (New York: Free Press, 1997), 49.

54. See Pipes's attack on conspiracy theory, esp. 40–41, and Hofstadter,

Paranoid Style, 3–40. See also my discussion in Dean, "Declarations of Independence."

55. Žižek, *Plague of Fantasies*, 54.

56. For a more thorough discussion, see Jodi Dean, "Webs of Conspiracy," in *The World Wide Web and Contemporary Cultural Theory*, ed. Thomas Swiss and Andrew Herman (New York: Routledge, 2000).

57. Žižek, *Plague of Fantasies*, 47.

58. In *Aliens in America* I consider alternative explanations for the abduction program, in particular the more positive interpretation of consciousness transformation suggested by Harvard professor John Mack.

59. Fenster writes, "Conspiracy theory's resistance is limited to interpretation and narrative, relegating its opposition to the problems of the dominant political order to the realm of a limited hermeneutical resistance to a prevailing, linguistic order." *Conspiracy Theories*, 141.

5

"My Body Is Not My Own"

Alien Abduction and the Struggle for Self-Control

Bridget Brown

THE ALIEN ABDUCTION PHENOMENON is unique to the last thirty or so years, its emergence marked by the publication of *The Interrupted Journey* in 1966. Written by UFO investigator John Fuller, the book tells the story of Betty and Barney Hill, a couple from New Hampshire who struggle, with the help of a therapist who takes them through a series of hypnotic regressions, to account for several hours of "missing time" lost during a car trip. In the process of reconstructing the hazy details of these lost hours, the Hills remember, to their horror and surprise, being taken aboard an alien spacecraft and subjected to a series of medical experiments against their will.

While under hypnosis, Betty Hill recalls having been given a "complete physical examination by intelligent, humanoid beings" during which the aliens stuck a needle into her navel:

> I see the needle, and it's bigger than any needle that I've ever seen. And I ask him what he's going to do with it . . . and he said he just wants to put it in my navel, it's just a simple test and I tell him, no, it will hurt, don't do it, don't do it. And I'm crying and I'm telling him, it's hurting, it's hurting take it out, take it out. . . . I don't know why they put that needle into my navel. Because I told them they shouldn't do it.[1]

Hill objects, but to no avail. When the exam is through, she asks her captors to explain the purpose of this forced procedure, and is told, to her astonishment, that it is a pregnancy test. She continues to seek information, attempting to assert some sort of control over her situation: "I asked what kind of pregnancy test he planned with the needle. He did not reply, but started to insert the needle in my navel with a sudden thrust. Suddenly I was filled with great pain, twisting and moaning."[2]

Though Barney is hazier about the details of his examination, he does remember "lying on a table" and "thinking that someone was putting a cup around my groin."[3] While Barney does not explicitly interpret the uses of the cup, he does sense a need to capitulate to the aliens' agenda in order to survive: "I will be very careful and be very still and will be cooperative, and I won't be harmed."[4] In order to assuage the terror he feels, he chooses a combination of prayer and dissociation, later recalling his decision to "just stay here and pretend that I am anywhere and think of God and think of Jesus and think that I am not afraid."[5]

In the forced medical exam, abductees are, during a state of paralysis and terror, subjected to a variety of technical violations by their emotionless alien captors; this has become since the 1980s the most prevalent and perhaps most puzzling feature of the abduction scenario. Many abductees believe that the central purpose of this exam is to initiate them against their will into an ongoing intergalactic, interspecies breeding project. They report stolen sperm, stolen eggs, stolen and implanted pregnancies. Under hypnosis they remember being with part-human/part-alien hybrid babies on the spaceship, babies that are suspended in tanks, and that fail to thrive for the lack of human nurturance. The often explicitly gynecological/proctological alien medical examination, including the anal probe, has come to be such a standard and ubiquitous feature of abduction that it has been successfully parodied on popular television comedies such as *The Simpsons* and *South Park*. In the 1990s, accounts of human reproductive violation at the hands of aliens are represented in a seemingly limitless variety of cultural sites, low and high: in self-published conspiracy literature; in tabloid newspapers; in best-selling paperbacks such as Whitley Strieber's *Communion*; on television talk shows; on shows devoted to the investigation of paranormal phenomena, including *Sightings, Strange Universe,* and *In Search of . . .*; on dramatic series focusing on the abduction phenomenon, most notably *Dark Skies* and *The X-Files*; on television comedies, including the animated series mentioned above as well as *Frasier* and *Kids in the Hall*; in advertisements for cars, airlines, and candy bars; in documentaries produced by the Learning Channel and for the high-minded PBS series *Nova*. Concurrent with this media explosion, the most popular, widely circulated accounts of the "truth" of alien abduction have come to emphasize the encroaching threat posed by aliens to human reproductivity and physical well-being. This scenario was, however, uncommon if not entirely absent from both science fictional accounts of human/alien contact and in UFO/alien lore during the postwar period preceding the turn to accounts of alien abduction.

In this essay I seek to explore how and why this new story of human contact with aliens—one that foregrounds capture, physical violation, and reproductive tampering—emerges in the mid-1960s and reemerges with a vengeance in the 1980s. It has become increasingly clear that current alien abduction stories, beginning with the publication of the Hills' story, are markedly different from the UFO and alien contact stories of the 1940s and 1950s. Pre-abduction accounts were, for the most part, centrally concerned with the possibilities of mass destruction or national invasion, thus reflecting the postwar, post-atomic context of their telling. Accounts of abduction are, in contrast, expressive of anxieties about the mass management and manipulation of creation, specifically the management of one of the most intimate and heretofore seemingly "natural" human functions, reproduction.

In the turn to abduction both alien and human are redefined, as are those forces that abductees believe are conspiring against them. Abductees are one among many subsets of a loose coalition of individuals and groups that compose the community of UFO believers, many of whom remain focused, as they have been since the late 1940s, on gaining access to classified government information about UFOs and their alien occupants. The theory of government cover-up, known among believers as the "cosmic Watergate," received a shot in the arm during the 1997 media frenzy surrounding the fiftieth anniversary of the alleged—and officially denied—flying saucer crash at Roswell, New Mexico. Abductees share with other members of the UFO community feelings of frustration and disenfranchisement that are explicitly tied to lack of access to knowledge. They are, however, less concerned than other subgroups with what the government knew and when it knew it. By their accounting, abduction is deeply personal and it is the abducting aliens themselves who have access to knowledge they do not, knowledge conferred by their superior intellect and technological advantage. And in a critical if paradoxical twist, the knowledge that abductees seek to wrest from their captors is knowledge of themselves: of who they are and what they are about—knowledge that the aliens' actions suggest can be gleaned through surveillance, dissection, and analysis of the human body.

In order to understand where this particular anxiety comes from—as distinct from atomic age anxieties about mass destruction expressed in other postwar science fictions—we need to look beyond science fictional representation of aliens, and outside the social history of UFO groups. We have to read the stories abductees tell, starting with the Hills, alongside other cultural narratives they resemble, in this case narratives about medical and technical surveillance and management of the human body and, more specifically, human reproduction. During the early 1960s such narratives filled the pages of lifestyle magazines. Images of the sort of clinical, intimate invasion first reported by the Hills were standard fare in magazines announcing the new biotechnical revolution, accompanied by text more fantastic, science fictional, awesome, and often more horrifying than anything Hollywood had yet conjured. These popular accounts of scientific progress bear close analysis; in them, the stuff of science fiction is made real, and the lines between science fact and science fiction, between the present and the future, collapse with interesting consequences.

THE HUMAN BODY AND/AS THE NEW FRONTIER

In the early 1960s, popular lifestyle magazines rendered America's "science explosion" as evidence of the country's sustained national vigor. In its twenty-fifth anniversary issue (1960), *Life* takes stock of the nation's scientific achievement. The Sputnik crisis conspicuously absent from its overview, this anniversary issue heralds "Man" as having conquered "the last of the extreme heights, deeps and wastelands of this earth" and thus ready "to leave it."[6] While the text most explicitly references space travel, in the pages of this and other magazines from the same period another "new" frontier is figured prominently for conquest: the biological frontier of the human body. In "Explosion of Science," articles on the inner space of individual cells, on the mysterious behavior of viruses, and on the miraculous mapping functions of DNA all conspire to tell this story. Likewise, an article in the June 1964 volume of *Reader's Digest* explores "The Wondrous Inner Space of Living Cells." The article begins with what must have been a startling and confound-

ing claim: "They saw cells walking–and it was a fascinating performance."[7] It goes on to describe cells as "complex entities, each with a specific mission in life that it strives mightily to carry out."[8] Throughout,
cells are rendered as actors: they "bulge," "creep," and "perform." Each
cell has a surface that is its "face": it "swallows," "gulps," and "calls"
out to other cells. What's more, "DNA is the dictator of them all."[9]
Human beings in their complex entirety are merely observers of this action. In the context of the science explosion, readers of lifestyle magazines learn, to see a life form is not only to know it, but also to invest it
with human qualities. At the same time, these cells, viruses, and genes
exist outside and somehow separate from "us." In such discourse about
biological progress we see the blurring between "them" and "us" that
results in a defamiliarization of the body, an alienation of self from self.

Nowhere during this period is this sense of familiar and "natural"
relationship with one's own body more profoundly disrupted than in
popular discourse about new reproductive technologies. Five years
after the anniversary issue of *Life* discussed above, another special issue
of *Life* was published, devoted specifically to the explosion of biotech-
nology. "Control of Life" includes a series of features that together explore the possibilities of genetic engineering, fetal surgery, and what
would be called, by 1969, in vitro fertilization. "Control of Life" exemplifies the ways investigations into new scientific and medical break-
throughs were reported in such magazines in the early to mid-1960s. It
tells a story of technical progress in the futuristic, space age idiom characteristic of its historical moment, a story about the exploration and colonization of human bodies by science, and the implications of that project for the human future.

These articles also make evident a powerful and exclusive alliance
between doctors, technology, and fetuses, now made visible and thus
"real" through the miracles of new imaging technologies. Fantastic images accompany stories about the magic of medicine, the miracles of
doctoring, and the body as fallow terrain onto which a fantasy future is
mapped. As the passive title and accompanying cover photo of an ex-
pressionless woman lying prone on an examination table suggest from
the start, the human being is the object, not the subject, of control. The
penetrating entities here are doctors and clinicians, the fetoscopes and
other visualization technologies that they wield, and the staring, breathing fetus itself, who the pictures suggest may be quite capable of looking back. Each invasion is authorized, so it seems, by the naturalized

march of "progress," and must be endured, we are to believe, for the good of humankind—for the future itself.

Readers of "Control of Life" meet a number of expert (male) doctors who, in rapturous and sensational language, forecast the possibilities of the "profound and astonishing biological revolution" announced on its cover. Readers are first introduced to a Dr. Hafez, who rhapsodizes about techniques of gestation outside the human body. Dr. Hafez reports that such techniques are particularly suitable to the space age as a potential means for colonizing other planets. This article is accompanied by a picture of what the reader learns are "dummy vials"—mock-ups of vials containing various animal embryos. The text reads,

> When you consider how much it costs in fuel to lift every pound off the launch pad . . . why send full-grown men and women aboard spaceships? Instead why not ship tiny embryos, in the care of a competent biologist who could grow them into people, cows, pigs . . . anything we wanted—after they get there? After all, we miniaturize other spacecraft components. Why not the passengers?[10]

While the text suggests "man" as colonizer, the subtext and accompanying images suggest man—in this case most often represented by the prone body of the woman—as colonized, reduced through the intervention of technology, to the level of sheep, cattle, swine, or rhesus monkey. In the space age, the text suggests, human life has the equivalent value of a "spacecraft component"; distinctions between man and animal and man and machine are simultaneously collapsed. Perhaps most important, in this future scenario, for the good of future society, it is the "competent biologist," not the human parent, who is equipped to oversee not only the reproductive process, but also the care and nurturing of the young. Already existing gender and knowledge hierarchies are reinscribed, with men/experts clearly superior to women/nonexperts, even in their ability to scientifically manage the family.[11]

Throughout "Control of Life," the identity of mothers—and fathers—is upstaged not only by technical experts, but also by the proposed agency of the fetus itself. Readers of *Life*, as well as of advice columns such as "Tell Me Doctor" in *Ladies Home Journal*, were just beginning to be told in the early 1960s, in language that has become commonplace through the pro-life rhetoric of the 1980s and 1990s, that the fetus in utero was not so much a thing as a person. Indeed, a 1965 piece in *McCall's*, "The Secret World of the Unborn," happily reports that the fetus "is neither a quiescent vegetable nor a witless tadpole, as some have in the past conceived him to be, but rather a tiny individual human being, as real and self-contained as though he were lying in a crib with a blanket, instead of his mother, wrapped around him."[12]

The discourse of fetal patienthood, or personhood, pervades "Control of Life" as readers learn about doctors busy "perfecting other ingenious methods of observing and treating unborn children."[13] In the feature on fetal surgery, we witness a monkey fetus, lifted out of its mother's uterus, which has in turn been lifted out of her. The accompanying text informs us that "isolated in its mother's womb, the human fetus until recently has been inaccessible to direct medical and surgical care."[14] As techniques improve, we are told, "fetuses will undoubtedly be removed for transfusions, medication, or correction of defects."[15] We are assured that at this point the "patient within a patient will have come into his own," not only treatable, but already socialized. This is particularly striking in contrast to the accompanying photographs, which suggest not so much socialization and therapeutic treatment as autopsy and vivisection. While the fetuses are repeatedly represented as children, people, and patients, the mother is not so much an actor in as a setting for this human drama; the human father is entirely absent from the narrative of conception and reproduction.[16]

Throughout "Control of Life," value is placed on the optimistic yet dispassionate management of bodies; like the aliens who operate on Betty and Barney Hill, the doctors here express only the most perfunctory concern for the well-being of the people they treat. The Hills' alien captors still bear traces of other postwar anxieties, and Barney initially describes them as looking like Nazis. Upon further reflection, however, he characterizes the entities as clinicians, or medical tinkerers. If alien abductors are Nazis, then, they are Nazi doctors—miniature Mengeles—historically and emotionally fraught icons upon which to project one's worst dystopian anxieties about the misuse and abuse of science and progress.[17] Their dispassionate, clinical demeanor is emphasized by both Betty and her husband, Barney, who remembers being led into an examining room and told, "Don't be afraid. You don't have any reason to be afraid. We're not going to harm you, but we just want to do some tests."[18] When Betty struggles and protests against the repeated insertion of the needle into her navel, she remembers that her captors "looked very startled, and the leader bent over me and waved his hand in front of my eyes. Immediately the pain was completely gone, and I relaxed."[19] Like Betty Hill, the women who recede into the literal and figurative background of "Control of Life" have no recourse to respond to the particular vision of the future that drives the actions of the technical experts. Betty seems to give voice to the fact that awareness of one's disempowerment—in fact even protest against it—is no guarantee of rights or power. All efforts at assertion of self are ineffectual in the face of the totalizing, therapeutic gesture: only the doctor can take pain away.

So too for Barney Hill, and male abductees to follow. Indeed, one of the most noteworthy and striking features of the abduction narrative is the extent to which the gendered model of power relations suggested in prescriptive literature of the sort discussed above has been appropriated by men. In alien abduction, men too find themselves objects of the technological gaze, and are equally subject to intimate, bodily violations. In *The Interrupted Journey* Barney remembers in particular the violation of the aliens' eyes, remarking, "Oh those eyes! They're in my brain!"[20] The cross-gendered nature of these accounts suggests that for abductees, in the face of technical power—of the knowledge, access, and advantage conferred by it—we are all exposed, reduced, known: we are all equally likely to fall victim.[21]

In stories of abduction, the spaceship/clinic is the site of struggle between technically advanced alien clinicians and captive, immobilized human patients.[22] This story emerged as the power conferred by the doctor's expertise was augmented by a number of converging social forces in the United States. From the postwar period through the 1970s, a growing technical-professional new class extended its control from the management of military and state institutions to the management of social, domestic, intellectual, and personal spheres. It often did so at the behest of—and with funding provided by—the state, and in the service of Cold War, national security imperatives.[23] The space age rhetoric of futurism, as seen in "Control of Life," only served to enhance the scope of medical authority: accordingly, the doctor surveys and controls not only the present but also the future space of the body.

In the tradition of technocratic ideology in place since at least the Progressive Era, those possessed of scientific authority and technical expertise have long insisted on their own political disinterestedness and neutrality. Yet this insistence has been met with skepticism and suspicion invigorated many times over during the latter half of the twentieth century. The sheer destructive potential of technology was made manifest in the United States' use of the atom bomb; the increasing power and status of a postwar military–industrial elite became a focal point for antiwar protest during the war in Vietnam.[24] Articles such as those found in "Control of Life" dramatized the ways military technologies born of war were being brought to bear in the management of creation: it was the invention of sonar, for example, that enabled peering into the womb, and the impression of being peered back at. This irony, it seems, is not entirely lost on abductees.

Through the Hills' story and stories of abduction that follow in the 1980s and 1990s, the power/knowledge struggle between expert and nonexpert assumes a particular, if fantastic, form and location.[25] By positing the alien as part medical technician, part bureaucrat, part fetus, abduction narratives begin to give shape to anxieties about the increasing power of a growing technical-professional class to control all spheres of human activity, no matter how intimate. By positing humans as prone patients/victims, they remind us that disinterestedness and neutrality often mask abuses of power and authority. From the mid-1960s forward, abduction narratives pose and repose the question, If "technology" will bring us to a new frontier of human development, where does that leave me? And more important, what if I am the new frontier? The nature of the conspiracy suggested by alien abductees lies in the shared belief that only the aliens know the "true" answers.

ALIEN TECHNOLOGY AND THE INTERSPECIES BREEDING PROJECT

In one sense the story-form set up by the Hills remains the same in the 1980s and 1990s: average people in the course of daily activities such as cleaning house, sleeping, or driving are paralyzed, taken, examined, returned, and made to forget everything that has happened in the interim. At the same time, the story is elaborated on and expanded in critical ways by abductees and investigators, illustrating how assimilative and flexible the abduction belief is, how sensitive to changing historical circumstance, while offering abductees a narrative means for positioning themselves within that changing history. Abductees—male and female—continue to talk about forced reproductive experimentation, but with increasing explicitness. Their accounts detail the precise nature of the alien intervention into human reproduction; abduction experts catalogue and interpret their findings. Abductees fetishize fetuses in story after story of lost or stolen pregnancies and the subsequent presentation of hybrid alien/human offspring. A close look at how these more recent accounts are told by abductees and anthologized by investigators suggests how, in the context of the last ten to fifteen years, the politics of alien abduction have become increasingly complex. In these accounts the abducting aliens manage human bodies, sexuality, and ability to procreate. In the process they—along with the abduction experts and therapists to whom abductees turn for help—trouble abductees' sense of themselves as "normal" men and women.

The collective anxiety expressed by these abductees about the encroachment of technology into "natural" human functions has no doubt been occasioned by the realization since the 1960s of what were then only scientific and technological possibilities. In contemporary accounts of abduction one sees the degree to which reproductive technologies, while no longer entirely "new," nonetheless remain both alienating and awesome. Abductees continue to experience themselves—in contrast to the aliens—as confused and powerless nonexperts. A central facet of the interspecies breeding project remembered and reported by abductees is the forced in vitro fertilization of women. This includes, as in actual in vitro, now commonplace, the removal of ova from female abductees, their fertilization ex utero with human sperm, and the reinsertion of the embryo into the female body for gestation. Abductees report that in abduction, the alien doctors add one extra, critical step to this process: in creating the embryo, the aliens somehow manipulate it in order to include their own DNA, resulting in what Harvard psychologist and abduction expert John Mack colorfully calls "the altered conceptus."[26] Each step of the process—all forced and, like other traumas inflicted on the abductee, remembered only through hypnotic regression—is painstakingly detailed in most published abduction narratives. In abduction, gestation outside the human body *happens*, whether we want it to or not. And as Dr. Hafez playfully and speculatively predicted in 1965, it is a fantastic version of the "competent biologist," in this case the ultracompetent but unemotional alien, who controls this process, still not the male or the female human parent.

Intruders: The Incredible Visitations at Copley Woods (1987) is the book first, and most centrally, concerned with proving that the purpose of abduction is an interspecies breeding project (see fig. 5.1). Budd Hopkins opens his exploration with a revisionist reading of the Hill narrative, noting that "a decade or so later" after the publication of Interrupted Journey, "a device similar to the needle described by Betty is commonly used in Western medicine." He goes on to explain that

> The laparoscope is a long, flexible tube containing fiber optics which are magnified for internal viewing. The instrument is inserted directly into the patient's navel, not for pregnancy tests per se, but for a variety of related reasons—including the removal of ova. So-called test-tube babies are produced by using laparoscopy to locate and remove ova from the female for later fertilization outside the uterus with "the sperm of one's choice."[27]

Hopkins's ironic bracketing of the "so-called test-tube babies" is curious; there is a sense that even when the product of in vitro is real, its definition is provisional, fictional, does not mean any one real thing: what are they really? He suggests that we can only tentatively name and know them; they are human but somehow also altered or manufactured by the intervention of technology. This rhetorical ambiguity resonates with commentary about "superbabies" in the "Control of Life" essays, entities whose imminent arrival was heralded on the cover of that issue of Life, and who were accorded "a kind of immortality." This is not a wholesale endorsement—doubt edges in to the most optimistic assessments of such progress. Technical intervention disrupts both our sense of what is natural and our ability to name, to know, or to have any connection with the products of such technical intervention. At the same time, the "sperm of one's choice" is also literally bracketed by Hopkins, suggesting that it is not only the intervention of technology, but also the intervention of choice that disrupts an assumed natural order in the 1980s.

By the time Intruders was published in 1987, "so-called test-tube babies" were also a reality. Serious work on human in vitro fertilization began at roughly the same time as the emerging abduction phenomenon in the mid-1960s, most notably through the work of two British doctors, Robert Edwards and Patrick Steptoe. Early results of Edwards's work on maturing eggs in vitro were published in the

FIGURE 5.1. Cover image from Budd Hopkins's *Intruders: The Incredible Visitations at Copley Woods*, 1997. Reprinted by permission of Ballantine Books, a division of Random House.

Lancet, Scientific American, and *Nature* in 1965. By 1969 Edwards and Steptoe had succeeded in fertilizing a human egg with human sperm outside the human body.[28] In 1978 Louise Brown, the first "test-tube baby," was born to Lesley Brown, a young woman who, upon agreeing to be part of Edwards and Steptoe's experiments, did not realize that she was the first to do so, but in fact thought that the practice was already commonplace. In *Our Miracle Called Louise* Brown recalls, "I just imagined that hundreds of children had already been born through being conceived outside of their mother's womb."[29] Brown's ignorance is important to note: it suggests the difficulty with which the nonexpert can know what is scientifically possible or actual at any given time. At the same time it points to the science fictional nature of a process like in vitro that, while discussed extensively in mass media up through the late 1970s, was nonetheless quite remote to the experience of most people.

In their accounts of forced in vitro fertilization at the hands of aliens, abductees take this sort of confusion about scientific possibility and its personal ramifications to its imaginative extreme. So too do investigators such as Budd Hopkins and David Jacobs, who in turn use these accounts as the evidential centerpieces in arguments about the "truth" of alien abduction. In *Secret Life* Jacobs argues, following Hopkins, that "egg harvesting" is a "constant feature of the abduction experience," one that is "ultimately directed to the production of offspring."[30] Jacobs describes the procedure as follows:

> With one hand he [sic] presses on the woman's abdomen in the region above the ovaries, and with the other he inserts a variety of instruments into her vagina. The first is a speculum-like instrument that creates an opening large enough to work with. Then he inserts a long, thin, flexible tube that women report goes in very far. . . . Most women in some way know that he is taking an egg.[31]

Even Mack, who offers an alternative interpretation of abduction in his book *Abduction: Human Encounters with Aliens* (1994), assumes assisted reproduction as a central facet of the perceived experience.[32] Mack confirms that "it seems that some of the same women have been taken at later times during ovulation for the removal of ova from the Fallopian tubes. After the ova are retrieved by this process they are then apparently fertilized and brought to term outside the womb."[33]

Once the eggs are moved outside the womb—outside the natural space of the human body—the alien intervenes. In the abduction scenario, while ex utero, the human egg is combined with human sperm taken from male abductees by force. The sperm is taken by a variety of techniques hinted at in Barney Hill's memory of a cup over his groin. Male abductees have variously reported "a suction device of some sort," "some sort of tube or container," a "faucet thing, like a suction." Scott reports to Mack that it was the "wires that were applied to his testicles, in combination with the suction device over his penis that stimulated his erection and were 'making it happen.'" All the "stuff" the aliens were taking from him was being used, Scott knew, to "make babies."[34]

Outside the womb the human egg is also combined with alien DNA. As Mack's patient Jerry reports, "she has been given information from the aliens that, . . . [a]fter combining the male and female germ substance, the aliens alter the embryo in some way, perhaps adding a genetic principle of their own."[35] The ex utero vulnerability of the embryo to forces beyond human control suggests the strangeness—indeed the alienating effect—of assisted reproduction.

Once this fertilization process is completed, according to Mack, "the altered conceptus is reinserted in the uterus during a subsequent abduction, allowed to gestate for some weeks" only to be re-removed later in the pregnancy. Hopkins walks us through these steps:

> A fertilized egg is eventually "planted" back inside the uterus; if all goes well the embryo develops normally and a healthy, normal baby is born. . . . Now all of this leads to the unwelcome speculative inference that somewhere, somehow, human beings—or possibly hybrids of some sort—are being produced by a technology obviously—yet not inconceivably—superior to ours. . . . With our own current technology of genetic engineering expanding day by day, is it not conceivable that an advanced alien technology may already have the ability to remove ova and sperm from human beings, experimentally alter their genetic structure, and then replant altered and fertilized ova back into unknowing host females to be carried to term? Ova that can be removed can also be replaced, even by our own present day medical technology.[36]

For Hopkins, what is technically possible becomes not only probable, but real. Female abductees, or "host females," provide a collective forum for his leaps in logic and dystopian imaginings about genetic engineering, and for the assertion of his own expert status.

For many female abductees this in-and-out—intrusion, extraction, reinsertion—continues, seemingly ad infinitum: Jerry, for example, remembers something being implanted or removed from her vagina by the aliens fifty times.[37] Male abductees also recall exhaustion at their repeated violation: Mack's patient James remarks, "I feel like a lab animal, just sort of lying there and taking it."[38] Accompanying the repeated penetration/violation of abductees, and often as its result, comes a profusion of fetuses invested with varying degrees of power. In abduction narratives produced and published since the 1980s fetuses are everywhere: abducting, operating, implanting, being implanted, being removed, incubated, incubating. Jerry observes herself "naked on a table, unable to move her arms and legs" in a room lined with "lots and lots . . . of rectangular shaped containers." She remembers that "inside of these drawers, or incubators . . . were hundreds of, I don't know if you can call it babies or not, but little just I guess fetuses."[39] What's more, abductees beginning with the Hills have suggested that the abducting aliens themselves resemble fetuses. Barney and Betty described their captors as having "rather odd-shaped heads, with a large cranium, diminishing in size as it got toward the chin. And the eyes continued around to the sides of their heads. . . . Mouth . . . like a straight line. The texture of the skin . . . was grayish . . . I didn't notice any hair."[40] In more recent accounts abductees consistently describe their captors as fully fetal-looking, with large heads, large black eyes, necrotic skin, smooth, sexless, and hairless bodies. The fetal alien is understood by believers to be one of many species of alien: the Gray, or Zeta Reticulan. An amalgam of doctor and fetus—both creator and created—the abducting alien Gray once again elides, rendering virtually useless, the human parent.

As with the superbabies and test-tube babies discussed earlier, the hybrid babies—and abducting aliens themselves—are confounding: they inhabit an ill-defined border area between the real and imagined. Sometimes the aliens force abductees to hold and nurture the hybrid babies, which they describe as weak and listless. As Susan remembers,

> She's too small. The skin is very thin . . . you know newborn babies' hands, like tissue paper? Thinner than that. . . . I see her face, now. . . . Features are concentrated down in the lower part. . . . So the skin is not

robust in color . . . it's not baby-pink at all. It's a funny . . . grayish . . . pallor. . . . It's all concentrated down . . . the head goes down to a point.[41]

These dubious progeny embody the ways the promises of technology backfire—interventions of technology into a "natural" process bear Frankenstein's monsters, for whom abductees have difficulty showing love or nurturance. At the same time, concerns about these abandoned, ailing, unlovable fetuses reveal a sort of parental guilt, guilt about improper parenting, lack of desire to nurture. This in a culture that has, for decades if not centuries, suggested some form or another of "family values," and the assumption of traditional gender roles associated with those values, as the hallmark of normalcy and social acceptability.

The "relationship" between mother and fetus suggested by the rhetoric about reproductive technologies that emerged during the early 1960s provides ideological fuel for the sort of guilt expressed in these accounts. With the increased circulation of photographic images of the fetus in utero since the 1960s the fetus has increasingly been attributed human agency. The mother's body has come increasingly to be understood in contrast as abject vessel—that mass which surrounds the living, breathing "baby" inside.[42] The medical community now justifies the use of ultrasound to monitor even low-risk or "normal" pregnancies on the basis that visualizing the fetus enables both "reassurance" and mother/child "bonding."[43] By the turn of the millennium, the image of the fetus in utero has become domesticated—a commonplace addition to the family photo album, it provides a sort of technologically enabled prehistory of baby's life on earth (see fig. 5.2).

Perhaps a more critical ideological source for the gender guilt expressed in alien abduction narratives since the 1980s is the successful manipulation of both images of the fetus and scientific discourse about fetal personhood by members of the religious and political Right in the service of a conservative, pro-life agenda. If in the mid-1960s the images in *Life* suggested the female body as fallow terrain for the penetrating technical gaze, since the 1980s the woman's body has become an embattled terrain in debates over reproductive rights and in the wider-ranging morality campaign that seeks to police "normal" male and female behaviors. The fetus has come to play a critical iconographic role in these contests.[44]

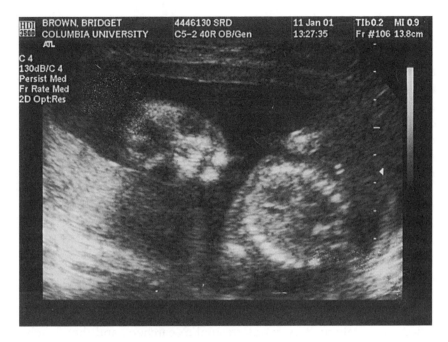

FIGURE 5.2. Author's 20-week ultrasound.

Obsessive concern with missing or stolen pregnancies in contemporary abduction narratives expresses a good degree of anxiety and confusion about the agency of mothers, fathers, and fetuses, and the politics of "choice." Kathie, as Hopkins reports, realized she was pregnant early in 1978: "Positive blood and urinalysis tests confirmed the fact. . . . Things were proceeding happily . . . until one day in March when Kathie awoke with what seemed to be a normal menstrual flow. . . . [A] visit to her doctor confirmed her fear: She was no longer pregnant. Yet there had been no apparent miscarriage. . . . She just wasn't pregnant anymore."[45] Kathie remembers her confusion and distress: "I knew I'd lost the baby. . . . I went in to have the test, but I knew what it would show. . . . I kept saying they took my baby . . . they took my baby, and I cried so hard they didn't know what to do with me. But I knew somebody took my baby."[46] In these scenarios women do not have abortions or choose to terminate pregnancies. Their babies are simply aborted, taken, disappeared with the same results: the women are no longer pregnant. The abduction narrative also enables male abductees to latch ill-defined feelings of disenfranchisement onto a preexisting discourse about the oppression of women. Through accounts of physical and reproductive violation, men can participate in conversations about bodily "choice" from which they have often been excluded and in which they have often been rendered patriarchal oppressors. In the abduction scenario, female abductees can displace guilt for choosing, or desiring to choose, abortion onto their alien captors. So too can male abductees displace guilt for any possible witting or unwitting collaboration in the oppression of women, or for their own ambivalence about the oftentimes heteronormative project of family planning.

THE LIMITS OF RESISTANCE TO ALIEN INVASION

The emergence of the abduction scenario in the mid-1960s signals a pronounced and critical shift in the ways we imagine the invading alien other and the ways we imagine the notion of invasion itself. The abduction scenario suggests that humans are among the data being collected and catalogued by extraterrestrial researchers, and that the objective detachment of invading extraterrestrials is not necessarily a benign detachment. Unwilling encounters with the Grays place abductees in the position of vivisected lab animals, such as the fetal monkeys, pigs, and cows featured alongside prone women in "Control of Life." The result is account after account of human experience told from the perspective of the laboratory rat. Mack's patient Ed articulates this perspective when he argues with his captor, shouting, "I'm not just your laboratory rat, guinea pig."[47] In trying to articulate the nature of the horror his alien captors represented for him, Barney Hill struggled to find the right words. He noted that they were frightening not in a "horrible sense, like a distorted, unhuman type of creature." Rather, according to Hill, "he was more—the frightening part was the military precision of—as if he was a person who knew what to do, could do it, and was willing to carry it out."[48] Contact with abducting aliens thus comes not through cataclysmic military conflict, but through the ability of those in power—those possessed of the knowledge and technology to create and destroy—to get in, on a regular basis, to the most mundane and intimate spheres of our everyday lives: our homes, our cars, our beds, our bodies. Indeed, abduction suggests that the body itself is an object of technical conquest and colonization by entities driven less by lust for global, intergalactic, or national dominance than by an inexplicable and overweening interest in skin, sperm, and frontal lobes—in human beings, human bodies, the very stuff of humanity itself.

Since the Hills, abductees have tried to "talk back" to their captors and object to forced procedures. In 1966 Barney Hill remarked, "I don't want them to operate on me."[49] In 1987 Whitley Strieber, author of the best-seller *Communion: A True Story*, more forcefully asserted, "I'm not going to let you do an operation on me. You have absolutely no right." In Strieber's account the aliens respond, "We do have a right."[50] In each case, protest is met with puzzlement and palliatives at best, or with the invocation of total authority at worst. Strieber is horrified by this bold assertion of power: "Five enormous words. Stunning words. We do have a right. Who gave it to them? By what progress of ethics had they arrived at that conclusion?"[51] Abductees rehearse, again and again, the difference between the right to protest and the ability to effect change over the conditions of one's own disempowerment. Abductees are left, in the end, with stories. These stories can be read, as I read them, as richly imaginative alternative histories of life in America since the mid-1960s; accounts that give voice to otherwise unexpressed or inexpressible critiques of existing power imbalances. Yet in the end, abductees do not read their own experiences this way. Abductees are left with bodily wounds and considerable frustration with both their alien captors and the experts who appropriate their stories into best-sellers. It is the realness of abduction for abductees, the realness of the terror experienced in and through them, that ultimately results in a deferral of blame for their own very real suffering onto an alien abductor. This deferral results, ironically, in renunciation of the possibility of social or collective response to the abuses of scientific, political, and moral authority that abduction narratives imaginatively critique.

NOTES

1. John Fuller, *Interrupted Journey: Two Lost Hours aboard a Flying Saucer* (New York: Dial Press, 1966), 164.

2. Ibid., 299.

3. Ibid., 123.

4. Ibid., 117.

5. Ibid., 123.

6. "Explosion of Science," *Life*, 26 December 1960, 15.

7. Rutherford Platt, "The Wondrous Inner Space of Living Cells," *Reader's Digest*, June 1964, 195.

8. Ibid., 195.

9. Ibid., 196. For more on how popular culture and science interact to imbue DNA with meaning and agency, see Dorothy Nelkin, *The DNA Mystique: The Gene as Cultural Icon* (New York: W. H. Freeman, 1995).

10. "Control of Life," *Life*, 10 September 1965, 76.

11. For discussion and debate between feminist historians on the relative empowerment of women in the face of medical expertise, see Barbara Ehrenreich and Deirdre English, *For Her Own Good: 150 Years of the Experts' Advice to Women* (Garden City: Anchor Press, 1978); Carroll Smith Rosenberg, *Disorderly Conduct: Visions of Gender in Victorian America* (New York: Knopf, 1985), especially her chapter on the American Medical Association; Elaine Tyler May, *Homeward Bound: American Families in the Cold War Era* (New York: Basic Books, 1988); Regina Morantz-Sanchez, *Sympathy and Science: Women Physicians in American Medicine* (New York: Oxford University Press, 1985).

12. "The Secret World of the Unborn," *McCall's*, 1963, 75.

13. "Control of Life," 64.

14. Ibid., 62.

15. Ibid.

16. Feminist historians of science have investigated the historic circumstances through which the fetus has been redefined as patient, and the (pregnant) female body subjected to medical and social surveillance and management. As Rosalind Petchesky notes in *Abortion and Woman's Choice: The State, Sexuality, and Women's Reproductive Freedom* (Boston: Northeastern University Press, 1984), the post–Baby Boom fertility decline that began in 1958 and continued through 1973 drove obstetrician/gynecologists to find the "new patient population of the fetus" (273). During this period, an increasing number of women were entering college and the labor force, marrying and bearing children later in their lives, and divorcing more frequently. New technologies such as amniocentesis, in vitro fertilization, electronic fetal monitoring, ultrasound, magnetic resonance imaging, and fetoscopy all "[carved] out more and more space/time for the obstetrical management of pregnancy" (273). In *Disorderly Conduct*, Smith Rosenberg considers the historical emergence of this particular redistribution of power in the nineteenth century. Smith Rosenberg notes that the American Medical Association then succeeded in creating "a new Oedipal triangle, linking the male physician with the female fetus against the mother" (242).

17. Nazi science and Nazi scientists figure prominently in a number of alien conspiracy theories that have emerged in the 1980s, all of which extrapolate, as do most conspiracy theories, from actual historical events. In this case, the postwar influx of German scientists to head up newly state-sponsored sci-

ence initiatives, including the rocket program, some of whom were indeed Nazis, is construed as a government-sanctioned cabal in charge of overseeing government-sanctioned experimentation on American citizens by abducting extraterrestrials. The *X-Files* episode "Project Paper Clip" (first broadcast 29 September 1995) offers one retelling of this story.

18. Fuller, *Interrupted Journey*, 159.

19. Ibid., 299.

20. Ibid., 93.

21. See Carol Clover, *Men, Women, and Chainsaws: Gender in the Modern Horror Film* (Princeton: Princeton University Press, 1992), and Kaja Silverman, *Male Subjectivity at the Margins* (New York: Routledge, 1992) for examples of how feminist film theorists have begun to challenge the argument that the filmic gaze is always a male gaze with which spectators identify, thus collaborating in the objectification of the female body. The locus classicus of this argument is Laura Mulvey's "Visual Pleasure and Narrative Cinema," *Screen* 16 (1975): 6–18.

22. Medical institutions have long been sites of power, and the gaze of the doctor—his ability to look in and through mere mortal flesh—has long been the coordinator of this power. See Michel Foucault, *Birth of the Clinic: An Archaeology of Medical Perception* (New York: Vintage, 1973). Foucault observes of nineteenth-century medical discourse that "in medical space . . . one began to conceive of a generalized presence of doctors whose intersecting gazes form a network and exercise at every point in space and at every moment in time, a constant, mobile, differentiated supervision" (31).

23. See, for example, Ellen Herman, *The Romance of American Psychology: Political Culture in the Age of Experts, 1940–1970* (Berkeley: University of California Press, 1995); Stuart Leslie, *The Cold War and American Science: The Military–Industrial–Academic Complex at MIT and Stanford* (New York: Columbia University Press, 1993); and Stuart Leslie, ed., "The Cold War and Expert Knowledge: Essays on the National Security State," special issue of *Radical History Review* 63 (1995).

24. For defenses of technocratic neutrality and objectivity from the first half of the century, see Frederick Winslow Taylor, *The Principles of Scientific Management* (New York: Norton, 1911); and Thorstein Veblen, *The Engineers and the Price System* (New York: B. W. Huebsch, 1921). For a postwar, postindustrial version of the same, see Daniel Bell, *The Coming of Post-Industrial Society: A Venture in Social Forecasting* (New York: Basic Books, 1976). For critiques of technocracy, see C. Wright Mills, *The Power Elite* (New York: Oxford University Press, 1956); and Theodore Roszak, *Making of a Counter Culture: Reflections on the Technocratic Society and Its Youthful Opposition* (Berkeley: University of California Press, 1968). For discussions of growing popular criticism of scientific and medical authority in general, see Charles Rosenberg, *No Other Gods: On Science and American Social Thought* (Baltimore: Johns Hopkins University Press, 1997),

and Malcolm Goggin, *Governing Science and Technology in a Democratic Society* (Knoxville: University of Tennessee Press, 1986).

25. A handful of abduction accounts were published in the 1960s and 1970s, one of which centrally concerns human reproduction as part of the alien agenda. As in the Hills' account, reference to alien attention to human reproduction is relatively understated in *The Andreasson Affair* (Englewood Cliffs, NJ: Prentice Hall, 1979) by UFO investigator Raymond Fowler; in Fowler's book abductee Betty Andreasson notes only that her captors at one point "measure [her] for procreation" (59).

26. John Mack, *Abduction: Human Encounters with Aliens* (New York: Scribner's, 1994), 414.

27. Budd Hopkins, *Intruders: The Incredible Visitations at Copley Woods* (New York: Ballantine, 1987), 18.

28. For more on Steptoe and Edwards, see Gina Maranto, *The Quest for Perfection: The Drive to Breed Better Humans* (New York: Scribner's, 1996).

29. Lesley Brown and John Brown, *Our Miracle Called Louise* (New York: Paddington Press, 1979), 106.

30. David Jacobs, *Secret Life: Firsthand Documented Accounts of UFO Abductions* (New York: Simon and Schuster, 1992), 107.

31. Ibid., 107.

32. Mack de-emphasizes victimization of abductees and stresses, in his New Age–inflected interpretation of the phenomenon, the consciousness-raising effects of abduction on abductees.

33. Mack, *Abduction*, 82.

34. Ibid., 99.

35. Ibid., 132.

36. Hopkins, *Intruders*, 118.

37. Mack, *Abduction*, 132.

38. Ibid., 200.

39. Ibid., 132.

40. Fuller, *Interrupted Journey*, 260.

41. Hopkins, *Intruders*, 240.

42. For discussion of the ways new reproductive technologies, especially fetal-imaging technologies, have influenced ideas about fetal and maternal agency, see Ann Oakley, *The Captured Womb: A History of the Medical Care of Pregnant Women* (New York: Blackwell, 1984); Sarah Franklin, *Embodied Progress: A Cultural Account of Assisted Conception* (New York: Routledge, 1997); Marilyn Strathern, *Reproducing the Future: Essays on Anthropology, Kinship, and the New Reproductive Technologies* (New York: Routledge, 1992); Petchesky, *Abortion and Woman's Choice*; and Faye Ginsburg and Rayna Rapp, eds., *Conceiving the New World Order: The Global Politics of Reproduction* (Berkeley: University of California Press, 1995).

43. See Janelle Taylor, "The Public Fetus and the Family Car: From Abortion Politics to a Volvo Ad," *Public Culture* 4 (1992). As cited in Taylor (23), during the 1980s the number of women getting ultrasounds for pregnancy increased drastically: from 35.5 percent to 78.8 percent between 1980 and 1987 alone.

44. Since the 1980s, the fetus has been redefined as a person not only in scientific discourse but also in legal discourse and anti-abortion legislation, oftentimes itself informed by scientific authority. In an essay on reproductive discourse in the 1980s, Valerie Hartouni details how abortion became a centerpiece during the 1980s for a wider-ranging campaign to "revitalize the country politically and rehabilitate it morally." Hartouni, "Containing Women: Reproductive Discourse in the 1980s," in *Technoculture*, ed. Constance Penley and Andrew Ross (Minneapolis: University of Minnesota Press, 1991), 3. The official legislative campaign to chip away at abortion rights began in 1981, when Senator Orrin Hatch spearheaded Senate Judiciary Subcommittee hearings, the goal of which was to locate life at the moment of conception and thus legally define the fetus as a person. In 1989, as a result of this campaign, the Supreme Court's decision in *Webster v. Reproductive Health Services* declared the fetus a person with rights.

45. Hopkins, *Intruders*, 79.

46. Ibid., 168.

47. Mack, *Abduction*, 60.

48. Fuller, *Interrupted Journey*, 207.

49. Ibid., 83.

50. Whitley Strieber, *Communion: A True Story* (New York: William Morrow, 1987), 107.

51. Ibid.

THE ENEMY WITHIN

6

Injections and Truth Serums

AIDS Conspiracy Theories and the Politics of Articulation

Jack Bratich

THE SPRING 1999 ISSUE of *Paranoia: The Conspiracy Reader* featured an article entitled "The AIDS-ET Connection."[1] This essay, written by Phillip S. Duke, Ph.D. (we are not told in what), provides a "unifying scientific hypothesis" that purports to explain the simultaneous emergence of two different HIV strains in the geographically diverse areas of Africa and the United States. Even more, this hypothesis claims to explain the phenomena of reported alien abduction experiences and cattle mutilations. According to Duke, this unifying hypothesis is "the gray alien agenda," which, in essence, is to depopulate the earth and establish an alien settlement. In his conclusion, Duke, in good scientific fashion, limits his speculative claims by stating that the "AIDS–ET Connection must still be considered a hypothesis" (because there is not enough confirming data to render it a theory). He ends his article with a request for information, questions, and comments from the readership.[2]

Splicing together different strains of conspiracy narratives (AIDS as biowarfare agent, the ufological phenomenon of abductions, cattle mutilations), "The AIDS-ET Connection" obviously has all the hallmarks of an AIDS conspiracy theory. In most commonsense approaches, this alone would be grounds for disqualification. But what element of the narrative is the crucial one that defines it as such? Is it the interjection of the "gray alien agenda," or would it be the same if we kept the agenda terrestrial? Furthermore, even if we could settle on the categorization of this hypothesis as "conspiracy theory," would that be the same as considering it "paranoid"? And what does this have to do with the truth-effects of the claims? In this essay, I will examine some of the political stakes involved in the production and problematization of

"AIDS conspiracy theories." Before addressing that specific strain of conspiracy accounts, however, I want to make some general methodological remarks on the very object of study, "conspiracy theories."

DIAGNOSING AND ASSESSING

Since the spring of 1995 a myriad of books and articles on conspiracy theories have been published, both for academic and popular audiences.[3] With the amount of prominent scrutiny paid to conspiracy theories of late, it is obvious that "political paranoia" has become a significant object of concern in political discourse.[4]

What is common among almost all of these public discussions is the disparaging application of the term "paranoid" to discredit certain kinds of knowledge-claims on the world. That is, they employ a seemingly easy and commonsensical transposition of a medical framework to the field of politics. In essence, these approaches *psychologize* politics. They decode a clinical term (paranoia) and, more important, a form of analysis (diagnosis) and translate them to the political sphere. Knowledge-claims, especially of a certain political kind, are treated as a symptom of a particular (though generalized) psychological condition. Their status as political-claims-to-be-addressed is relegated to an epiphenomenon-to-be-studied. The diagnostic model invokes the authority of science as it erases the politicality of the knowledges diagnosed. Given my commitment to take these claims more seriously, I do not want to psychologize this phenomenon out of its politics, and therefore refrain from the diagnostic judgment.

Aside from this rather traditional psychological approach (perhaps most famously articulated by Richard Hofstadter in his seminal essay, "The Paranoid Style in American Politics"),[5] a more recent form of analysis has emerged, which one might refer to as a sociological/cultural approach.[6] This more nuanced approach does not seek to dismiss conspiracy theories out of hand (as irrational), but rather looks for their origins in social, cultural, and economic conditions.[7] This may not sound terribly problematic at first, as this framework seeks a more complex historical basis for these theories, even giving them a veneer of rationality (however misguided).

However, in most cases the conspiracy accounts take on the status of being a kind of cultural folklore, whose claims have no truth-value other than expressing the truth of their storytellers. They have no explanatory power to tell others about their objects; they can only explain themselves as objects-for-us. Within this recent form of "root" analysis[8] or cultural-historical approach,[9] conspiracy accounts are still symptoms to be read, a result of social and cultural conditions rather than of a collective mental disorder. Conspiracy narratives are thus an expression of frustration, oversimplified and channeled in the wrong direction. Concerned intellectuals and activists, it follows, need to address the theorists' "real" grievances (unknown, of course, to them). Now, while I do not doubt that there are instances of conspiracy research that are infused with this motivation and narrative form, I want to argue that it is not politically efficacious to tell others condescendingly what their "real" grievances are or should be. Rather, as political intellectuals we need to address their claims as having a stake in *determining* the real.

My approach, then, begins with the question "What is a conspiracy theory?" while recognizing that this determination is made *elsewhere*, and is not inherent in the narrative *itself*. Given their discredited status, I will characterize "AIDS conspiracy theories" as "subjugated knowledges" in the sense Michel Foucault uses the term.[10] In his inquiry, Foucault wonders if there is anything to these knowledges outside their subjugation: "Is the relation of forces today still such as to allow these disinterred knowledges some kind of autonomous life? Can they be isolated by these means from every subjugating relationship? What force do they have, taken in themselves?"[11] I want to locate my approach in the gap opened by these questions, that is, between the force of subjugation and the knowledge "in and of itself."

Thus, it should be apparent that my approach does not seek to assert the "truth" of the subjugated knowledges (i.e., to treat them as suppressed truths requiring liberation) but rather to trace their relations to the regime of truth, to institutional practices, and to their productive deployment. We move from affirming the validity of the object's claims to problematizing the politics of truth surrounding (and forming) this object. Rather than positing the unity of conspiracy theories (under a term such as "political paranoia") in order to get at its deep meaning, this approach entails analyzing the practices of power that channel, shape, incite, and deploy conspiracy theories as *meaningful*. With regard, then, to my "object of study" I want to move from, in Deleuzo-Guattarian terms, tracing an object (locating, isolating, delimiting, interiorizing, unifying) to mapping a field (drawing, tracking, chasing).[12]

What matters here is how these narratives are "problematized" in contemporary American political discourse.[13] My inquiry is less concerned with what a conspiracy theory *is* and more with what it *does* and what is done to it. In other words, this approach is one that takes "articulation" seriously. According to Lawrence Grossberg, "the concept of articulation [describes] the process of forging connections between practices and effects, as well as of enabling practices to have different, often unpredicted effects. Articulation links this practice to that effect, this text to that meaning, this meaning to that reality, this experience to those politics. And these links are themselves articulated into larger structures, etc."[14] It "often involves delinking or disarticulating connections in order to link or rearticulate others. Articulation is a continuous struggle to reposition practices within a shifting field of forces, to redefine the possibilities of life by redefining the field of relations—the context—within which a practice is located."[15]

I immerse myself in these discursive conflicts surrounding and deploying conspiracy narratives in order to map the contingency of the official discourses of power and knowledge. In Foucauldian language, research and criticism are done "in such a way that the lines of force and the lines of fragility come forth; the points of resistance and the possible points of attack; the paths marked out and the shortcuts."[16] That is, I am not interested in explaining or interpreting conspiracy theories *as such*, but rather in explicating the forms of rationality and politics that lead us to be concerned with explaining these narratives. In John Fiske's terms, I will evaluate "the strategies by which . . . disbelief is validated and . . . counterknowledge is discredited."[17] It is apparent, then, that the methodological formulation of the object itself is at stake, insofar as conceptualization and articulation are political matters.[18]

MAPPING THE REAL ANALYSIS

In this essay I will map a particular problematization of AIDS conspiratorial accounts (especially its assumed political effects). I choose this because it is one of the most widely disseminated and visible conspiracy theories, and because it is perhaps the most fiercely debated political one (due to the urgency and life-and-death issues involved). "AIDS conspiracy theories" come in a variety of forms and political stripes. I have provided a chart, which, while certainly not exhaustive, does list the most prominent versions of this account (see fig. 6.1).[19] In general, I have found that AIDS conspiracy theories crystallize the stakes involved in the problematization of conspiracy theories, especially with regard to left politics.

The problematization of AIDS conspiracy theories by political and educational activists is not new. John S. James argued in 1986 that conspiracy theories were not useful.[20] Germ warfare conspiracy theories were unlikely to be proven, and, "even if proved, we could only punish the guilty, not save lives." This theory "distracts from a better use of our energies," which is to inform the public about what the author repeatedly calls the "neglect and mismanagement of treatment research." For James, the conspiracy is a "conspiracy of silence," a pattern of ignorance and mismanagement of AIDS treatment research by scientists, government officials, doctors, and journalists.[21]

A more recent argument, found in the fall 1996 issue of *Covert Action Quarterly*, makes an even stronger claim: that conspiracy theories are politically disabling and health-endangering beliefs.[22] By diverting attention from the social conditions and economic structures that make up the contemporary context in which AIDS endures, this article asserts, conspiracy theories are antagonistic to leftist concerns. In the following sections I will assess the article's articulations (how does it define a conspiracy theory? who are cited as examples?) as they link knowledge and practice. How is a theory translated into behavioral practice, in this argument? What forms of political thought and action are espoused, and which ones exiled? Given that some political organizations have formed around conspiracy narratives, what activist possibilities do the articulations leave out? This will be a fairly long and detailed reading of the article; I wish to convey with specificity both the article's arguments (especially for those unfamiliar with it) and the assumptions and political stakes that emerge from it.

"Tracking the *Real* Genocide: AIDS—Conspiracy or Unnatural Disaster?" by David Gilbert was the cover story of *Covert Action Quarterly*. The author has "been involved in the struggle against racism and imperialism since the early 1960s," is "currently serving a life sentence in New York State . . . as a white ally of the Black Liberation Army," and has been a "leading activist and educator on AIDS in prison" (55).[23] Gilbert begins his article by citing statistics that demonstrate that "the correlation between AIDS and social and economic oppression is clear and powerful" (55). He then argues that this pattern "meshes neatly

FIGURE 6.1. AIDS Conspiracy Theories

Author/Key Text	Origin/Source	Spread	Historical Context/Purpose	Prescription
Dr. William C. Douglass, *AIDS: The End of Civilization*	Artificial splice between visna virus and HTLV-1 at Ft. Detrick, MD. Deliberate introduction into populace.	WHO in Africa/CDC in United States. Both via vaccine programs. Casual contact.	CBW. Communist plot to destroy Western civilization.	Boost law and order; dismantle WHO/UN; fight communism.
Drs. Jakob and Lilli Segal, "AIDS: USA Home-Made Evil" (self-published pamphlet, 1986)	Artificial splice between visna virus and HTLV-1 at Ft. Detrick, MD. Accidental introduction into populace.	Tested on U.S. prison inmates, who accidentally spread it to New York's gay community. Not casual contact.	CBW. General U.S. malfeasance (accused of being KGB disinformation).	More scientific research.
Dr. Alan Cantwell, Jr., *AIDS: The Mystery and the Solution; AIDS and the Doctors of Death; Queer Blood: The Secret AIDS Genocide Plot*	Human-made, probably artificial splice, but could be old virus. Deliberate introduction into populace.	WHO in Africa/CDC in United States. Both via vaccine programs. Not casual contact.	CBW, military-medical-industrial complex. Genocide, especially against gays, and then "Blame the victims." Possible introduction of New World Order.	Become better health practitioners and healers; educate selves; fight back against power.
Jon Rappaport, *AIDS Incorporated: The Scandal of the Century*	Multifactorial: source is anything that suppresses immune system, including malnutrition, poverty, pharmaceutical and street drugs, pesticides, African swine fever. Deliberate introduction.	Poor environmental conditions and behavioral practices. Some treatments (AZT) contribute to problem. Not necessarily viral.	Collusion between pharmaceutical corporations and medical establishment; unaccountable institutions; sloppy and unethical research; possible CBW. Potential martial law.	Take better care of immune system (including safer sex). Open up newlines of AIDS research (nonviral). Activism: revolution in health care.
The Strecker Group (Dr. Robert Strecker et al.) *The Strecker Memorandum*	Artificial splice between visna virus and bovine virus. Deliberate introduction into populace.	WHO in Africa/CDC in United States. Both via vaccine programs. Can be carried by mosquitoes; condoms will not prevent spread. A viral cancer—contagious.	CBW, history of unethical experimentation on populace. Trial experiment, communist plot to exterminate U.S.	Research into electromagnetic cures, no intravenous drugs, reduce sexual promiscuity, no blood products, and start questioning official reports.

Author/Key Text	Origin/Source	Spread	Historical Context/Purpose	Prescription
Dr. Peter Duesberg, *Why We Will Never Win the War on AIDS; Inventing the AIDS Virus*	Nonviral: social factors, lifestyle, drug use.	Poor behavioral practices and continued unethical scientific practice. Some treatments (AZT) contribute to problem.	Collusion between pharmaceutical corporations and medical establishment; power of "virus hunters" (research establishment elite), greed.	Change behavioral practices (especially stop drug use); open up new lines of AIDS research (nonviral).
Dr. Leonard Horowitz, *Emerging Viruses: AIDS and Ebola – Nature, Accident, or Intentional?*	Artificial splice. Possibly accidental, but probably deliberate introduction into populace.	Vaccine programs, with CIA and military-medical-industrial complex backing.	CBW, military-medical-industrial complex, CIA human experiments and foreign subversion, postwar Nazi International. Genocide, against gays in U.S.; blacks in Africa. Population control/New World Order.	Broaden social, political, and scientific perspective. (Horowitz heads Tetrahedron, Inc., an educational/activist organization.)
Haki R. Madhubuti, "AIDS: The Purposeful Destruction of the Black World?" in *Black Men: Obsolete, Single, Dangerous?*	Human-made, synthesized from smallpox and hepatitis B vaccines. Deliberate introduction into populace.	WHO in Africa, via vaccine programs. Also can be carried by mosquitoes. Virus can live outside body.	CBW, history of unethical experimentation on black populace, including Jonestown massacre. Genocide against "the black world."	Educate selves; be understanding of those who are ill; be activists; seek preventative health; fight for that which is good, just, and right.
G. J. Krupey, "AIDS: Act of God or the Pentagon?" in *Secret and Suppressed*	Artificial splice by U.S. military and civilian research nexus. Deliberate, but possibly accidental introduction into populace.	WHO in Africa/CDC and NIH in United States. Both via vaccine programs. Not casual contact.	CBW, military-medical-industrial complex, Cold War politics, militarization of health research. Justification for suspension of civil liberties and imposition of martial law.	Cause is secondary: need to prevent and cure AIDS; fight bigotry and reactionary panic; need radical cure—not just medical, but political (make government accountable).

with an extensive history of chemical and biological warfare (CBW) and medical experiments which have targeted people of color, Third World populations, prisoners, and other unsuspecting individuals" (55–56).[24] Because of this context, Gilbert argues, "there are good reasons why so many prisoners as well as a significant portion of the African-American Community believe that government scientists deliberately created AIDS as a tool of genocide" (56–57).

We can already see at work here the above-described sociological approach to conspiracy theories. This framework finds "good reasons" for these conspiratological beliefs (in the conditions of social/political oppression), giving them an understandable, rational basis. However, this approach still finds these narratives to be misguided in their *apprehension* of those conditions.[25] That is, the conspiracy narratives cannot have a purchase on *explaining* those conditions of oppression, but they can be *explained by* an appeal to those contexts. Even at the discursive moment when the analysis invokes a shared historical context (of oppression), there is still a distancing effect produced between the author and his objects. The analyst authorizes himself with a clearer, truer perspective, which will dietrologically explain how another set of claims has been misguided in its analysis of the "same" context.

"SIMPLY WRONG": THE SCIENTIFIC CRITIQUE

Gilbert continues for the next few pages with a two-tiered critique of these beliefs (the scientific and the political). First, Gilbert announces that there is a "problem with this almost perfect fit [AIDS and deliberate genocide]: It is not true" (57). The splice theories of HIV's origin "wilt under scientific scrutiny" (58).[26] And what is this rigorous scrutiny that triumphs over the human-made splice theory origin story? Gilbert cites two scientists. First, he refers to his friend Janet Stavnezer ("a professor of molecular genetics and microbiology specializing in immunology"), who states that the "splice theory is scientifically impossible" (57–58). Second, he cites a Dr. David Dubnau who, in a *Covert Action Information Bulletin* article nine years earlier, stated that the HIV splice theories "are simply wrong" (58). No findings from any studies are produced. Rather, Stavnezer's statement comes from "personal correspondence and discussions" and Dubnau, whose specific scientific credentials we are not given, is simply cited from a previous article (59 n. 8).

This appeal to expertism is followed by a brief attempt to further scientifically dismiss the human-made HIV origin story. Gilbert argues that the spacing and timing of the epidemic "eliminate the possibility that scientists deliberately designed such a germ to destroy the immune system" (59). Without going into too much detail about his argument, let me just point out that his claims rest on a couple of assumptions. One, he assumes the fixed truth of certain scientific hypotheses that, especially in 1996, were highly contested.[27] Two, Gilbert places a considerable amount of credence in the publicity of scientific practice, claiming that up to "the end of the 1970s the search for human retroviruses was propelled by speculation that they might cause cancer, not that they would target the immune system" (59).[28] By believing that HIV arose before it could be considered a CBW (chemical–biological warfare) genocidal agent, Gilbert invests trust in the visibility of science. He prefers to believe in the official record of science's history rather than in the institutional secrecy endemic to scientific practice in a CBW context. That is to say, Gilbert eschews his *own* critical sensibility employed in the beginning of the article when he discussed the history of covert medical warfare. Instead he chooses to use that very same official science as a way to discredit the AIDS-as-genocide conspiracy accounts. In his first prong of attack, then, Gilbert seeks to legitimate his framework on conspiracy theories through an alliance with scientific authority (though not necessarily with scientific procedures). By appealing to expertism and investing an excess of faith in the official scientific record, Gilbert tries to use science's power to authorize his own position, ignoring even his own discussion of the complicity of that science's history with the context of oppression.

"DANGEROUS TO YOUR HEALTH":
THE POLITICAL CRITIQUE

Gilbert then dissects what he calls "the most common source of the conspiracy theories circulating in New York State prisons" (59), the work of William Campbell Douglass, M.D.[29] But a few pages before he performs this thorough analysis, he establishes the frame under which we are to read his interpretation. The second part of his two-tiered critique (the political-activist) occurs in a section entitled "Dangerous to Your Health." Here, Gilbert states (in the same vein as James a decade earlier) that "conspiracy theories divert energy from the work that must be done in the trenches if marginalized communities are to survive this epidemic: grassroots education, mobilization for AIDS prevention, and better care for people living with HIV" (57). These theories "distract from the urgent need to focus a spotlight on the life-and-death issue of AIDS prevention and on the crucial struggle against a racist and profit-driven public health system" (57). In his experience as a prison AIDS educator, the author has found "these conspiracy theories to be the main internal obstacle . . . to implementing risk reduction strategies" (57), and briefly mentions a study at the University of North Carolina, Chapel Hill, that confirms his belief.[30]

It is at this point that Gilbert's argument makes three crucial articulations that will guide his reading of Douglass's conspiracy theory, as well as determine his perspective on conspiracy theories in general. First, he conflates HIV origin stories with accounts of the means of HIV transmission (something he later takes Douglass to task for). Gilbert finds that the mindset of "denial" among prisoners is a result of their adherence to conspiracy theories. He asks in their voice, "What's the point of all the hassles of safer sex, or all the inconvenience of not sharing needles, if HIV can be spread, as many conspiracy theories claim, by casual contact such as sneezing or handling dishes?" (57). While I agree that there are some conspiracy theories that do have a casual-contact version of transmission (Douglass being the premier example), it does not follow that all chemical–biological warfare AIDS origin stories or HIV splice theories contain them (see fig. 6.1). Based on this conflation, Gilbert then makes the second articulation, that between origin stories and behavioral practices. "People whose activities have put them at risk of HIV are often petrified and turn to conspiracy theories as a hip and seemingly militant rationale for not confronting their own dangerous practices" (57). In essence, belief in conspiracy theories leads to risky behavior and resistance to AIDS education.

The third important articulation Gilbert makes is less about preventative health education and more about what we might call preventative *political* education. Gilbert argues that "[conspiracy] theories provide an apparently simple and satisfying alternative to the complex challenge of dealing with the myriad of social . . . factors that propel the epidemic" (57). Harkening back to his opening treatment of conspiracy theories as having "good reasons," Gilbert finds these origin stories to be overly simplified misrecognitions of the "real" conditions of oppression. Rather than locate origin stories as one possible factor in this "myriad," Gilbert chooses to describe them as a competing analytic framework, one that is too simplistic and ignorant of "real" conditions to have legitimacy as political analysis. Gilbert himself doubts the possibility of knowing the origin of AIDS anytime soon, but is personally "convinced that humans did not design HIV" (57). Origin stories about AIDS in this account are, at best, unknowable and thus unrelated to political and educational struggles, and, at worst (when they take the conspiratorial form), a deadly diversion from urgent prevention practices and from real political analysis.

After the author has articulated AIDS origin stories to transmission stories, unsafe behavioral practices, and political ignorance, the principal assertion of the piece can be made (extracted and highlighted by the editors): "The false conspiracy theories are themselves a contributing factor to the terrible toll of unnecessary AIDS deaths" (56–57). It is with this urgent proclamation that readers are to understand the subsequent reading of Douglass's conspiracy theory, as well as the political and educational effects of conspiracy accounts in general.[31]

RIGHT WOOS LEFT: DOUGLASS AND POLITICAL SEDUCTION

The article proceeds with an elaborate and detailed explication of William Douglass's theory. I do not have much to say regarding Gilbert's interpretation of Douglass, as it seems thorough and accurate. However, there is much to say about the *significance* of Douglass in Gilbert's argument. As I have mentioned earlier, Gilbert focuses on Douglass because he is the "most common source of the conspiracy theories circulating in New York State prisons" and his works "are prime sources for many black community militants and prisoners who embrace the conspiracy theory out of a sincere desire to fight genocide" (59). But Douglass's theory also confirms all the fears about conspiracy narratives that Gilbert has already alarmed us about. For one thing, Douglass's origin story (the splice theory) is bound up with the casual-contact transmission account (AIDS is not a sexually transmitted disease, it is an airborne virus, it can be transmitted through eating utensils), which can lead to severely destructive behavioral practices.

Douglass also has perhaps the strongest right-wing politics of all the conspiracy theorists, believing AIDS to be part of a communist plot to destroy Western civilization (even after the collapse of the Soviet Union). In addition, as Gilbert notes, his prescriptions for action primarily involve establishing and strengthening law-and-order policies.[32] Furthermore, Douglass offers a hodgepodge of general reactionary calls to save Western civilization (including military action against Russia, the abolishment of the United Nations and the World Health Organization, and anti–Mexican immigration policies). Thus, Douglass functions as an excellent representative of the worst of conspiracy theories, especially for the left-leaning readership of *CAQ*. His well-deserved repugnance, however, begins to function as representative of conspiracy theories in general, as the next section on politics develops.

Gilbert uses Douglass's reactionary theory as a springboard for a discussion of contemporary populist struggles. Linking Douglass to Lyndon LaRouche through their mutual reliance on the prominent AIDS conspiracy theorist Robert Strecker, M.D., Gilbert begins to articulate AIDS conspiracy theories firmly to the contemporary right-wing movement in the United States. The familiar figure of Bo Gritz is then trotted out, linking these theories to the then-hyped militia movement and further entrenching the articulation to right-wing politics.[33] After a brief meditation on the danger of being seduced by the Right's populist, "attractive mantle of 'militant anti-government movement,'" Gilbert restates his main thesis: "Whatever the right's motives, the practical consequences are clear: There is a definite correlation between believing these myths and a failure to take proven, life saving preventive measures. In the end, the lies promulgated by the likes of Douglass, Strecker, and LaRouche kill" (62). The argument cements its articulation between AIDS conspiracy accounts and a particular political position within the deadly effects that necessarily flow from believing in these theories.

The rest of the article goes on to elaborate thoroughly on what the "real" genocide is, providing a meticulous account of the numerous factors contributing to the horrific living conditions facing poor African Americans today, and the criminally negligent public health and political system's role in furthering the AIDS epidemic. The article concludes with a call for grassroots organizing and peer education, while decrying "the fundamentally right-wing conspiracy theories of Dr. Douglass and the like that lead us on a wild goose chase for the little men in white coats in a secret lab," and which (once again) "divert people from identifying and fighting back against the real genocide" (64). Through condescension (one is reminded of people talking about "little green men") and an urgent political warning, Gilbert reiterates his articulations with a sense of alarm and an appeal to the authority of the "real."

In summary, why spend so much time on one article? Gilbert, I believe, has provided the most cogent and serious treatment of the topic of AIDS conspiracy theories from the Left that I have come across. It encapsulates in an impassioned and persuasive manner the assumptions and articulations made offhandedly by others in the sociological approach to conspiracy theories. Unlike the mainstream articulations performed on conspiracy theories, Gilbert's argument does not dismiss them out of hand through a transposed clinical term like "paranoia." He takes them on as a significant set of political claims, ones that sprout from and respond to the same conditions as his own analysis (and by extension, the Left's). Unfortunately, he quickly depicts them as a *competing* set of claims (in fact a competing *framework*), ones that mistakenly and simplistically assess their own conditions. Furthermore, he attributes deadly effects to these mistaken beliefs, giving them the power of life and death in altering behavior. Finally, he locates these beliefs in a right-wing political position, turning his perceived competitor into an enemy. The reader needs to tease out these linkages from this article to foreground the politics of articulation, and to elaborate the political stakes involved in these particular conceptual procedures.

One of the stakes of this article's articulations is most prominent in Gilbert's discussion of the contemporary right wing in the section entitled "Sign of the Times." This section is a surprisingly tangential moment in an otherwise cogently structured argument. But its very "straying" gives us an insight into what is at issue in this entire meditation on AIDS conspiracy theories. In a "Right woos Left" logic reminiscent of Chip Berlet's account of LaRouchite politics, Gilbert depicts the Right as a seductive force on the terrain of radical politics.[34] In his own conspiratological moment, Gilbert asserts that "the 'Populists' use anti-business rhetoric to try to recruit from the left," having "the attractive mantle of 'militant anti-government movement,'" and claims that "the right has co-opted the critique of big government and big business" (62). AIDS conspiracy theories, then, are merely one more instrument that the Right uses to appear radical and divert energies away from "real" problems (i.e., those that come under the Left's domain).

The "dangerous diversion" that AIDS conspiracy theories present, then, is not primarily a distraction from AIDS activism or prevention, but from "real" analysis and politics (i.e., left politics). Gilbert is concerned with a loss of discursive authority; his articulation of conspiracy theories to the Right is a preventative maneuver. It positions conspiracy theories in the opposition's camp so as to reduce their powers of seduction to those who are Left-identified. Rather than exploring a way to link AIDS origin stories to the concerns and strategies of a left politics, Gilbert finds that not only are origin stories unarticulatable to left concerns, they are in this case *antagonistic* to those concerns. Rather than assessing if and how an origin story could contribute to an ongoing project of defining the contemporary social-political-economic context, this articulation claims that an origin story produces an entirely different context, one that diverts attention from the real one. As such, this diversion needs conceptual policing: it is thus positioned as belonging to the enemy, as life-threatening, as *left-threatening*.

At stake in Gilbert's article, then, is the very identity, stability, and legitimacy of the Left in the chaotic contemporary political structure. The political spectrum anchored by Left and Right finds itself in jeopardy, often through the emergence of conspiracy theories.[35] Eschewing a politics of articulation, Gilbert's article performs articulations through an identity politics, in which certain narratives have at their core a determined set of effects, and which are located in an identifiable and essential position in the political field.[36] Rather than open the Left up to critique and rearticulation with other subjugated knowledges, this article wishes to place the Left squarely within the dominant regime of truth (as having authority, even scientific, against competing subjugated claims). The article seeks to position the Left as the sanctioned bearer of correct analysis, as well as the legitimate judge of the truth of radical politics.

CRITERIA AND ARTICULATION

Thus far my analysis has focused on foregrounding the articulations and the attendant political stakes of one problematization of AIDS conspiracy theories. I have concentrated on this argument by Gilbert as a way of explicating the conceptual procedures that further contribute to the subjugation of a subjugated knowledge, in the name of preserving the Left's identity. But this is only half of Foucault's framework for comprehending subjugated knowledges (i.e., analyzing the subjugating practices). The second part would be to try and answer the question, "What is there to the knowledge outside its subjugated status?" That is, what can we say about the knowledge's positivity, or, within the concerns I have here, how do we judge the politics and articulability of a conspiracy theory? What criteria can be employed in evaluating a set of political claims?

First, I would reiterate the methodological value discussed at the beginning of this essay. There may be no *general* criteria for the *general* category of "conspiracy theory," as the question of what a conspiracy theory *is* is already a matter of articulation (i.e., it has no identity as an object). General criteria would still adhere to "a principle of interiority or essentialism which locates any practice in a structure of necessity and guarantees its effects even before it has been enacted."[37] A different framework is needed, one that would not be something like interpretation (guided by the traditional metaphysical question "What is?"), but evaluation ("Which one?").[38] It "never consists in interpreting, but merely in asking what are your lines . . . and what are the dangers on each?"[39] And this evaluation is performed "not in the manner of a moralist, but that of a metallurgist or an assayer: the question is never simply one of good or bad, but the specificity of each case."[40] Thus it is important to not assume a narrative's identity, effects, and politics, but to assess accounts and groups on a case-by-case basis.

This approach based in a politics of articulation would need to employ a different set of criteria. It would not necessarily work to establish the validity or the desirability of conspiracy theories, but neither would it assume an agenda of identifying and differentiating them from left politics *at the outset*. It would assume that there is no necessary relation between an AIDS origin story and political effects, nor between the *desire* for an origin story and political effects. A particular conspiracy theory could be a diversion from a set of political concerns, but it could also be a complement, even a catalyst for new forms of analysis and activism.[41] Thus, this approach is not a call to embrace conspiracy theories, but to embrace a politics of articulation, one that brings into question the very desire to *avoid* conspiracy theories and the aspiration to identify with a regime of truth.

In the limited space I have left here, I wish to provide a brief sketch of what a politics of articulation-oriented criteria might look like. This would offer a set of questions by which the political effects of a narrative could begin to be assessed, but only after some serious attention to the specificities of the account itself, as well as how it has been articulated elsewhere. The overriding concern here is the degree of openness/closedness of any particular account. That is to say, these questions begin to address a narrative's articulability.

1. Narrative Composition
- How does it compose its narrative? What is its metanarrative (i.e., the story provided about how it came to be an account)?

2. Community and Interests
- What is its construction of community, the interests represented, its assumed audience? Which identifiable groups does it align itself with? Against? How does it create an Us/Them?
- What are the identifiable conceptions of context, history, power?

3. Authorization Procedures
- What are its sources of authority? How does the account try to legitimate itself? Is there room for argumentation and debate? How does its authority depend on the community it constructs?
- What is the account's relationship with scientific authority? Does it seek authorization through science, or does it acknowledge that "even scientific characterizations of the reality of AIDS are always partly founded upon prior and deeply entrenched cultural narratives"?[42]
- How does the narrative indicate its sources, where its information came from and how it arrived? Who are its contacts? Are these channels open enough for intervention and articulation? To what degree is the informational network sealed?
- Does it define itself as "alternative" or oppositional? How so? What does it position itself against?

- To what extent are power relations and culture recognized as being involved in meaning production? How does it enter contemporary "contests for meaning" around AIDS?[43]

4. Location
- Extratextual research: Where does the account appear? What kind of forums and sites? What is its position in the larger discourse (is it a local, mainstream, and/or discredited position)? What are its institutional affiliations?
- How has the account been responded to, accepted, redirected, circulated? Have other attempts at articulation to the account been made?

5. Prescriptions
- What does the account call for: education, activism, understanding, apathy, further research? What behavioral practices does it promote and discourage?
- Whom does it call upon? What subjects is it trying to hail? What effects are desired for other accounts?

6. Instrumentalization
- What possible articulations are to be made to/with this account?
- What does the account open up; what does it foreclose? How strong is either impulse?
- Which elements of this account are articulable? Which are unacceptable? Are these separable, or does one entail the other?
- Finally, does the account challenge certain assumptions of ours? Is it trying to make something thinkable that we previously did not consider so? Does this weaken political efficacy, or does it open up new avenues of political activism? Can this account do something *to* us, as well as *for* us?

ARTICULABILITY

It may very well be the case that many, if not most, narratives that are deemed to be AIDS conspiracy theories would have low degrees of articulability. Very often, the desire for recognition within the dominant regime of truth (i.e., their desire to be a science) prevents conspiracy accounts from defining themselves as a construction, as an articulation. Instead, the truthful authority of a narrative is assumed because it is based in science. Bracketing the articulations that compose a narrative negates the politics of cultural construction as such.

In addition, I would argue, many genocide-oriented accounts do not open up spaces for other alternative, subjugated knowledges. This is a particular version of conspiracy theory characterized by a lack of openness (to debate, alternate accounts, further research, alliance possibilities), an assured sense of origin and telos (the deliberate plot to exterminate certain identities), and a nonrecognition of the politics of knowledge construction. More important, this version leaves other subjugated knowledges (especially other conspiracy theories) open to *further* disqualification. For instance, a closed genocide account could give chemical–biological warfare narratives a bad name. By articulating the CBW context so tightly to a racial genocide context, to a foreclosure on discussion, and often to poor behavioral advice, any origin story that includes it is susceptible to immediate dismissal, as this case study "proves" where the CBW narrative can get us.[44] This narrative's potential danger is its ability to be used as a straw synecdoche for a variety of subjugated AIDS accounts.

The concern I have is with the effects something like the black genocide account may have on political articulation. As I mention above, this particular AIDS account (in its will to closure, in which belief in a piece requires buying into the entire narrative) may preclude (for non–like-minded thinkers) the possibility that *any* of the elements of this narrative may have truth-effects, or political-effects that the Left could articulate to. For what is it that we are skeptical of in reading this narrative (insofar as it is a conspiracy theory)? Is it the way CBW is articulated to a specific telos and its articulation to action (political activism and preventative behavior)? Or is it something much more unsettling, something like the very *thinkability* of CBW as a context for AIDS?

We need to ask ourselves if there are certain elements that in and of themselves are unacceptable to the goals and values of a left-wing political project. What assumptions do we hold that are secured, not open to negotiation? How are these assumptions anchored by and through a regime of rationality? What kind of rationality is promoted and assumed by leftist political projects? My argument is that a political project that involves a consideration of cultural constructions of meanings has an obligation to at least foreground these assumptions (even politicize them). Does this kind of self-critique weaken political strategy (i.e., "it doesn't get anything done") or might it open up new possibilities for political activism? If the Left is committed to a politics of articulation, then analysis and strategy cannot assume the givenness of a narrative's truth-effects and political efficacy. In making politics an issue of contingent strategies through a self-critical articulatory practice, we must recognize the significant connection between "what is linkable" and "what is thinkable."

NOTES

1. Phillip S. Duke, "The AIDS–ET Connection," *Paranoia: The Conspiracy Reader* 6, no. 1 (spring 1999): 51–54.

2. Ibid., 51, 53, 54.

3. Examining the *Readers' Guide to Periodical Literature* (1990–99), one sees that in the first five years of the decade (1990–94) there were twenty articles published on the topic of conspiracy or paranoia. In 1995 alone this number was eclipsed, as twenty-two articles were produced. This trend has continued, as the latter five years (1995–99) have already seen eighty-eight listings.

4. Among the more prominent scrutinizations include Daniel Pipes, *Conspiracy: How the Paranoid Style Flourishes and Where It Comes From* (New York: Free Press, 1997); Chip Berlet's numerous works on conspiracy theories and militias for the left-wing press and mainstream news media—see, for example, Berlet and Matthew N. Lyons, "Militia Nation," *Progressive* 59, no. 6 (June 1995): 22–25; Robert Robins and Jerrold Post, *Political Paranoia: The Psychopolitics of Hatred* (New Haven: Yale University Press, 1997); a deluge of social research on militias—see, for example, Marc Cooper, "Montana's Mother of All Militias," *Nation*, 22 May 1995, 714–21, and the entire issue of the *Progressive* 59, no. 6 (June 1995); and copious other reports in journalistic publications and broadcasts (specifically around the CIA–crack–Contra connection and the crash of TWA Flight 800).

5. Richard Hofstadter, "The Paranoid Style in American Politics," in *The Paranoid Style in American Politics and Other Essays* (New York: Knopf, 1965).

6. Though these are not necessarily consistent, fully formed approaches, I would include such things here as Elaine Showalter's work on recent American myth making in *Hystories: Hysterical Epidemics and Modern Media* (New York: Columbia University Press, 1997); the repeated journalistic efforts to locate the Oklahoma City bombing in a "culture of hatred and violence"; and the *Covert Action Quarterly* article on AIDS conspiracy theories that I will address later.

7. Showalter stands somewhere in between, employing a kind of hybrid between social psychology and folklore studies.

8. Gilles Deleuze and Felix Guattari, *A Thousand Plateaus*, trans. Brian Massumi (Minneapolis: University of Minnesota Press, 1987), 3–25.

9. See, for example, Peter Knight, *Conspiracy Culture: From the Kennedy Assassination to "The X-Files"* (London: Routledge, 2000), and the essay in the present collection by Bridget Brown.

10. Michel Foucault, "Two Lectures," in *Power/Knowledge*, ed. Colin Gordon (New York: Pantheon, 1980), 78–108. In the first of his "Two Lectures," Foucault distinguishes "official knowledges" from subjugated knowledges. Subjugated knowledges "have been disqualified as inadequate to their task or insufficiently elaborated: naïve knowledges, located low down on the hierarchy, beneath the required level of cognition or scientificity" (82). A subjugated knowledge is a "popular knowledge," but "far from being a general commonsense knowledge . . . [it is] on the contrary a particular, local, regional knowledge, a differential knowledge incapable of unanimity and which owes its force only to the harshness with which it is opposed by everything surrounding it" (82).

11. Ibid., 86.

12. Deleuze and Guattari, *A Thousand Plateaus*, 12–14.

13. I take the concept "problematization" from Michel Foucault, who describes it in the following manner: it is "not the representation of a pre-existing object, nor the creation by discourse of an object that does not exist. It is the totality of discursive and nondiscursive practices that introduces something into the play of true and false and constitutes it as an object for thought." Michel Foucault, "The Concern for Truth," in *Politics, Philosophy, Culture*, ed. Lawrence D. Kritzman (New York: Routledge, 1988), 257.

14. Lawrence Grossberg, *We Gotta Get Outta This Place* (New York: Routledge, 1992), 54.

15. Ibid., 54. On articulation, see also Stuart Hall, "On Postmodernism and Articulation: An Interview," *Journal of Communication Inquiry* 10 (1986): 45–60; Ernesto Laclau and Chantal Mouffe, *Hegemony and Socialist Strategy: Towards a Radical Democratic Politics* (London: Verso, 1985), 105–14.

16. Michel Foucault, "The Question of Power," in *Foucault Live*, ed. Sylvère Lotringer, trans. John Johnston (New York: Semiotext(e), 1989), 189.

17. John Fiske, *Media Matters: Everyday Culture and Political Change* (Minneapolis: University of Minnesota Press, 1994), 192.

18. According to Paul Patton, "the Deleuzian view of concepts implies a commitment to certain politics of conceptual form." Patton, "Conceptual Politics and the War-Machine in *Mille Plateaux*," *Sub-Stance* 13 (1985): 61.

19. One might ask here why, after having spent time arguing against describing the "object" as such, I have decided to organize certain narratives

under the category of "AIDS conspiracy theories." This provisional chart is an attempt to show the wide variety of narratives that could be labeled a conspiracy theory, and thus demonstrate how problematization requires *selectivity* as a moment of articulation. That is, which narrative is held up in an analysis as a synecdoche for conspiracy theories in general? The theories in the chart have either been problematized somewhere as a conspiracy theory (even the nonviral, non–germ warfare ones like Duesberg's), or have appeared in a forum (like the zines *Paranoia* or *Steamshovel Press* or on conspiracy-oriented Web sites like *Conspiracy Nation* or *The 70 Greatest Conspiracies*) that has been discursively positioned as a site for conspiracy theories.

20. John S. James, "AIDS Conspiracy—Just a Theory?" *San Francisco Sentinel*, 12 September 1986; available from <http://www.immunet.org/atn/ZQX01301.html>.

21. Ibid., 1–5 (from printout of Web site article).

22. David Gilbert, "Tracking the *Real* Genocide: AIDS—Conspiracy or Unnatural Disaster?" *Covert Action Quarterly* 58 (fall 1996): 55–64. Further page references to this article are cited in parentheses in the text. I wish to thank Paula A. Treichler for bringing this article to my attention.

23. I cite this in order to locate the author's political affiliations squarely with the Left, in case that wasn't apparent from the magazine's title.

24. Gilbert discusses here the genocidal use of smallpox-infested blankets against Native Americans, the Tuskegee experiment, and more recent examples of vaccination testing fiascos against African Americans.

25. In this way, the conspiracy theory is no longer deemed "outside" the regime of truth, but is brought to judgment within the regime of truth. That is, it can be rendered true or false, rather than "irrational" (as in the psychological dismissal). For more discussion on being "in the true," see Michel Foucault, "The Order of Discourse," in *Untying the Text,* ed. Robert Young, trans. Ian McLeod (London: Routledge, 1981).

26. In essence, the splice theory argues that HIV is a result of the scientifically engineered artificial splicing of two or more already existing viruses (usually a visna or bovine virus with a human one).

27. I'm referring here to the geographical pattern of vaccination campaigns and first appearances of HIV, and, more importantly, the "compelling evidence for the earlier genesis of HIV." Gilbert, "Tracking the *Real* Genocide," 59.

28. Gilbert's faith in the stated purpose of retrovirus studies ignores military biowarfare research, which is very often classified. He doesn't seem to be aware of the document considered a "smoking gun" in many AIDS biowarfare accounts. It is a transcript of once-classified testimony by Dr. Donald MacArthur, a deputy director of the Department of Defense, to a House of Representatives subcommittee on military appropriations. In it, MacArthur

requests funding "to make a new infective microorganism which . . . might be refractory to the immunological and therapeutic processes upon which we depend to maintain our relative freedom from infectious disease." House Committee on Appropriations, *Hearings on Department of Defense Appropriations for 1970*, 91st Cong., 1st sess., H.B. 15090, Part 5, Research, Development, Test and Evaluation, Dept. of the Army, 1969. In Leonard Horowitz, *Emerging Viruses: AIDS and Ebola* (Rockport, MA: Tetrahedron, 1996).

29. I do not doubt Gilbert's experience of Douglass's prominence, but I do want to mention the former's selectivity among the variety of AIDS conspiracy theories, as it allows him to make generalizing statements about AIDS conspiracy theories.

30. Unfortunately, Gilbert does not give a citation for this study. However, I did come across a similar one done at the University of California, Davis (and here again I am greatly indebted to Paula Treichler for bringing this to my attention in her ceaseless efforts to keep me abreast of AIDS conspiracy theory developments): Gregory M. Herek and John P. Capitanio, "Conspiracies, Contagion, and Compassion: Trust and Public Reactions to AIDS," *AIDS Education and Prevention* 6 (1994): 565–75. This study purported to correlate AIDS-related distrust to beliefs about casual-contact transmission, and to personal risk reduction behaviors. Though it did find that "the distrust is strongly associated with AIDS-related beliefs and attitudes," this distrust was limited to distrust of doctors and the fact that information about AIDS was being withheld (572). It found that "[b]eliefs about casual contact were not related" to beliefs in "the genocidal purpose of AIDS," and "distrust was unrelated to whether or not respondents reported behavior changes" (572). The authors, however, still speculated that the lack of trust in health educators "springs from suspicions" about "malicious intent" on the part of the government (573). Rather than question the relation between health practitioners and the state, this study, in its will to resecure the authority of those health practitioners, still seeks to locate conspiratological beliefs as the source of the problems.

31. The use of the phrase "false conspiracy theories" appears to be a redundancy in this argument. But read another way, it could signify the possibility of *true* conspiracy theories. Perhaps, on this reading, we need better, truer conspiracy narratives?

32. These proposals include mandatory HIV testing, quarantining HIV-positive people, removal of HIV-positive children from school, and antiprostitution measures ranging from harsher imprisonment to execution.

33. This article appeared during a time when much media attention (from both the mainstream press and left-leaning journalism) was focused on the American militia movement (of which Bo Gritz was a key member/metonym). Since the Oklahoma City bombing in April 1995 much conceptual work was being performed to unequivocally locate this multifarious assemblage of

groups and interests within the right-wing camp. As I have argued elsewhere, this approach abandoned a political project of articulation in favor of preserving the Left's identity. Jack Bratich, "Democratic Fallout: Militias and Right Monitors" (paper presented at the 46th annual meeting of the International Communications Association, Chicago, May 1996).

34. See, for example, Chip Berlet, "Friendly Fascists," *Progressive* 56, no. 6 (June 1992): 16–20; Chip Berlet and Joel Bellman, "Lyndon LaRouche: Fascism Wrapped in an American Flag," *A Political Research Associates Briefing Paper*, 10 March 1989.

35. This troubling of the Left/Right distinction by conspiracy theories has even been given a name, "fusion paranoia." See Michael Kelly, "The Road to Paranoia," *New Yorker*, 19 June 1995, 60–75.

36. Interestingly enough, Gilbert's article even demonstrates the various political positions espoused by conspiracy theories. At one point, when Gilbert discusses Jakob and Lilli Segal, early proponents of the HIV splice theory, he places them in a communist context, even hinting that this theory was promoted as Soviet disinformation. Later, however, Douglass's appropriation of this splice theory is firmly rooted in an anticommunist framework. Even in the starkly divided political context of the Cold War, there is no necessary relation between an AIDS origin story and a political position.

37. Grossberg, *We Gotta Get Outta This Place*, 52.

38. Gilles Deleuze, *Nietzsche and Philosophy*, trans. Hugh Tomlinson (New York: Columbia University Press, 1983), 75–76.

39. Gilles Deleuze, "Toward Freedom," in *The Deleuze Reader*, ed. Constantin V. Boundas (New York: Columbia University Press, 1993), 253.

40. Patton, "Conceptual Politics," 79.

41. Take, for example, Tetrahedron, Inc., a nonprofit educational corporation headed by Dr. Leonard Horowitz, author of the above-mentioned conspiracy narrative tome *Emerging Viruses*. This group, according to its letterhead, provides employee assistance and education, professional development seminars, and health education products and programs, and organizes Horowitz's extensive lecture tours. Or consider the Brotherly Lovers, an AIDS activist group based in Philadelphia, who have attempted to spearhead a class-action lawsuit in which they would petition for a government investigation into the possible artificial origin of HIV. See Eric Taylor, "PWAs vs. the USA," *Paranoia: The Conspiracy Reader* 2, no. 4 (winter 1994–95): 52–54.

42. Paula A. Treichler, "AIDS, Gender, and Biomedical Discourse: Current Contexts for Meaning," in *AIDS: The Burdens of History*, ed. Elizabeth Fee and Daniel M. Fox (Berkeley: University of California Press, 1988), 233. My gratitude goes to Treichler for prompting me to think in these criteria-oriented terms.

43. Ibid., 190.

44. See, for example, G. J. Krupey's conspiracy account, which deploys the CBW context (see fig. 6.1). He, too, believes that the condition of AIDS is a result of human creation, planning, and introduction. The telos? To create a panic that would justify martial law. The effects on behavior? Krupey states that a radical cure is needed, one that is not just medical, but political. A structural change in governing practices is required in which access and participation are opened up on a far more democratic scale. This double call does not necessarily preclude a cultural politics of science (much less prescribe hazardous preventative practices), it just argues that it can coexist with a cultural politics of power. It might have a higher degree of articulability to left politics, but that would require a more extensive evaluation of his account.

7

White Hope

Conspiracy, Nationalism, and Revolution in The Turner Diaries *and* Hunter

Ingrid Walker Fields

We believe that the future is what we make it; That we have a responsibility for the racial quality of the coming generations of our people; That no multi-racial society is a healthy society; That if the White race is to survive, we must unite our people on the basis of common blood, organize them with a progressive social order, and inspire them with a common set of ideals; That the time to begin is now.

THE BUSINESS CARD of William Pierce's publishing company, National Vanguard, articulates the separatist tenets and mission of his white supremacist group, the National Alliance. This vision of a white America is the basis for two of Pierce's novels, *The Turner Diaries* (1978) and *Hunter* (1989), each of which portrays a different means to National Vanguard's desired end.[1] What Pierce's protagonists "make" of the future is a white America—literally, in *The Turner Diaries*, and ideologically, in *Hunter*. Both novels imagine the end of the twentieth century through a racial imperative that employs conspiracy as a narrative form to assert white supremacy as a nationalizing force. In the 1990s America envisioned in each novel, the Anglo-Saxon race is the subject of a systemic "multicultural" conspiracy. Because these novels use conspiracy narratives to imagine white identity as a field of political contention, they conceive of a defensive discourse that demands revolution—militant or ideological—as its end. Furthermore, these texts project racial revolution as a means of politicizing and policing the eroding boundaries of racial identity *as* national identity. This article explores why Pierce formulates this social goal within a conspiracy narrative by considering how this particular narrative informs and empowers the white nationalism found in *The Turner Diaries* and *Hunter*. Pierce's use of conspiracy to fulfill white nationalism in *The Turner Diaries* evolves in *Hunter* as a means of introducing this ideology as a legitimate part of American popular discourse.

In late-twentieth-century America, the term "conspiracy" does not necessarily signal a belief that a group literally colludes to control events. Conspiracy has become a metaphor representing feelings of disenfranchisement, signifying a sense of betrayal. More important, the metaphor asserts a desire for direct causality and accountability, suggesting that we wish to believe that someone, some group, is responsible for the way things are.[2] While this sense of betrayal and causality is intrinsic to the worldview of each text, *The Turner Diaries* and *Hunter* respond to the perceived racial conspiracy in the United States in significantly distinct ways. Each posits the answer to a conspiracy against white racial integrity with a contrasting plan to inspire social change.

The fundamental difference between these two texts' racial discourse is how narrative forms of conspiracy envision and instruct social action. Of particular interest here is the logic of conspiracy as a narrative that proposes two potential teleologies.[3] *The Turner Diaries* successfully adopts a classic conspiracy narrative to produce a violent revolution. This narrative—one typical of the American government's various anticommunist campaigns, for example—identifies and calls for the purge of a domestic enemy in order to preserve national security and unity. The classic conspiracy narrative is employed in *The Turner Diaries* to declare white supremacy to be a much-needed nationalizing ideology. The novel's call for the elimination of all nonwhites and their sympathizers renews the racial purity and, thus, the unity and integrity of the nation.[4]

Hunter modifies a populist conspiracy narrative to effect social change by reeducating Anglo-Americans to embrace their white superiority. By populist conspiracy narrative, I mean what are generally called conspiracy theories about the government or other powerful entities, narratives marked by the implication of their own political impotence.[5] The primary commonality of populist narratives is the perception of the public (or some subgroup) as the victims of a conspiracy, who, despite having little agency against the conspirators, expect to seek political recourse. The populist narrative's telos is characterized by the irony of the bankruptcy of conspiracy as a political discourse: in recognizing disenfranchisement, the narrative nevertheless seeks a solution through the system it denounces. While the classic conspiracy narrative emphasizes restoration of national unity through the elimination of a public enemy, the populist conspiracy narrative de-emphasizes political action, focusing instead on raising social awareness about the conspiracy as the means by which citizens will reclaim political power. Thus, these two forms of conspiracy narrative establish specific teleological expectations: whereas *The Turner Diaries* imagines a mass population in need of culling and violent inspiration, *Hunter* imagines a mass population in need of ideological reprogramming through the media. The evolution from a genocidal revolutionary logic to a more calculated manipulation of mass media suggests a shift in the conception of the nature and threat of the racial conspiracy and the discourse employed to identify and counter it.

REBIRTH OF A NATION

Published a decade apart, *The Turner Diaries* and *Hunter* both imagine a 1990s America, each from a different historical and ideological moment in our history.[6] *The Turner Diaries* synthesizes the concerns of white supremacist and gun rights discourse in its depiction of a national—and eventually global—race revolution. This version of late-twentieth-century America is severely intolerant of a specific "racism"—defined as acts perpetrated by whites against people of color—and has created a climate in which white people are under scrutiny for racist transgressions while people of color exploit the situation. The seemingly liberal government ("the System") extends its oppressive influence with the Cohen Act, a law that repeals the Second Amendment right to own firearms. The consequent insurrection is chronicled by one of its unassuming heroes, Earl Turner, whose fellow patriotic militant white supremacists ("the Organization") have prepared to fight the System's despotism. Turner's diary describes his experiences as he organizes small resistance cells and goes about the daily labor of domestic terrorism. The plot leads to Turner's induction into the Organization's inner circle (The Order)—a transcendence that concludes with Turner's suicide mission and subsequent martyrdom as the Organization's savior.

Turner's diary begins in 1991, after the Cohen Act's gun raids precipitate the Organization's first act of political terrorism in what becomes a national (and eventually a global) race war. In its opening paragraph, the novel celebrates the dynamic nature of action: "After all these years of talking—and nothing but talking—we have finally taken our first action. We are at war with the System, and it is no longer a war of words."[7]

This novel presents as fact the dire social circumstances and the necessity for white nationalism. Turner does not question what becomes a holy war; his role in the revolution is clear. This certitude is reflected in the political discourse of *The Turner Diaries'* America: it exemplifies the politics of resistance inherent in the polarizing language of conspiracy narratives (the System vs. the Organization). In *The Turner Diaries*, conspiracy functions as a narrative trope loosely employed by various groups, but most directly associated with the System's and the Organization's political engagement with each other. *The Turner Diaries* elicits a history of classic government conspiracy narratives in which the preservation of national security depends on the eradication of a public enemy, but it revises who constitutes "national" and "enemy." For Turner and the Organization, the classic conspiracy form describes the insidious threat of the System's multiracial tyranny, the domestic enemy Turner calls a "Jewish-liberal-democratic-equalitarian" plague. Yet, early in the novel, the System attempts to employ its traditional conspiracy narrative, characterizing the Organization's resistance to the Cohen Act as that of a "Fascist Racist Conspiracy" and describing the Organization as a public enemy that must be crushed (*TD*, 4). However, Turner asserts that the government's ability to produce public enemies has lost its currency. He imagines that the American public rejects this narrative because "[N]ot even the brainwashed American public could fully accept the idea that nearly a million of their fellow citizens had been engaged in a secret, armed conspiracy" (*TD*, 4). Within the logic of the Organization's nationalizing ideology, the disenfranchised and disillusioned (white) public detects the government's fabrication of this public enemy. For Turner, the resulting public dissent suggests a collective righteous will, not a paranoid conspiracy. Ultimately, the System's conspiracy narrative about the Organization's illegal activities propels the Organization's own narrative toward a teleology that prescribes the means of the nation's dissolution and rebirth.

The novel emphasizes the Organization's irrevocable ideological divergence from the System; its struggle constitutes more than a mere contest for political power. Specifically, Turner claims that the stake of this conspiracy is the white race's existence: "much more than our freedom is at stake. . . . our history, our heritage, and all the blood and sacrifices and upward striving of countless thousands of years. The Enemy we are fighting fully intends to destroy the racial basis of our existence" (*TD*, 34). By characterizing the System as the source of a genocidal conspiracy, the Organization legitimizes the extremity of its narrative's teleology—that is, the reciprocation of that genocidal attitude. In confronting a potential mutineer, hardline members of the Organization denigrate the moderate's desire to reclaim an idyllic political past, insisting on the obligatory casualties of revolution in building their utopian future:

> We are forging the nucleus of a new society, a whole new civilization, which will rise from the ashes of the old. And it is because our new civilization will be based on an entirely different world view than the present one that it can only replace the other in a revolutionary manner. There is no way a society based on Aryan values and an Aryan outlook can evolve peacefully from a society, which has succumbed to Jewish spiritual corruption. (*TD*, 111)

Mere political reform cannot be effective where mass lynchings, bombings, and murders are needed to purify a nation's polluted populace. Although Turner acknowledges that there is no point to an extermination of all Americans, he recognizes the practicality of "eliminat[ing] the consciously evil portion of the population—plus a few hundred thousand of our morally crippled 'good citizens' across the country, as an example to the rest" (*TD*, 166). Through such distinctions, *The Turner Diaries* articulates the difference between a populist conspiracy narrative, which, in indicting the government as a public enemy, seeks political reform, and a classic conspiracy narrative, whose hegemony ensures the destruction of a public enemy.

The force of the Organization's ability to assume the narrative and political authority of what has typically been the System's conspiracy narrative (the power to identify and destroy a public enemy) is represented in its opening act of war—the demolition of the national FBI headquarters. In attacking this particular arm of the System, the Organization destroys the government's ability to contain the seditious group because the bomb destroys a computer system designed to track all Americans by domestic passport. Symbolically and literally, this act terminates a history of the FBI's unparalleled political dominance. Turner expresses surprise at the ease with which the Organization usurps the source of the System's power to control political opposition, claiming, "We never would have gotten away with it back in the days of J. Edgar Hoover" (*TD*, 7). His reference to the source of the FBI's history of dominance—the man who built an empire through the powerful concept of the conspiring public enemy—plays on his narrative's revision of the classic conspiracy narrative in its demonstration of the System's political bankruptcy.[8] Pierce underscores the irony of a minority group marshaling the resources required for such a grand-scale revolution as a Cold War satire. The Organization uses America's biggest public enemy to bring about the anticipated nuclear holocaust. By aiming its few nuclear missiles at the Soviet Union, the Organization forces the Pentagon to mount a full-scale nuclear attack on the Soviets in order to forestall reciprocation. The Soviet missiles destroy much of the United States and its government strongholds, bringing about the initial victory in the Organization's white New World Order.[9]

THE REVOLUTION WILL BE TELEVISED

In his second novel, *Hunter*, Pierce moves away from the working-class constituency of *The Turner Diaries* to what the book jacket calls a "comfortable yuppie" demographic. Oscar Yeager, a talented engineer whose patents have made him modestly wealthy, works as a consultant to the Pentagon (thus funding his racial plan with defense budget dollars). He is represented as a highly educated, sensitive, and extremely rational person. When we first meet Yeager, he is being uncharacteristically reactionary, literally hunting black and white "miscegenating" couples in his disgust about the decline of the race. The less tumultuous social climate of *Hunter*'s 1990s America combined with Yeager's comfortable class status creates a more ambiguous situation for Yeager. Initially, Yeager doesn't even identify himself as a white supremacist. Unlike Turner, he seeks a deeper, intellectual contextualization of his white supremacism as well as a solution that speaks to the social ambiguities he perceives. *Hunter* is a truncated *bildungsroman* chronicling Yeager's hunt for a philosophy, his subsequent education about the Jewish media conspiracy, and his own answer to the racial conspiracy of multicultural America.

Yeager's education is initiated by two white supremacists: Harry Keller, of the professionally oriented white supremacist group the National League, and Jack Ryan, a high-ranking FBI agent. Ryan catches Yeager "hunting"; but rather than arrest him, he employs Yeager in his own career advancement plan to rid the FBI of powerful Jews. Through several well-planned assassinations, Ryan becomes head of a new security agency that eventually suspends civil liberties for the sake of domestic control. Keller, a mild-mannered political thinker, and Ryan, a power-hungry official, offer distinct yet kindred perspectives about racial reform in America. Neither philosophy fully satisfies Yeager; while Keller's peaceable promotion of his racial agenda through the dissemination of educational materials is not aggressive enough, Ryan's emphasis on containing the race problem through martial control is too limiting. Through his own research and extensive discourse with both men, Yeager rejects the two models to design his own racial philosophy and plan of action.

As the novel's extremist, Ryan provides the narratological bridge from *The Turner Diaries* to *Hunter*: his vision of reform echoes the martial law enacted at the end of *The Turner Diaries*. Although Yeager declares that "it's my world, my race, and it's being gang-raped," he balks at Ryan's solution because it won't salvage the race.[10] Ryan responds,

> If it offends your humanist sensibilities to reform the behavior of the American people with hunger and the toe of a boot and the threat of a bullet, then there are gentler methods. . . . If you had the television networks under your control you could . . . partly reprogram the herd . . . [but] you'd still need to give the majority of the people a good kick in the ass to make them break a lot of the bad habits they've picked up. (*H*, 142)

This tele-education is exactly what Yeager adopts as the centerpiece of his plan to resurrect the white race. With help from the National League, he engineers a media coup d'état: the League challenges televangelist Jimmy "Braggart" with its own charismatic fire-and-brimstone preacher, steals Braggart's fundamentalist audience on Easter Sunday, and goes on to depose the Jewish media monopoly by attacking the multicultural ideology it promotes—all while gaining the largest market share of the viewing audience. By devising an influential religious and racially progressive mouthpiece, the National League succeeds in reaching white America and eroding the Jewish/multicultural hold on the American imagination.

Because Ryan wants to write off the white public in the name of national security and blackmails Yeager into furthering his megalomaniacal agenda, Yeager is driven to assassinate him. In this climactic moment, Ryan assails Yeager's idealism about the race:

> You imagine that when the Blacks rise up and start the wholesale burning and looting and raping and killing, hundreds of thousands of these heroic White men which exist in your mind will materialize, along with their heroic women, and you'll organize them into a disciplined force for mopping up the Jews, the queers, the feminists, the nigger-loving liberals, the politicians and the other race traitors, the nut-case Christians, the spics, the gooks, the towel-heads, and what's left of the Blacks after I've crushed the rebellion. But it won't happen, Yeager. It's only a dream. (*H*, 247)

Although it's not really Yeager's vision, that dream is precisely *The Turner Diaries'* vision. Through the ensuing argument, both Ryan and Yeager describe the impossibility of *The Turner Diaries'* teleology—a race war—and implicitly agree that it is not a plausible solution. Interestingly, Pierce declines to offer a fait accompli in *Hunter*; rather, the novel closes with Yeager continuing in his group's work to educate white America even as he pursues what he calls "political flux" by plotting to assassinate other powerful men like Ryan. While his efforts at affecting white racial uplift are largely invested in education rather than violent revolution, Yeager cannot quite abandon the hunting that limits the government's ability to intercede and ensures the National League's success. He seems to subscribe to the classic conspiracy narrative's pragmatic "eradicate the enemy" methodology even as he promotes the populist conspiracy narrative's agenda of social awareness. In the difficult transition period, however, this violence is understood as an evil necessary to the future of the white race in America.

In *Hunter*, Pierce depicts the ambiguity of causal power relations, particularly in terms of white racial decline. In this sense, the novel is less certain than *The Turner Diaries* about systemic conspiracies against Anglo-America. Pierce's portrayal of racial conspiracy in *Hunter* reflects the metaphorical understanding of conspiracy as a betrayal and disenfranchisement. Yeager's quest for a historicized ideology and a plan of action implies racial conspiracy while recognizing that culpability for the betrayal of white America extends beyond the terms of conspiracy's "us/them" polarity. Yeager finds multiple sources of miscegenation and white apathy. Instead of arguing which sources pose the greater threat, he narrows his focus to satisfy his own questions and encourage education within his race.

Like Turner, Yeager undergoes a significant refinement of his ideas about racial superiority. The difference between the education of Turner and Yeager is the difference between dogma and dialectic. When we meet Turner at the beginning of *The Turner Diaries*, he has already adopted wholesale the crusade of white supremacy. The conflict of the novel is not Turner's, but the nation's. By contrast, Yeager struggles with white supremacism; he resists others' anti-Semitism and labors to assimilate what he learns about Judaism, media politics, and the white American public. Yeager is relentless in his ideological reflection, the need to understand his actions on behalf of the race in terms of a comprehensive theoretical context. He hunts for revenge, then for a philosophy, and finally to employ that philosophy in a specific political movement to reeducate and reform white America.

Both texts focus on mobilizing a constituency; thus each text's conspiracy narrative and its envisioned teleology are situated as an issue of audience and class. *The Turner Diaries* imagines its social project to be the fabrication of a white nation. The text invokes a classic conspiracy narrative, proposing the violent purge of a sociopolitical system that conspires to infect and debilitate white America. It targets a militant working-class audience with characters whose labor skills allow them to organize and carry out a revolution. *Hunter* addresses an audience of well-educated, upper-middle-class white Americans. Its readers imagine themselves in the role of inspiring others to racial consciousness—not with terrorism, trench warfare, and personal sacrifice, as Earl Turner does, but with the ideas they transmit from a comfortable, anonymous distance. "It's a shame we have to use trickery to persuade people to do what's right," Yeager comments. "It makes me uneasy. . . . These people—most people—*have* to be tricked. They just aren't developed enough to recognize the truth or to distinguish between right and wrong" (*H*, 223). *Hunter*'s privileged audience observes white America's television revolution from behind the scenes.

In the shift from *The Turner Diaries'* war to *Hunter*'s ideological de-bate, Pierce increasingly concerns himself, discursively and philosoph-ically, with racial supremacy and its political currency—as implied by his conspiracy narrative. Although *Hunter* expresses an ideology simi-lar to that of *The Turner Diaries*, it rejects the fantasy of violent racial rev-olution and examines both the individual's efficacy in fulfilling racial goals and the possibility of reeducating Anglo-America. No "mass" can be imagined to take action: nearly everyone is entwined in America's 1990s race relations. While *The Turner Diaries* shares this general view of the pervasive damage caused by a multiracial America, it envisions no potential redemption for most Anglo-Americans. In *Hunter*, however, revolution takes place on parallel planes consisting of those who take action against racial conspiracy by becoming educators and those who need to, and can, be educated. At the same time, *Hunter* exemplifies the populist conspiracy narrative form by emphasizing the limitations of any group's ability to realize its racial aspirations. Yeager's individual-ism is essential to his success; while he ardently supports the necessity of his group's communal effort to educate white America through its televangelist forum, he must maintain his vigilantism by hunting ene-mies, as well. In *Hunter*, Pierce doesn't use racial conspiracy to orches-trate a national, genocidal revolution; instead, he uses it as a basis from which to launch a more complex discourse on individual agency and ideology in racial revolution.

THE COLOR OF CONSPIRACY: REVISITING
WHITE NATIONALISM

Pierce's use of conspiracy narrative to project racial identity as a na-tional issue is enhanced by the relation between these novels and vari-ous contemporary groups and events. *The Turner Diaries* has been iden-tified as having a significant role in the discourse of antigovernment groups, from "new orders" to militias. In the early 1980s, a group called The Order—a self-styled model of the novel's internal secret society—included reading *The Turner Diaries* as an initiation requirement. The Order's real-world activities included counterfeiting, robbing armored cars, and the assassination of Alan Berg, a Jewish talk show host.[11] Re-cently, former Klansmen calling themselves The New Order (after the

1980s group) have allegedly "plotted to bomb every state capitol building in the country, strike at post offices and communication systems,
poison the water supplies of five major cities and blow up the Southern
Poverty Law Center."[12] Perhaps most striking, however, is that the
bombing of the Murrah Federal Building in Oklahoma City replicates in
detail *The Turner Diaries'* first terrorist act, the bombing of national FBI
headquarters.[13]

Despite the fact that Pierce takes no credit for inspiring these actions and disassociates himself from the Oklahoma City bombing, he
clearly sees the novel as doing important social work. He claims that
The Turner Diaries is "a novel with a message in the venerable tradition
of *Uncle Tom's Cabin*."[14] By locating his novel in the tradition of *Uncle
Tom's Cabin*, Pierce alludes to the legendary influence of Harriet Beecher
Stowe's novel in instigating the Civil War. Pierce's comparison self-consciously invokes the political power of literature, raising questions
about what he imagines the social work of *Uncle Tom's Cabin* and, thus,
The Turner Diaries—and *Hunter*—to be. The irony of associating his first
novel with an abolitionist text somewhat contrasts the issue common to
the resolution of both texts: what to do about the "race problem." One
potential result of both novels' concluding visions is, essentially, to render North America a white continent through ethnic nationalism. At the
end of *Uncle Tom's Cabin*, George Harris proposes African repatriation
as a political solution to slavery: "The desire and yearning of my soul is
for an African nationality. I want a people that shall have a tangible, separate existence of its own. . . . On the shores of Africa I see a republic
. . ."[15] Pierce's commentary is more pointed: "I don't have time to write
for entertainment. It's to explain things to people. I'd like to see North
America become a white continent."[16] Of course, *The Turner Diaries'* vision far exceeds that of *Uncle Tom's Cabin*; Pierce moves beyond nationalism and imagines war and white supremacy on a global scale. Pierce
uses a classic conspiracy narrative as the vehicle for this ideology because only in this narrative form can he imagine *The Turner Diaries* to be
the little novel that started—and won—the big war.

If *The Turner Diaries'* social project is racial revolution for a white
America, what is *Hunter's* social project? The novel is more of a call for
self-awareness than a call to arms. *Hunter* presents a discriminating
marketing of white supremacist ideology sublimated in a dialogue
about self-awareness and personal action. In the evolution from *The
Turner Diaries* to *Hunter*, Pierce has taken a step away from the former

novel's vision of national and global race war as the solution to the racial conspiracy toward a complex and less definitive reassertion of white dominance. *Hunter* is the more reflective text: the ongoing education of Oscar Yeager—the protracted dialogues with similar yet not entirely like-minded white supremacists—suggests a need for self-reflexivity in white supremacist ideology. The potential in America for a white supremacist professional class to influence other Americans is, *Hunter* suggests, predicated on this sort of individualistic intellectual, ideological, and spiritual growth.

As in his fiction, Pierce's nonfiction and interviews have articulated radically different means of producing white nationalism. On the one hand, Pierce asserts that "a violent uprising in which marches and demonstrations are accompanied by terrorism and street fighting [cannot] achieve success—so long as the major elements of the power structure remain in the hands of our enemies." His prescription, instead, is to "build structures with certain military and police functions which have as their immediate task the co-ordination of recruiting inside the government's military and police agencies."[17] Pierce's politics suggest that to achieve a lasting success, white supremacists must infiltrate and appropriate the very government they have rejected—in effect, institutionalizing white nationalism. Elsewhere, however, Pierce has contextualized that social vision by claiming that "[w]e are in a war for the survival of our race . . . that ultimately we cannot win . . . except by killing our enemies."[18] Pierce's conflicted rhetoric employs both the restrained separatist and fascist discourses that describe the two social projects he explores more fully in his novels' fin de siècle national vision.

Nevertheless, one might read a significant development in the revision of *The Turner Diaries'* genocidal view of late-twentieth-century racial politics to *Hunter's* less widespread violence and media-controlled cultural/racial revolution. While *The Turner Diaries'* teleology calls for concerted violence, *Hunter's* teleology legitimizes white supremacism as racial discourse in the American media. *Hunter* promotes education and ideological understanding as a requisite basis for action. Thus, this evolution from reactionary violence toward an emphasis on the core concepts supporting occasional violence is a subtle one: on the whole, *Hunter* encourages extremist thought rather than extremist violence. A skeptical view of this revision might find that Pierce has merely decentered his text from any direct liability for readers' acts. However, *Hunter* is more exploratory than that: it begs the question of the role of violence, stopping short of a radical call to arms in its emphasis on the importance of debate and media control in legitimizing and promoting white supremacism in mainstream American political discourse. Rather than envision mass violence, *Hunter* isolates within one figure the potential violence in the discourse of racial supremacy within a multiethnic society, projecting instead a silent, relatively bloodless revolution through religious and political institutions.

While Pierce would like to align *The Turner Diaries'* political influence with that of *Uncle Tom's Cabin*, his novels more accurately echo a different literary history of white nationalistic racial discourse. The function of racial conspiracy narrative as a call to arms but also as a political and philosophical movement has its roots in two of Thomas Dixon's early-twentieth-century novels, *The Leopard's Spots* and *The Clansman*.[19] The politics of Dixon's South exemplify a history of racial discourse in which white supremacy is expressed as a means of realizing national identity. The late-twentieth-century white supremacism of Pierce's novels emulates the narrative strategies of Dixon's fiction: *The Leopard's Spots* articulates and enacts its white supremacism within the American political system, whereas *The Clansman* depicts the rise of the Ku Klux Klan as a more militant, revolutionary force representing white nationalism in Reconstruction America.

In *The Leopard's Spots*, the federal government's plan for Reconstruction is understood as a conspiracy against the purity of the white South, specifically an attempt to destroy the democratic ideals at the heart of American identity:

> With the Anglo-Saxon race guarding the door of marriage with fire
> and sword, the effort was being made to build a nation inside a nation
> of two antagonistic races. No such thing had ever been done in the his-
> tory of the human race, even under the development of the monarchi-
> cal and aristocratic forms of society. How could it be done under the
> formula of Democracy with Equality as the fundamental basis of law?
> And yet this was the programme of the age.[20]

Walter Benn Michaels argues in "The Souls of White Folks" that the antagonism inherent to Dixon's Reconstruction forges a relationship between racial identity and national identity.[21] He writes that Dixonian (southern white) America conceives of itself as the victim of Reconstruction's imperialism. Thus, the legacy of Dixon's vision of white

America for *The Turner Diaries* is precisely the reenactment of this Reconstruction reading of the government as an imperial power.

Although *The Leopard's Spots* provides Pierce with a racist, imperialist characterization of the federal government, Dixon's second novel, *The Clansman*, emphasizes the violent promotion of racial supremacy that distinguishes *The Turner Diaries*' apocalyptic vision. Dixon wrote that "*The Clansman* develops the true story of the 'Ku Klux Klan Conspiracy' which overturned the Reconstruction régime." The story recounts

> [h]ow the young South, led by the reincarnated souls of the Clansmen of Old Scotland, went forth under this cover and against overwhelming odds, daring exile, imprisonment, and a felon's death, and saved the life of a people, form[ing] one of the most dramatic chapters in the history of the Aryan race.[22]

In *The Clansman*, Dixon develops the Ku Klux Klan's representation as a distinct, forceful response to Reconstruction's conspiracy to annihilate the white South. Having identified the internal enemy, the Klan acts in secret to expose and destroy it. By the novel's final scene, the Klan forcefully establishes its supremacy, successfully defeating its foes throughout the southern countryside. Ben Cameron, a favorite southern son in the new generation, exclaims, "Look at our lights on the mountains! They are ablaze—range on range our signals gleam until the Fiery Cross is lost among the stars!" (*C*, 374).

By contrast, *The Leopard's Spots* focuses on a political revolution in which white nationalism is effected through democratic channels. Its conclusion demonstrates the power of political rhetoric, rather than the muscle of the Ku Klux Klan, as a catalyst for racial reform. Dixon imagines the state and national administrations poised to "nullify the Fourteenth and Fifteenth Amendments to the Constitution of the Republic" (*LS*, 446). An entire chapter details Klan hero Charles Gaston's speech, a political performance that galvanizes the Democratic Party and inspires this radical transformation of America's racial future:

> When Gaston spoke at Independence, five thousand white men dressed in scarlet shirts rode silently through the streets in solemn parade and six thousand negroes watched them with fear. There was no

cheering or demonstration of any kind. The silence of the procession gave it the import of a religious rite.

   Like scenes were enacted everywhere. Again the Anglo-Saxon race was fused into a solid mass. The result was a foregone conclusion. (*LS*, 446)

In *The Leopard's Spots*, the imperial government is overthrown within the political process: white supremacism is embraced as a Democratic Party platform at both state and federal levels. The Klan's passive presence during Gaston's speech distinctly contrasts with the closing pages of *The Clansman*, which, although also anticipating the results of a key election, emphasizes the embattled Klan's glorious victory. In keeping with the telos of each novel, *The Leopard's Spots* portrays the disbanding of the Klan after it has served its purpose—relying instead on political power to effect white nationalism. *The Clansman*, however, imagines no such abbreviation of the Klan's power or its militancy.

   For Dixon, the heart of the conspiracy against the white race, and thus the provoking factor of political and militant white action, is the government-sponsored aggression of Reconstruction Negroes. Dixon exploits the southern mythos of miscegenation—the sexual violation of white women by black men—as the precipitating factor in the Ku Klux Klan's formation. "A gale of chivalrous passion and high action, contagious and intoxicating, swept the white race. The moral, mental, and physical earthquake which followed the first assault on one of their daughters revealed the unity of the racial life of the people" (*C*, 341). In both novels, the exaggerated threat and fear of miscegenation is not only the source of Reconstruction's moral bankruptcy, but it motivates southern whites to fulfill their destiny.[23] The Ku Klux Klan's response to a black man's attempt to kiss a white woman graphically demonstrates southern white hysteria about this "threat." Tim Shelby's corpse is left in public, its mouth pinned shut with a placard explaining, "[t]he answer of the Anglo-Saxon race to the Negro lips that dare pollute with words the womanhood of the South. K.K.K." (*LS*, 150). In Dixon's Reconstruction America, the Klan successfully polices the bounds of white purity.

   Nearly a century later, Pierce's novels recall the charged sexual politics of Dixon's racialized state. In the opening scene of *The Turner Diaries*, the black Equality Police's abusive invasion of Turner's apartment building recalls scenes of monstrous aggression by renegade black officers of the Reconstruction military depicted in both *The Leopard's Spots* and *The Clansman*. Pierce gestures toward the miscegenation mythos with events such as the motivating factor for Turner's girlfriend's white supremacism and gun ownership: her roommate's rape and murder at the hands of a "Negro." Later, when the Los Angeles area is invaded by the Organization, Pierce tropes the lynching of black men for the alleged rape of white women with mass hangings in which race traitors (government officials and college professors) and race defilers (white women and men who had sexual partners of color) wear signs declaring the category of their crime. This devastation, called "the day of the rope," incorporates mob violence and the political charge of miscegenation in ways that recall and amplify Dixon's racial context (*TD*, 160). Clearly, Dixon's racial revolution has failed to transpire in Pierce's late-twentieth-century America. In a more complex racial context, Pierce's novels fulfill white nationalism with less simplistic solutions.

Michaels argues that during the late nineteenth century, Dixon's fantasy of white Reconstruction America "confers on national identity something like the ontology of race."[24] *The Turner Diaries* and *Hunter* construct a systemic conspiracy that elicits this Dixonian reading of the government as the imperial power, reintroducing the need for white supremacy *as* nationalism in racial discourse. Pierce's more thorough development of conspiracy as his narrative form raises questions about its implications. Does it reflect a paranoid view of the multicultural demographic and politics of twentieth-century America—that is, does it express an actual perception of a national conspiracy against white separatism or supremacism? Or is it a means by which Pierce is able to recapture an ontology in which race is inextricably linked to national identity? Dixon's white nationalism expresses a paranoia about the future and racial purity of Anglo-America that romanticizes white supremacist activities by individuals and groups such as the Ku Klux Klan at the turn of the century, when the Klan's actual activity was waning. Pierce expresses his white nationalism in the late 1970s and 1980s, periods in which Americans responded to a problematic history of racial inequality both with the mainstream ethnic awareness of multiculturalism and, to a lesser extent, the resurgence of white supremacism. Conspiracy not only signifies the disenfranchisement of white supremacy in this social context, it creates the dire necessity for resistance.

In Pierce's work, racial conspiracy provides a social context, the issue of patriotism provides the rationale for the Organization and the National League's action, and the issue of racial purity provides their ideal. For *The Turner Diaries*, the logic of Dixon's imagined America can be extended to total racial revolution as the teleology of its conspiracy narrative. A decade later, however, the political climate has changed. The conspiracy narrative in *Hunter* presents a nationalism more typical of the logic of Dixon's racial ideology as it calls first for political reform, a reform Pierce ultimately locates not in the war-torn streets but in middle America's television viewing. Pierce's imagined America changes— from a racial civil war intended to catalyze the creation of a white planet to a mitigated sense of what might viably revive and sustain white nationalism—which suggests that the use of conspiracy narrative is less an expression of paranoia than it is a strategy for white supremacy as a legitimate nationalist discourse. *Hunter*'s revision of *The Turner Diaries'* America within a different conspiracy narrative signifies an awareness of the prevalence of this populist conspiracy narrative in American culture, as well as an awareness of the growing unpopularity of militant white supremacism.[25] Pierce's use of the populist conspiracy narrative as a vehicle makes political sense in this cultural moment because it addresses the unparalleled power of the media and their mobilization of powerful political constituencies, such as the Christian Right. Rather than promote the fantasy of a global race war, Pierce uses conspiracy narrative to address more viable means of racial reform.

NOTES

Many people have been influential in the writing of this essay. My sincere thanks to Anthony Vital, Hilene Flanzbaum, Sean McCann, Chris Zinn, Scott Fields, and Walter Benn Michaels for their encouragement and guidance. The essay originated in a seminar supported by the National Endowment for the Humanities. I would also like to thank the Walter and Betty Jones Foundation for its support of this project.

1. National Alliance, Hillsboro, WV. Pierce writes under the pseudonyms Andrew Macdonald and Randolph Calverhall. *The Turner Diaries* and *Hunter* are published under Macdonald; *Serpent's Walk*—a novel about the Nazi Party and World War II—is published under Calverhall.

2. My use of the pronoun "we" refers to a basic demographic: the employment of conspiracy as a general term in popular, mainstream American discourse. The form covers many conceptions of conspiracy, ranging from

reference to governments and political events (Watergate) to reference to the dynamics of our daily lives (e.g., that the lack of reliable news media is a conspiracy). In this essay, I hope to make a distinction between conspiracy as a term of analysis and as a term being analyzed. In other words, I imagine many constituencies for the most common vernacular referent, conspiracy theorist. The phrase suggests an analysis—which is what many conspiracy theorists offer. In my reading, however, this primary "analysis" becomes a narrative, one with specific strategies and teleologies. I don't consider myself a conspiracy theorist; rather, I am interested in why conspiracy is a narrative mode employed in many ways in American popular discourse.

3. I have described more fully these two distinct and politically significant forms of conspiracy narrative in Ingrid Walker Fields, "*Libra, JFK,* and the Paranoid Politics of History," *Thresholds: Viewing Culture* 11 (1998): 1–12.

4. The classic conspiracy narrative has had many expressions, from Red Scare pre- and post–World War I to the anticommunist era typified by the House Un-American Activities Committee, anticommunist legislation, and the various spy trials of the 1940s and 1950s. *The Turner Diaries'* assumption of this narrative form is significant because the narrative has traditionally been employed by the state, which has the power to identify and purge public enemies and to renew national unity.

5. I take "populist" at its literal meaning, "of the populace," rather than its reference to the early-twentieth-century political movement (Populism). The populist conspiracy narrative imagines itself to speak on behalf of the populace in its resistance to a conspiring government or system.

6. *The Turner Diaries* was originally serialized and illustrated in *National Vanguard's* predecessor, *Attack,* beginning in January 1975. (My thanks to Martin Durham for this information.) In May 1996, Barricade Books republished *The Turner Diaries,* making it available to readers through mainstream publishing distribution.

7. Pierce, *The Turner Diaries* (Arlington, VA: National Alliance/National Vanguard Books, 1978), 4. Additional references will be noted in the text (*TD*).

8. The term "public enemy" originated with the FBI's first Public Enemy campaign in the early 1930s. Because of strong public support for a series of famous bank robbers, J. Edgar Hoover and Attorney General Homer Cummings designed a campaign to cast the gangsters as enemies of the public. The Justice Department's 1933 campaign centered around the publication of a "Public Enemies" list of the top ten criminals wanted by the FBI, such as John Dillinger, Charles "Pretty Boy" Floyd, George "Machine Gun" Kelly, Lester Gillis, alias "Baby Face Nelson," and Bonnie (Parker) and Clyde (Barrow). The crucial subtext of the Public Enemies campaign was the narrative of containment, which evidenced the necessity to fully empower and arm the FBI while garnering public support for the agency as its super police force. Congress passed several bills

in Cummings's Twelve Points Program in 1934, allowing FBI agents the right to carry firearms and make arrests and giving them wider jurisdiction. Richard Gid Powers, *G-Men: The FBI in Popular Culture* (Carbondale: Southern Illinois University Press, 1983), 39–48, 119–20.

9. Turner recognizes the irony of the concept of public enemy in the changing political landscape. In his view there are various declensions of "public enemy": the Soviets, the Organization, and—for Turner—the System.

10. Pierce, *Hunter* (Arlington, VA: National Alliance/National Vanguard Books, 1989), 56. Additional references will be noted in the text (*H*).

11. John Kifner, "Bomb Suspect Felt at Home Riding Gun-Show Circuit," *New York Times*, 5 July 1995, A1, A18.

12. The group also allegedly plotted to assassinate Center cofounder Morris Dees. Southern Poverty Law Center, *Intelligence Report* 90 (spring 1998): 4.

13. *The Turner Diaries* enjoyed mainstream national celebrity because of its relation to convicted Oklahoma City bomber Timothy McVeigh. McVeigh reportedly admired the novel and espoused its ideological position, following its tactic of bombing federal buildings. While *Hunter* was found in convicted coconspirator Terry Nichols's home, no connection has been made by the news media. It is worth noting that Nichols purports to have had a behind-the-scenes role in his part in the Oklahoma City bombing, much like Yeager's role in *Hunter*.

14. Peter Applebome, "A Bombing Foretold, in Extreme-Right 'Bible,'" *New York Times*, 26 April 1995, A22.

15. Harriet Beecher Stowe, *Uncle Tom's Cabin*, ed. Elizabeth Ammons (New York: Norton, 1994), 274.

16. Marc Fisher and Phil McCombs, "The Book of Hate: Did the Oklahoma Bombers Use a 1978 Novel as Their Guide?" *Washington Post*, 25 April 1995, D1.

17. Carl Mollins, "At Home with a Racist Guru: William Pierce Anticipated the Oklahoma Bomb," *Maclean's*, 8 May 1995, 42.

18. "Patriots and Profits," Kathy Slobugin, CNN, October 29, 1995. Quoted from *Klanwatch* Web site, Southern Poverty Law Center, <http://www.splcenter.org/klanwatch/alliance.html> (18 June 1998).

19. Ironically, *The Leopard's Spots* was conceived as a direct response to *Uncle Tom's Cabin*'s influence in the American imagination. Upon seeing a dramatization of Stowe's novel, Thomas Dixon was driven to write "the true facts" of the South's Reconstruction experience. In a letter to the *New York Times* defending the controversial novel, he wrote that authoring it was "the most important moral deed of my life." Raymond A. Cook, *Thomas Dixon* (New York: Twayne, 1974), 65, 67. Dixon ensured a connection between the two works by using one of Stowe's characters, Simon Legree, as a significant figure in his novel.

20. Dixon, *The Leopard's Spots* (New York: Doubleday, 1902), 201. Additional references will be noted in the text (*LS*).

21. Walter Benn Michaels, "The Souls of White Folks," in *Literature and the Body: Essays on Populations and Persons*, ed. Elaine Scarry (Baltimore: Johns Hopkins University Press, 1988), 185–209.

22. Dixon, *The Clansman* (Lexington: University Press of Kentucky, 1970), xix, xx. This discourse was made famous by D. W. Griffith's treatment of *The Clansman* in the film *Birth of a Nation* (1915). Additional references will be noted in the text (C).

23. In *The Clansman*, Marian Lenoir and her mother preserve white honor by leaping to their deaths after she is raped by a malicious Negro. *The Leopard's Spots* portrays a similar scene at Annie Camp's wedding: as she is dragged away by Negro rapists, Annie is mortally wounded by a bullet intended for her assailants. It's telling that Dixon portrays Annie's inadvertent death as preferable to her potential rape. Her father says, "Let us thank God she was saved from them brutes" (*LS*, 126).

24. In "The Souls of White Folks," Michaels crystallizes the issue at stake for writers of Dixon's Progressive Era:

> Insofar as the question, Are you white? has been and continues to be successfully replaced by the question, Are you American?—insofar, that is, as a question supposedly about biology has been preserved as a question supposedly about national identity—one might say that the very idea of American citizenship is a racial and even racist idea, racist not because it embodies (a more or less concealed) preference for white skins but because it confers on national identity something like the ontology of race. (192)

25. The late 1980s is a period intolerant of many neo-Nazi activities, from the social outrage regarding the Alan Berg case to the trial of Tom Metzger for sponsoring skinhead activities.

8

"All Eyez on Me"

The Paranoid Style of Tupac Shakur

Eithne Quinn

IT IS LITTLE WONDER that the life and death of Tupac Shakur have received such relentless media attention, for his story is both extraordinary and intriguing. In 1971 Tupac was born into the Black Panther Shakur family. His mother, Afeni, was one of the famous (and chic) Panther 21, tried for and acquitted (just one month before Tupac was born) of conspiring to blow up several New York department stores. When Tupac was ten, his stepfather, Mutulu Shakur, left the family to go into hiding and remained on the FBI's "Ten Most Wanted" list until his capture in 1986. As a young man and rising star, Tupac was involved in numerous run-ins with the law, including his both celebrated and condemned "shoot-out" with two off-duty police officers in Atlanta (for which he was acquitted of all charges). To mention only the most notable and notorious events that followed, he was robbed and shot five times at a New York recording studio in 1994, imprisoned for sexual assault in 1995, and in September 1996, aged twenty-five, he was fatally wounded in a drive-by shooting in Las Vegas. At the time of his death, Tupac and his record label, Death Row, were at the center of the media-fueled antagonism between East and West Coast rap personnel (the "beef" between Suge Knight's Death Row and Sean "Puffy" Combs's Bad Boy Records, which many fans and pundits held responsible for his death).[1] As an artist Tupac explored a range of styles, personas, and forms (including poetry, theater, film, and music) over the course of his curtailed but highly productive career. After a stint in the acclaimed Oakland rap group Digital Underground (debuting on its 1991 single "Same Song"), he went on to produce five solo albums and numerous collaborative cuts during his lifetime, and best-selling material continues to be compiled and released posthumously.[2] He enjoyed a successful and critically lauded movie career, starring in six films, which fed into his controversial celebrity image.[3] In all, as critics are at pains to point out, he was a contradiction: a "tabloid bogeyman," a heartthrob, an activist, a talented artist, a thug, and so on.

However, to mention these sensational events up front is in many ways to get them out of the way. Though fascinating, the actual and alleged conspiracies and exploits of Tupac's story are not the focus of this chapter. I do want to keep hold of the context of Tupac's real life insofar as it has had such a powerful influence on his publicity image. His stormy life informed and shaped his own evolving oeuvre, and greatly influenced how he and his music were constructed by critics and understood by audiences. Though we must be careful not to read his music as straight personal testimony (which is always the temptation and one to which he played, at times sincerely, at times as a marketing strategy), the boundaries between fact and fiction, between reality and fantasy in this case are particularly insecure, as commentators have frequently observed.

This essay explores Tupac's cultural output and publicity image, specifically in terms of what I am calling his "paranoid style." Through an analysis of exemplary and representative tracks, and then a wider look at his publicity image, I will examine the ways his work mobilized themes of paranoia and narratives of conspiracy to animate many of the pleasures and predicaments of his own cultural identity and celebrity status. Tupac has always been constructed as exemplary, as a representative of his generation. Historically locating this overbearing construction allows for a more complex understanding of the social specificity and undoubted generational resonance of the Tupac phenomenon in the "post-revolutionary era."[4] At the heart of Tupac's paranoid aesthetic seems to be a complex and contradictory interrogation of the operations of cultural power, particularly in regard to two fundamental and difficult relationships: between structure and agency, and between individual identity and group identity. I want to suggest that in his explorations of the expressive possibilities of psychological disturbance, Tupac grappled with and vividly enacted Marx's aphorism that "men make their own history, but not in conditions of their own making"—a paranoia-inducing predicament if ever there were one.

THE POLITICS OF PARANOIA

In her study of racial rumor and black urban legend, *I Heard It through the Grapevine: Rumor in African-American Culture*, Patricia Turner largely avoids the term "paranoia." Instead, her folklorist methodology sets up the exploration of a less charged set of questions about long-standing racial rumors revolving around contamination, cannibalism, conspiracy, and castration. She defines her favored term *contemporary legends* as "unsubstantiated narratives with traditional themes and modern motifs that circulate orally (and sometimes in print) in multiple versions and that are told as if they are true or at least plausible."[5] As we shall see, this serves as an apposite description of recurring themes and motifs percolating in Tupac's rhymes. However, there are two main reasons I insist on the more contentious term "paranoia" in this essay. Most important, it is central to the Tupac lexicon: he frequently characterizes the personas he adopts as "paranoid," and critics repeatedly use the word to describe him and his music. For instance, *Q* magazine describes Tupac as "a gun-toting paranoiac"; and, quoted in *Vibe* magazine, an industry insider (present on the night of Tupac's 1994 shooting) airs the oft-repeated view that Tupac "made it seem like niggas had a plot against him. Like he was so important that street niggas wanted to kill him, industry niggas wanted to kill him. He's believing his rap. He's believing the movie scripts that he's played." Once he became a celebrity, stories of setups, allegations, plots, and feuds—both proven and rumored, plausible and implausible—proliferated in and around him in the various realms of law enforcement, sexual relations, street gangs, the legal system, and the music business. In terms of Tupac's music, critic David Toop describes it as "skirting close to self-pity and paranoia"; and *New York Times* critic Jon Pareles speaks of his "songs' paranoia and anger."[6]

The second reason for holding on to the term "paranoia" relates to methodology. As evidenced by this edited collection, there is a venerable tradition of paranoid narrative in U.S. culture. To sidestep the important area of *black* paranoid poetics, in an attempt to avoid the difficult questions and contentious issues it raises, would be to sell short the rich expressive repertoires of black conspiracy culture.

The fact remains, however, that the term "paranoia," especially when used in association with African Americans, is a difficult one.

According to the *Oxford English Dictionary*, *paranoia* is the "tendency to suspect and distrust others or to believe oneself unfairly used." In terms of blacks as well as other historically exploited groups of Americans this definition amounts to little more than a rational posture of skepticism. More problematically, the *O.E.D.* provides a second definition: "a mental illness characterized by delusions of persecutions, unwarranted jealousy, or exaggerated self-importance."[7] The discrepancy between justified suspicion and irrational paranoia calls up the broad and polarized ideological contention between Left and Right over the reasons for continuing black poverty and disadvantage in post–civil rights America. Conservative and neoliberal commentators and policy makers have cast black political and economic frustrations firmly in terms of the second, "defective" meaning of paranoia. In crude terms, proponents of the "culture of poverty" and "color-blind" schools of thought, which have held such sway since the 1970s, focus on the behavior and attitudes of individuals and groups in their explanations of persisting economic inequity and black social dislocation (a discourse that has justified massive reductions in federal spending and welfare support). Put bluntly, to speak of black paranoia falls dangerously close to the conservative supposition along the lines that black people cannot get ahead because they have "chips on their shoulders," and need to dispense with their "politics of blame" and instead face up to the purported "declining significance of race."[8] Liberal-left critics, on the other hand, foreground structural problems—institutional racism and prejudicial power structures in a radically restructured economy, the retreat from social justice and the rolling back of welfare, and, more radically, the problem of the late-capitalist economic system itself in which "underclass" poverty is inherent—in their explanations of continuing black poverty in the post–civil rights era. Leftist critics, then, reject arguments that focus on the social pathology of groups or individuals. At the center of this discussion, of course, is a debate about systemic forces versus personal responsibility, about structure versus agency.

In the rightwardly realigned climate of the 1980s and 1990s, conservative positions on black disadvantage, and the charge of racial paranoia, have been absorbed and reproduced by the establishment press and mainstream intellectuals. For instance, the *Ethnic Newswatch* reported in 1996 (the year of Tupac's murder) on the mainstream press's predilection for stories about "the tendency of black Americans to embrace conspiracy theories." The *Ethnic Newswatch* criticized the elitist, self-serving posture of the establishment press, dubbing this kind of coverage "the 'dumb and paranoid' theory" in which the black urban poor are constructed *en masse* as conspiratorial dupes.[9] Many intellectuals have supported conservative consensus readings of racial suspicion. Take Daniel Pipes in *Conspiracy: How the Paranoid Style Flourishes and Where It Comes From*, who quotes a "clinical psychologist" who remarks that there is "probably no conspiracy involving African-Americans that is too far-fetched, too fantastic, or too convoluted."[10] In her provocative book on contemporary hysteria, public intellectual Elaine Showalter takes up (an ostensibly liberal version of) the same centrist position. She contends that individuals and groups are increasingly cloaking psychic troubles behind conspiratorial explanations. In many ways, Showalter's position accords with neoconservative discourses on race, in that she lays blame for social problems on self-determined psychological and cultural factors, rather than on the structural or external ones that the groups themselves hold accountable.[11] A starting point of such works is that conspiracy theories are by definition wrongheaded, foolish, and harmful. The conservative center defines its own political consensuality, rational and disinterested perspective, and rigorously considered arguments by setting up an easy opposition with the disaffection of those "dangerous extremists" or "lost souls" who resort to crude conspiratorial explanation.

Yet, returning to the two meanings of the word "paranoia," we might pose the following questions: Are socially marginal people more likely to be cultural dupes or cultural critics? Does a position of marginality open up a critical perspective and foster a robust skepticism, or, on the other hand, is such a social position too far removed from the political center, leading to the reliance on reassuring narratives, as a disaffected "opting out" of political and cultural engagement? And, the central question or tension in this case study: Is paranoid thinking evidence of a productive mistrust of authorized premises and conventional thinking, or the sign of a defective and harmful pathology? It is with this charged, fundamental debate in mind that I would like to turn to Tupac's paranoid poetics.

THE PARANOID STYLE OF TUPAC SHAKUR

To get a broad sense of Tupac's oeuvre, we can trace his cultural output across three loosely organized phases: first as "paranoid spokesperson," then as "paranoid individual," and finally an eclectic paranoid style that draws on the first two phases to produce an overblown free-play of interwoven conspiratorial motifs.[12] Though the analysis below identifies distinct phases, it will also draw out the crucial overlaps and inconsistencies between the various modes of his paranoid style. The first phase was inaugurated on his debut solo album, *2Pacalypse Now* (1991). Tupac's persona of this period was something of a "paranoid spokesperson" in that the hostile world was, as Richard Hofstadter put it, "not directed specifically against him," but was often "directed against a nation, a culture, a way of life whose fate affects not himself alone but millions of others."[13] His rhymes are indignant and accusatory, pointing the finger at the racist and exploitative social order and most defiantly at corrupt and aggressive law enforcement. A rhetoric of racial genocide is mobilized as he angrily expounds the difficulties of growing up black and male in post–civil rights America. "One by one, we are being wiped off the face of the earth," he asserts in the track "Words of Wisdom." His early hit single "Trapped" (1991) registers the generational sense of disappointment and betrayal at the integrationist dreams deferred ("Why did ya lie to me? / I couldn't find a trace of equality"). He berates the escalating levels of imprisonment of young black men ("Too many brothers daily heading for the big pen [penitentiary]"), a situation portrayed in the video clip featuring Tupac handcuffed and behind bars. The social commentary is apposite: the massive escalation of the prison-industrial complex during the Reagan/Bush years has led, since 1980, to a threefold increase in the number of African Americans in prison.[14]

Although Tupac specifically calls out the police and judiciary, the law emerges as only the most conspicuous, direct target. The undetermined, paranoid pronoun "they" (got me trapped) works to link the local situation and actual experience of imprisonment to the more abstract workings of social repression and to people in authority as a whole. In the same vein, the idea of entrapment stands for the physical space of a jail cell and simultaneously, to use Mike Davis's term, for the "carceral" geographies and social immobility of the urban ghetto (Tupac is "trapped in my own community"). The track, with its urgent and relentless repetition of the chorus refrain, invites the listener to connect the vivid local instance to the wider systems of social power. In productively unstable ways, the track hovers between a paranoid sense of *psychological* entrapment and a rational, indignant sense of *social* entrapment.

Such tracks fit within the kind of galvanizing politico-activist rap prevalent at that moment, in which there is a pervasive sense of explosive urgency. When Hofstadter suggests that the paranoid spokesperson "is sometimes disposed to set a date for the apocalypse," these rap artists give him one.[15] Tupac's album is entitled *2Pacalypse Now*, and Public Enemy's album of the same year is *Apocalypse '91: The Enemy Strikes Black*. Both titles temporalize social emergency in the immediate present (both playing on movie titles, demonstrating rap's proficiency in plundering and rearticulating pop cultural as well as political discourses).[16] This is a moment of insurrectionary political rap, understandably lauded by many critics for its social force, rhetorical exuberance, and sonic innovation.

In this phase, Tupac frequently referenced nostalgically the black nationalism and explosive insurgency that marked his early 1970s birth—a politicized era in which the declamations of the black paranoid spokesperson (and I mean this nonpejoratively as a spokesperson who adopts a morally charged rhetoric in the battle against systemic oppression) held great explanatory resonance.[17] This was the "golden age" of political conspiracy: of Richard Nixon, covert actions, and government informers. It was a time of conspiratorial actualities and political plotting (by black nationalists and government agencies)—according to his stepfather, young Tupac "had to keep secrets."[18] The residual sense of collective insurgency and of black political mobilization informed Tupac's politicized rhymes, which typically activated a sense of group belonging and communal resistance rather than individual identity.

Tupac epitomized the performative ways gangsta rappers—who were becoming highly marketable at this time, and developing an increasing awareness of their mass audience—started to play to white fears about black masculinity. Many critics have explored how social and political discourses have worked to stereotype and demonize black men in the public imagination.[19] Michael Rogin characterizes *demonology*, a strategy championed by Ronald Reagan, as "the creation of monsters as continuing features of American politics by the inflation, stigmatization, and dehumanization of political foes." Among the examples he offers are "the Indian cannibal, the black rapist," and, he might have added, the gangsta rapper."[20] In 1991, then Vice President Dan Quayle famously declared that Tupac had "no place in our society," activating the discourse of symbolic exclusion and sealing Tupac's status as a charged sign of the times.[21] Crucially, some rap artists actually embraced and rearticulated the very stereotypes they were served up. In what we might call a "self-demonologizing" move, gangsta rappers played up to mainstream paranoia by taking on the role of what Tupac calls "America's nightmare" (chanted repeatedly on "Words of Wisdom"). Equally, gangsta rapper Ice Cube is "The Nigga Ya Love to Hate," and Public Enemy conjures white paranoia with the title *Fear of a Black Planet* (1990). In Tupac's generically titled "Young Black Male" (1991), the answering refrain is "hard like an erection," tapping into the psychosexual anxieties and fantasies of white (as well as black) racial thinking.

The motivations for adopting this performative posture are numerous: to incite black masculinist resistance and pride; to goad and provoke black and white bourgeois society with the formidable and legendary "bad nigga" type; to adopt a mask of defiance in the face of intractable mainstream demonization; and, to be sure, to sell racially encoded rebellion to an eager youth market. The enactment and subversion of prevailing stereotypes involve a symbiotic dynamic: a two-way paranoid gaze exchanged through rap music. At the very least, self-demonology forcefully announces that black subjects have a powerful grasp of the double binds, of what Janice Radway describes as the "intricate interdependencies" of race.[22] Tupac provocatively asserted in a 1993 interview, "If a white bitch grabs her purse when I walk by, I'm snatchin' it. I'ma start acting on these stereotypes."[23] The anecdote is critically astute: in opting for the reactive tactic, Tupac is asserting that he understands that his personal agency is limited, that he is embedded in the social structures and caught up in the representational regimes that he wishes to critique. These artists demonstrate an acute awareness of the uneven power economy at play in and around their own cultural practice.

This self-demonologizing persisted in Tupac's second phase, but at the same time, Tupac redirected his persona toward that of "paranoid individual" (or what I term elsewhere "introspective badman").[24] There are a number of reasons Tupac dropped much of his overtly political rhetoric (his "motivated badman" status); the most compelling have to do with his changing personal circumstances (as he gained power, celebrity, and notoriety), and with record sales. The gangsta rap production trend came into mass market ascendance in 1991 with the chart-topping success of *Niggaz4Life* by NWA, after which time politicized rap faded. Tupac at once responded and contributed to this shift, as he increasingly adopted the "thug life" mantle on record and in life. The album titles signpost the shift from spokesperson to individual: his second album was titled *Strictly 4 My NIGGAZ* (1993); his third and most critically acclaimed release was called *Me against the World* (1995), signaling the increasing introspection and mistrustful isolation of his characterizations.[25] The mode of *Me against the World* is elegiac, comprising a series of "slow-jams" on which Tupac conjures psychological portraits of a troubled and bereft young man. Paranoid delusions preoccupy "Death around the Corner":

> *I no longer trust my homies*
> *Them phonies tried to do me*
> *Smoking too much weed*
> *Got me paranoid, stressed*
> *Pack a gat and my vest*

This may shed some light on the "real" Tupac: the album came out when he was in prison, and shortly after he had been robbed and shot. Before his imprisonment, he was widely reported to be carrying firearms and wearing a bulletproof vest ("pack a gat and my vest"). In any case, the consistency of the personas adopted on the album worked to encourage fans and critics to read the songs as autobiographical testaments, putting added strain on his "keepin-it-real" publicity image.

Tupac developed the persona of a psychologically disturbed individual, which was underwritten by his memorable role as Bishop in his 1990 debut movie, *Juice*. He had played the delinquent-turned-psychopath, Bishop, and this character furnished him with what became his signature phrase: "I *am* crazy. But you know what else? I don't *give* a fuck!" This line captures the total relinquishing of the paranoid spokesperson's moral responsibility, political authority, and broader perspective.

In some ways, however, the psychopathic Bishop stands in tension with Tupac's *Me against the World* mode in that the screen character is not prone to introspective rumination, nor does he emerge as a sympathetic character. The tracks on the album, by contrast, often begin with the consumption of alcohol and weed—a narrative device that stimulates rumination. These drugs function, by turns, to exacerbate paranoia ("weed got me paranoid"), to abate anxiety and alleviate mental suffering ("I smoke a blunt to take the pain out"), and to kindle a sense of righteousness and bluster ("Even though I know I'm wrong, man / Hennessee make a nigga think he strong, man").[26] The grain of Tupac's voice is thick and rough, the lyrics often delivered with impassioned strain underlining the sense of spiritual crisis. This work departs in several ways from orthodox gangsta rap. Where gangsta often projects an image of irreverent masculinist bluster, Tupac sheds light on how one tries to galvanize that image; where gangsta tends to steer clear of sentiment in favor of action, Tupac wallows in emotion, shedding "So Many Tears"; where gangsta revels in irreverent amorality, Tupac is grappling with his own moral ambivalence. He explores terrain powerfully pioneered in 1991 by the Geto Boys' "My Mind Is Playing Tricks on Me," which, according to the *Source* magazine, "took us on a terrifying trip through the mind of a gangster under the gun."[27] A shared feature of the Tupac and Geto Boys tracks—alongside insomnia, suicidal thoughts, paranoid delusions, and a preoccupation with death—is the mistrust of women. On "So Many Tears," Tupac raps, "Don't trust my lady," and "I'm hearing noises, think she's fuckin with my boys." Unusually for gangsta, the woman is described respectfully ("my lady") and emphasis rests on his own irrational jealousy rather than on her purported infidelity. Again, this draws attention to psychic strain, conjuring an image of emotionally inarticulate vulnerability. An important spin-off of gangsta, then, these personas of shell-shocked young men offer highly expressive psychological portraits.

However, this sense of emotional realism is in some ways problematic. It is here more than anywhere else in gangsta that the words *pathology* and *pathos* come uneasily together, stemming as they do from the same root (of suffering and disease). These songs offer a compelling cocktail of masculine sentimentalism, psychological disturbance, and social dysfunction, which holds great sway in the imagination of young male fans. Tracks like these, perhaps more than any others, lead white middle-class (usually male) critics into making the following type of untoward statement: "Rappers' posture of menacing danger appears mysteriously cool and soulful to the white listener, while sending a chilly frisson down his/her spine; whereas for the young black, the cold scariness of rap . . . is merely realism."[28] This critic's description of the "white" listener's responses, though highly generalized, may hold weight. (Certainly, among my mostly white students in Britain, Tupac fans are among the most ardent—

adamant that his performances are authentic and unself-conscious.) But it seems to be precisely the sense of "soulfulness" and "frisson" these songs elicit in the critic himself that leads him into making the second specious statement about the "merely" authentic responses of the generic "young black." Tupac's and Geto Boys' performances of the pathological gangsta tend to provoke fairly simplified notions of autobiographical expression, poetic voicing, and "ghetto authenticity." The danger is that Tupac's "paranoid individual" poetics serve to *close down* productive tensions and connections between the personal and political, between the specific instance and the abstract structural context. Instead they squarely locate the experience of psychological strain within local gangbanging pathologies and grim ghetto realities. Domestic suspicions, gang conflicts, suicidal rumination, and drug-induced disturbance all feature heavily in the densely coherent textual flow of Tupac's album. Though very powerful and affective, these tracks encourage the titillating mystification of black dysfunction.

Although these themes still run through Tupac's next two albums after he signed to Death Row Records, there is another distinct change of complexion in his paranoid imagery. As journalist Jon Pareles summarizes: where *Me against the World* "portrayed gangster life as grim and suicidal," *All Eyez on Me* (1996) is "slick, cocksure and utterly unrepentant."[29] Again, the titles intimate the shifts: *All Eyez on Me* communicates a move away from themes of individual paranoid persecution, toward a more grandiose sense of celebrity-self; and then *The Don Killuminati: The 7-Day Theory* signals an increasingly eclectic approach to conspiracy. On *Don Killuminati*, Tupac throws all sorts of plots into the mix, achieving an overblown, baroque conspiracist mode. He adopts the stage name "Makaveli"—a cross between the classic conspiratorial thinker Machiavelli and the black vernacular term "mack" (meaning pimp or street player). In discarding his regular name, Tupac complicates any simple sense of authorship, of personal testimony, disrupting a stable point of identification for listeners. Unlike the fairly stable first-person of *Me against the World*, this serves to draw attention to the unstable boundaries between authorial voice, persona, and characterization in the music. The album cover depicts Tupac martyred on a cross, and the title marries religion and numerology ("7-Day Theory"), the mafia ("don"), and ancient conspiratorial beliefs (the play on "Illuminati"). The track "Hail Mary" opens,

Makaveli in this—Killuminati, all through your body
The blow's like a twelve gauge shotty (Uhhh, feel me!)
And God said he should send his one begotten son
To lead the wild into the ways of the man
Follow me, eat my flesh, flesh of my flesh.

The widely divergent self-mythologizing images bear out the great narrative pleasures of conspiracy. Tupac's ready appropriation of competing motifs and rhetorics—sacred and secular, racial and international, contemporary and Renaissance, personal and political—stands in diametric opposition to the finely wrought, politicized conspiracy plot associated with the Cold War era and, in U.S. domestic terms, the early 1970s. There are no overriding antagonists, no reassuring meta-narratives, no Manichean conflicts. Instead, his paranoid style embraces the confusions of overlapping, conflictual, and commodified narrative. This seems to exemplify the turn to "insecure paranoia" (to use Peter Knight's term) arising from the confounding complexity of contemporary society marked by uncertainty, flexibility, information overload, and media saturation.[30]

Patricia Turner explains that groups modify their lore to accommodate the new challenges they face. In the postwar era, the shift in black rumor is toward stories about the commercial establishment and malevolent corporations.[31] In sweeping terms, the evolution of Tupac's paranoid style seems to illustrate this turn to the market in youth culture—specifically in black youth culture. The Makaveli track "Toss It Up" opens with the eerie chanting of Tibetan monks followed by Tupac's introductory lines: "The money behind the dreams / This big-ass conglomerati called Death Row—Killuminati!" The term "Conglomerati" saliently conjoins the mystique of gangsta entrepreneurialism and the vast, impenetrable complexity of multimedia conglomerates. The hallowed business enterprise is construed as an enshrined locus of power: above all, battles are fought and plots planned and executed in and between companies. By invoking a vestigial sense of the political spokesperson, but favoring the role of Death Row spokesperson—a shift from traditional cultural protest to an emphasis on cultural resources—Tupac captures something of wider trends in black cultural politics.

This account of Tupac's shifting style overschematizes the phases of Tupac's paranoid aesthetic, but what undoubtedly emerges starts to look very far removed from the coherent "interconnectedness" usually associated with paranoid film and fiction. There are few traces in Tupac's oeuvre of an overarching authorial voice, which comes to alleviate alienation, to redeem the paranoia through aesthetic creation. No such stable critical distance is afforded Tupac, who knows only too well that his own cultural output is as inescapably ordained by the marketplace and by his precipitous personal circumstances as by his artistry. Rather than standing outside, he is at pains to show that his music and image are embedded in the culture he critically comments on. As such, Tupac's vision is contingent, radical, and absurdist. Tupac asserts, "I haven't been out of the paper since I joined Digital Underground. And that's good for me cuz I don't want to be forgotten. If I'm forgotten then that means I'm comfortable and that means I think everything is OK."[32] At all times, then, his "real life" dramas were feeding into his publicity image and informing how his music was received and consumed, collapsing the bourgeois distinction between art and life. However individualist his paranoia became, Tupac always retained elements of the spokesperson mantle associated with his black nationalist parents. At the same time, in his early politicized tirades he never attempted to take on the role of authoritative race commentator as Public Enemy's Chuck D did; instead Tupac had already started to fashion his distinct enactment of psychological dis-ease, of dangerously rattled mindset.

Despite these overlaps and inconsistencies between phases, the trajectory from political spokesperson to apolitical individual compellingly animates the sweeping shift from revolutionary to postrevolutionary era, from spokesperson to individualist. Yet it is by no means a matter of simply applauding Tupac's politicized statements and decrying his move toward apolitical ones. Instead, what is significant about Tupac's paranoid vacillations between individual and spokesperson, between representative of group and of self, is the critical commentary they open up about representational politics and communal identity, and about the basis for political consciousness and group mobilization.

ALL EYEZ ON ME

ADARIO STRANGE: "What's the name of this album?"
TUPAC SHAKUR: "*All Eyez on Me*. Because they are. Everybody's watching for me to fall, die, get crippled, get AIDS, something."[33]

"All Eyez on Me" may well suggest a sense of paranoid self-importance, but for Tupac it was also an accurate statement of affairs by 1996. Surrounding his life and death were several popular contentions—or what we might call representational "burdens"—repeated to the point of cliché. Tupac's most onerous discursive burden was that of uplift and responsibility: the idea that Tupac should have inspired young black men to better themselves in various ways. A *New York Times* article provides an example of this when it contends that Tupac (single-handedly) "might have reconciled hip-hop's rivalry between the East and West coasts."[34] The sense of responsibility calls on another timeworn burden: that of representation as realism, representation as an act of authentic depiction. This discourse pervaded the reception of Tupac. It is signposted by the title of the same *Times* article, published after Tupac's murder: "In One Death, Mirrors of Our Times."

These representational burdens shaped the contours of his black public reception, as for instance the essays collected in *Tough Love: The Life and Death of Tupac Shakur* demonstrate. Tupac was repeatedly constructed as archetypal. Writing in *Rolling Stone*, hip-hop journalist Kevin Powell states, "To me, Shakur was the most important solo artist in the history of rap, not because he was the most talented (he wasn't) but because he, more than any other rapper, personified and articulated what it was to be a young black man in America."[35] Film director John Singleton puts the same point more dramatically: "Tupac is the original young, Black male."[36] In life, Tupac became an allegory for the shift away from the black nationalism and activism of his parent culture, which, as indicated above, he still represented vestigially. His publicity image was widely perceived as a combustible mixture of "Black Power" past and "thug life" present, the sense of his residual political commitment rendering the perceived changes all the more poignant. He became a symbol of post–civil rights malaise and political frustration. As Mumia Abu-Jamal asserts, "From revolutionary to thug—regression in the extreme, in one generation."[37] In his imprisonment, Tupac became a representative of the massively increasing number of incarcerated young black men. In death, he became an emblem of their desperately high murder rates: eleven thousand killed as a result of homicide in 1993 alone. "The tragedy of Tupac is that his untimely passing is representative of too many young black men in this country," asserted Quincy Jones (Tupac's prospective father-in-law at the time of his murder).[38]

The allegorical freight borne by Tupac surpassed other gangsta rappers in large part because he struck a chord with many more black people. The older generation often turned a hostile or, at best, deaf ear toward Snoop, NWA, and Geto Boys. Yet Tupac's frequent rap odes to his family—his biological family, especially his mother, Afeni, as on the "Dear Mama" single; his political black nationalist family, the Shakurs; and his extended "racial family," the black community—furnished him with an extraordinarily broad black constituency. To take one example, when the black scholar Wahneema Lubiano takes issue with Tupac's uplifting single "Keep Ya Head Up" (pointing to its celebration of conservative family values), her own appreciation emerges just as clearly: twice, almost despite herself, she calls the song "beautiful."[39] Also, unlike many gangsta artists, Tupac was a favorite with the ladies. With his good looks, charisma, and image of "tough vulnerability," alongside his popular female-centered tracks (including "Brenda Had a Baby" and "Keep Ya Head Up"), he enjoyed a loyal female following, even after his sexual assault conviction. The representational weight bearing down on Tupac was very heavy and pulled in different directions—all eyez were indeed on him.

Though gangsta rappers are constructed as representatives of black urban youth, the disparity between these celebrities and their purported constituency can be particularly difficult to negotiate. *Vibe* editor Alan Light explains,

> Last month, a rapper may have been on the streets, in school or yes maybe in a gang (an image record labels are all too eager to promote). Overnight, he's on MTV, his pockets filled with cash, kids rolling up on him, saying, "Yeah? You think you're bad?" He's getting positioned, hustled, sweated all the while needing to prove that he hasn't lost touch with the streets.[40]

Light vividly describes some of the pressures on newly famous rap stars, who are far removed from the experiences and problems of the average young person. As Robin Kelley and Phillip Harper's article title on Tupac tersely puts it, "Representin' What?"[41]

What is less often acknowledged, because less poignant and sensational, is that Tupac, along with other gangsta stars, became a beacon of black bootstrap uplift. If he was a "tabloid bogeyman," he was also a "poster boy" for the overcoming of poor and difficult beginnings in

America through sheer talent, aspiration, and hard work—a discourse energized by the individualist enterprise culture of the times. This representational status sits very uneasily with that of invisible, impoverished black youth. It forced Tupac into a highly paradoxical situation, which he seemed to understand very well.

In an MTV interview he asserted, "All society is doin' is leechin off the ghetto; they use the ghetto for their pain, for their sorrow, for their culture, for their music, for their happiness, for their movies."[42] In some ways, the very spectacle of his celebrity, his exceptionality, served to shift attention away from his putative constituency, to render even more invisible and unpalatable black urban poverty and actual imprisoned young men. Tupac came to symbolize for many the romantic notion of hedonistic thug life, sentimentalized macho pathology, and ghettocentric celebrity. Tupac afforded great opportunities for sensational press coverage about the "crisis of black men" and jeremiads about the state of American youth. But the discursive organization of these issues around such a telegenic and totemistic figure worked to displace attention away from the more mundane, intractable, but crucial questions of political economy.

The overblown selfhood and the extravagant psychic portraits of his music and image dramatically enacted some of the double binds of Tupac's stardom. His publicity image offered a resonant expression of both the power of spectacle and spectacular impotence. It laid bare the fractures produced by the combination of an inordinate sense of agency conferred by the media spotlight and a genuine sense of responsibility he bore as representative, coupled with his debilitating lack of autonomy in the face of wider industrial, discursive, and political forces. To be given or to take on some new version of the "race artist" mantle at a time when a sense of committed politics and social justice have little popular sway is a difficult status to negotiate meaningfully. It is probably to his credit that he felt and projected such discomfort with this mantle in light of its limited political salience (despite its persisting cultural resonance) in the post-soul 1990s.

"We're living in so much poverty and despair that by rapping about it, kinda making it seem like we controlling it, it makes us feel better about being here."[43] If Tupac's remark explains something about hip-hop bluster, it also provides an adept description of conservative "raps" about personal responsibility and self-help. In the post–civil rights era, these are popular discourses both *about* and *of* the black urban poor. As historian Robin Kelley argues, there has been a declining sense of entitlement and even of the *desirability* of government intervention and support among poor and working-class Americans.[44] Social inequality and economic inequality are less tangible and less noteworthy, not because they are less prevalent, but because they are taken for granted. This political dissipation and the sense of the intractability of social and economic conditions seem to have fostered a situation in which the only thing worth "rapping" about is self-help, a discourse of personal and community reliance (and of course by implication personal and group failing). Compounded by the free market zeitgeist of the post-seventies period, the discrediting of the need for government support and entitlement strikes a resonant chord with many black and white Americans.[45] In a neoconservative climate, press articles about personal uplift and self-help make for good copy just as raps about responsibility and family ("Dear Mama") or its self-conscious rejection ("Thug Life") sell records, and in so doing help to shift the focus away from wider material conditions and relations of power.

Armond White is probably right to argue that "[y]outhful black activism—essentially a dream of the past—was never more to Tupac than a role to play."[46] However, when he goes on to endorse songs like the "salvation-over-survival" of R Kelly's "I Believe I Can Fly" in order more forcefully to denounce Tupac's "religiosity by rote," he is doing little more than perpetuating the discourses of uplift.[47] Such rhetorical moves place an inordinate and inappropriate charge on young artists to act as race delegates, which is not only anachronistic, but is in danger of playing dangerously into the rhetorical hands of the Right.

Tupac's "bugged out" publicity image constitutes a salient expression of the complex interdependencies between economics and culture, between individual and society. To take one arresting example, the cover of the February 1994 issue of *Vibe* magazine carried a striking sepia-toned photo of Tupac in a straitjacket, with the accompanying title, "Is Tupac Crazy or Just Misunderstood?" (see fig. 8.1). Clearly this mobilizes his psychologically disturbed star image, and at the same time invites readers to see the straitjacket as a trope for the pathologizing racist society that confines young black men more generally. In the accompanying article Kevin Powell asks rhetorically, "Is he a young black man shackled by the system, or an individual young black man out of control?"[48] He calls up the familiar dialectics of spokesperson versus individual, structure versus agency, which are critically engaged

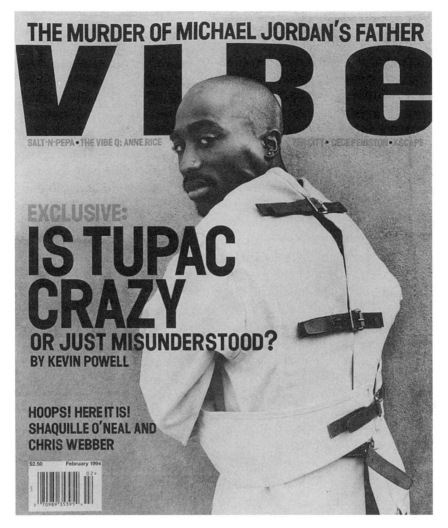

FIGURE 8.1. "Is Tupac Crazy or Just Misunderstood?" Cover reprinted by permission of *Vibe* magazine.

by Tupac. When *Vibe*—at that time a recently launched magazine struggling to get a viable foothold in the market—ran this cover, it achieved greater sales and reached a broader audience than ever before. This small episode crystallizes the double binds of Tupac's predicament. Despite the sheer spectacle and sensation of his star aura, he had relatively little control over his own image construction (he is said to have disliked this cover photo). At the same time, Tupac was partially complicit in the marketing of this media-fueled image of black pathology. Just as this cover sold copies of *Vibe*, so his sensational lyrics sold albums. The power of this iconic *Vibe* cover then rests not just on its intended meanings, but on its perhaps inadvertent commentary on the terms of its own representation: Tupac was "straitjacketed" by the media, by the hip-hop press itself; in short, by the commercial power of his own notorious image. The richness of his image lies in the fact that he exposes rather than conceals these complex cultural dynamics.

By the time of his death he had sold 20 million records for an estimated $75 million, rendering him a very important commodity for the record industry.[49] Tupac's notoriety served to enhance sales at the same time as it led to political pressures on record companies (from black community organizations, state bodies, and the government) to distance themselves from gangsta producers. Thus record corporations were in the disingenuous position of publicly censuring notorious artists while tacitly licensing and profiting from their activities. This produced a situation in which, as Keith Negus argues, "the genre culture of rap" has been ostracized by the record industry corporations—held at arm's length from industry power centers.[50]

Discriminatory power is exerted, maintained, and reproduced, not by the clandestine acts of conspiring corporate elites, but by the less conspicuous (and thereby of course less targetable and less accountable) interplay of prejudicial cultural practices and insidious structural dynamics. Such processes tend to prevent rap artists from entering into a corporate career in the record industry, serving to perpetuate the marginalization of rap's genre culture. In his recent account of hip-hop culture and film, S. Craig Watkins corroborates this view, breaking down in detail why it is that so many black youth are isolated from the informal networks and opportunity structures that facilitate mobility in the culture industry, despite their high visibility and commercial centrality.[51] Rap artists are given free rein, but only in invisibly circumscribed domains (again recalling Marx's maxim).

To be sure, the actions of quite visible individuals also played a part in the takedown of Tupac—not least himself. He must share some responsibility for the fact that, as David Sanjek remarks, "the public at large currently possesses a largely negative view of the African American participation in the music industry" by virtue of the murders, strong-arm tactics, parole violations, and so on, in and around Death Row Records.[52] In some ways, though, the Death Row imbroglio and especially Tupac's demise provide almost a grim parable. Tupac's paranoid style at once captures and feeds into the frustration born out of the mismatch between black America's great historic and ongoing cultural resources combined with their persisting low stock of political and economic capital. Tupac's expressive, even deathward-bound paranoia is a troubling but remarkably pointed outgrowth. The central point then is not that these forces made Tupac paranoid (though that may partially be true), but that his chaotic and commercial paranoid style offered a timely and astute pop-cultural expression of the pressures on working-class–oriented (or "ghettocentric") black male celebrity in the contemporary period.

CONCLUSION

Part of the importance of this case study is that it gives us clues about how people are actually using conspiracy narratives, about the ways individuals are approaching paranoid thinking. Tupac's paranoid imagination does not represent any simple blaming of external causes in an attempt to hide the "real" problems that are internal and psychic (as Showalter proposed). Instead, his star aura constitutes a persuasive blurring and sometimes even inversion of Showalter's symptom and diagnosis. Tupac's populist paranoia animates Peter Knight and Alasdair Spark's suggestion that "much conspiratorial thinking is an internalization via narrative of conflicts buried deep in the social realm."[53] Tupac's music and celebrity image offer frank explorations of psychic strain—a compelling pop-cultural enunciation of paranoia, which is in large part brought on by external factors. The evidence above certainly complicates the "dumb and paranoid" discourses percolating in mainstream critical and media spheres about black people's predilection for paranoia (whether actual or invented). On the whole, Tupac's critical paranoia does not close down complex understandings and theoretical questioning, but instead tends to use its possibilities for total explanation to glimpse profound connections between the personal and the political, the psychic and the social, the individual and the larger relations of power. Such critical thinking is of course essential to the production of political consciousness.

On the track "Only God Can Judge Me Now" Tupac recounts one of the increasingly common lyrical ruminations about his own shooting:

> *I hear the doctor standing over me, screaming I can make it*
> *Got a body full of bullet holes, laying here naked*
> *Still I can't breathe, something evil's in my IV*
> *'Cause every time I breathe, I think they're killing me*
> *I'm having nightmares, homicidal fantasies.*

In what critic Steven Daly calls "one of the most morbid artifacts of the pop era," the video for the single "I Ain't Mad at Cha" (filmed only one month before his death) includes scenes of Tupac being shot and going to heaven.[54] These recurring depictions of his own shooting emphatically informed the reception of his murder in 1996. In a postmodern turn of events, fictional and factual narrative resolutions developed an intertextual relationship to one another. Such fictive death scenarios fueled the conspiracy theory that he had staged his own death—just one more rehearsal in Las Vegas. This imposes a bathetic formal resolution to the story, which again suggests the power of the market forces: he staged his own death in order to sell more records! In any case, that was one of the ideas disseminated by Chuck D on his famous Web site "Thirteen Reasons Why Tupac Is Still Alive." Other intriguing reasons include the contention that Tupac died on Friday the thirteenth (which is true), and that "there was no autopsy" (which is incorrect).[55] The conspiracy theories suggesting that Tupac faked his own death confer a sense of agency on the fan and, by extension, the rapper; he is no longer the victim, no longer dead. Fans rewrite events with the same kind of wish fulfillment that they have bestowed on other celebrities who have died suddenly and prematurely, which provides the upbeat ending we all wanted. However, this reassuringly populist reading is, I have tried to argue, substantively overshadowed by the grimmer logic of structural forces.

NOTES

1. On Tupac's life and times, see Armond White, *Rebel for the Hell of It: The Life of Tupac Shakur* (New York: Thunder's Mouth Press, 1997); and Connie Bruck, "The Takedown of Tupac," *New Yorker*, 7 July 1997, 47–64. For an illustrated anthology of his hip-hop press reception, see the editors of *Vibe*

magazine's *Tupac Shakur* (New York: Crown, 1997); for personal and critical treatments of Tupac's death, see Michael Datcher and Kwame Alexander, eds., *Tough Love: The Life and Death of Tupac Shakur* (Alexandria, VA: Alexander Publishing, 1997).

2. "Same Song," *This Is an EP Release* (Tommy Boy). Tupac's five solo albums released during his lifetime are *2Pacalypse Now* (Interscope, 1991); *Strictly 4 My N.I.G.G.A.Z.* (Interscope, 1993); *Me against the World* (Interscope, 1995); *All Eyez on Me* (Death Row, 1996); and, as Makaveli, *The Don Killuminati: The 7-Day Theory* (Death Row, 1996).

3. Tupac's starring film roles are in *Juice* (Ernest Dickerson, 1990); *Poetic Justice* (John Singleton, 1993); *Above the Rim* (Jeff Pollack, 1994); *Gridlock'd* (Vondie Curtis Hall, 1997); *Bullet* (Julien Temple, 1997); *Gang Related* (Jim Kouf, 1997).

4. This term is from Clayborne Carson, "Rethinking African-American Political Thought in the Post-Revolutionary Era," in Brian Ward and Tony Badger, eds., *The Making of Martin Luther King and the Civil Rights Movement* (London: Macmillan, 1996), 115–27.

5. Patricia Turner, *I Heard It through the Grapevine: Rumor in African-American Culture* (Berkeley: University of California Press, 1993), 4–5.

6. *Q* magazine, April 1998, 56; *Vibe*, August 1995, reprinted in editors of *Vibe, Tupac Shakur*, 60; David Toop, "Farewell to Arms," *Face*, November 1996, 156; Jon Pareles, "In One Death, Mirrors of Our Times," *New York Times*, 22 September 1996, B30.

7. *The New Shorter Oxford English Dictionary* (Oxford: Oxford University Press, 1993 edition), s.v. "paranoia."

8. "Politics of blame" comes from Shelby Steele, an exemplar of the black neoconservative positions, at pains to discredit any sense of racial entitlement among black people; see *The Content of Our Character* (New York: HarperCollins, 1991). The "declining significance of race" comes from the groundbreaking work of neoliberal sociologist William Julius Wilson, *The Declining Significance of Race: Blacks and Changing American Institutions*, 2d ed. (Chicago: University of Chicago Press, 1980).

9. *Ethnic Newswatch*, 31 December 1996, 20. The media storm about reports of the crack/CIA/Contra connection, following the *San Jose Mercury News* series "Dark Alliance" by Gary Webb, offers a powerful illustration of the gatekeeping functions of the American establishment press (a story that, curiously, broke in the same month as Tupac's death).

10. Jewelle Taylor Gibbs, *Race and Justice: Rodney King and O. J. Simpson in a House Divided* (San Francisco: Jossey-Bass, 1996), 241, 237–38; quoted in Daniel Pipes, *Conspiracy: How the Paranoid Style Flourishes and Where It Comes From* (New York: Free Press, 1997), 2.

11. Elaine Showalter, *Hystories: Hysterical Epidemics and Modern Media* (New York: Columbia University Press, 1997).

12. My appropriation of hoary Hofstadterian terminology ("paranoid style," "paranoid spokesperson," etc.) is by no means intended to force a match between what are two widely divergent applications of paranoia in terms of content and function. There is an unbridgeable gap between the pejorative meanings proposed by Hofstadter in his classic 1966 article about extremist political groups and the paranoid *poetics* that I have in mind here. Still, stripped of their original ideological intent, Hofstadter's terms do offer a widely understood frame of reference and descriptive shorthand; see Richard Hofstadter, *The Paranoid Style in American Politics and Other Essays* (New York: Knopf, 1966).

13. Ibid., 4.

14. Statistics from the Bureau of Justice found that 700,000 black men were incarcerated in 1994, up from 25,000 in 1960; reported in *New York Times*, 18 September 1996, A20. On the explosion of the prison population and the privatization of prisons in the Reagan/Bush years, see Robin D. G. Kelley, *Yo' Mama's Disfunctional! Fighting the Culture Wars in Urban America* (Boston: Beacon Press, 1997), 97–100.

15. The paranoid or political spokesperson adopts a righteous rhetoric in the battle against systemic oppression.

16. Apocalypse is a resurgent theme in rap, notably in the predictions of global disaster on Busta Rhymes' best-selling albums, *When Disaster Strikes* (Elektra, 1997) and *Extinction Level Event* (Elektra, 1998); the mystical numerology of "living mathematics" advanced by Wu-Tang Clan on *Enter the Wu-Tang (36 Chambers)* (Loud/RCA, 1993) and the solo work of Method Man including *Tical 2000: Judgement Day* (Def Jam, 1998); and the futuristic style of video director Hype Williams, whose influential, award-winning clips include Tupac's "California Love," which depicts a dystopian future-desert of campfires and rusty cybertechnology reminiscent of the Mad Max films.

17. The political rhetoric of the Black Power movement often involved conspiracy rhetoric and imagery; see, for example, Stokeley Carmichael and Charles V. Hamilton, *Black Power: The Politics of Liberation in America* (New York: Vintage Books, 1967); and Eldridge Cleaver, *Soul on Ice* (New York: McGraw-Hill, 1967).

18. Bruck, "Takedown of Tupac," 49.

19. See, for instance, Tricia Rose, "Rap Music and the Demonization of Young Black Males," in Thelma Golden, ed., *Black Male: Representations of Masculinity in Contemporary America* (New York: Whitney Museum of Modern Art, 1994), 149–57; "Assassination of the Black Male Image," interview with Earl Ofari Hutchinson, *Louisiana Weekly*, 28 August 1995, A1; and Stephen Steinberg, *The Ethnic Myth: Race, Ethnicity, and Class in America* (Boston: Beacon Press, 1982), 279–84.

20. Michael Rogin, *Ronald Reagan, the Movie, and Other Episodes in Political Demonology* (Berkeley: University of California Press, 1987), xiii.

21. Quayle's politically opportunist remark was inspired by the contention of a defense lawyer that *2Pacalypse Now* had incited his client to shoot a Texas policeman.

22. Janice Radway, "What's in a Name? Presidential Address to the American Studies Association," *American Quarterly* 51 (1999): 10.

23. Quoted in Kim Green, "War Stories," *Source*, August 1993, 58.

24. Eithne Quinn, "Gangsta Rap and the Badman Figure from Stackolee to (Mr) Scarface," in S. Craig Watkins, ed., *Black Culture, Industry, and Everyday Life* (Malden, MA: Blackwell, forthcoming).

25. *Me against the World* entered the Billboard chart at number 1 when it was released in April 1995, and went on to sell two million copies, as reported in *New York Times*, 13 February 1996, C13.

26. Lyrics from the track "Lord Knows."

27. *Source*, January 1992, 20.

28. Ted Swedenburg, "Homies in the Hood: Rap's Commodification of Insubordination," *New Formations* 18 (1992): 59.

29. Jon Pareles, "Prison Makes Rap Tougher," *New York Times*, 13 February 1996, C13.

30. Peter Knight, "Everything Is Connected: *Underworld*'s Secret History of Paranoia," *Modern Fiction Studies* 45 (1999): 811–36.

31. Turner, *I Heard It through the Grapevine*, 82.

32. Quoted in White, *Rebel for the Hell of It*, 175.

33. *Source*, March 1996, 111.

34. Pareles, "In One Death, Mirrors of Our Times."

35. Cited in Cathy Scott, *The Killing of Tupac Shakur* (Las Vegas: Huntington, 1997), 180.

36. Quoted in *Source*, August 1993, 56.

37. Mumia Abu-Jamal, "2Pacalypse Now," *Louisiana Weekly*, 30 September 1996, A5.

38. Figures from Bureau of Justice Statistics, quoted in *New York Times*, 18 September 1996, A20. Quincy Jones, editors of *Vibe, Tupac Shakur*, book jacket quotation.

39. Wahneema Lubiano, "Black Nationalism and Black Common Sense: Policing Ourselves and Others," in Wahneema Lubiano, ed., *The House That Race Built* (New York: Pantheon, 1997), 246–48.

40. Editors of *Vibe, Tupac Shakur*, 33.

41. Robin D. G. Kelley and Phillip Brian Harper, "Representin' What?" *Frieze*, November–December 1996, 41–44.

42. Quoted in White, *Rebel for the Hell of It*, 52.

43. *Source*, March 1996, 111.

44. Kelley, *Yo' Mama's Disfunktional!* 78–102.

45. For his article on African American conspiracy theories, Theodore Sas-

son recorded a series of group discussions of neighborhood crime-watch groups in early-1990s Boston. The rejection of liberal explanations for the high rates of crime and poverty in these discussions is striking, leading Sasson to comment, "the widespread belief that through pluck and perseverance anyone can 'make it' militated against the liberal argument" (274–76). Theodore Sasson, "African American Conspiracy Theories and Social Construction of Crime," *Sociological Inquiry* 65 (1995): 265–85.

46. White, *Rebel for the Hell of It*, 162.

47. Ibid., 206–7.

48. Kevin Powell, "Is Tupac Crazy or Just Misunderstood?" *Vibe*, February 1994, 22.

49. Sales figures from "Tupac Shakur: Fans Still Mourn," *L.A. Sentinel*, 19 September 1996, A1.

50. Keith Negus, "Cultural Production and the Corporation: Musical Genres and the Strategic Management of Creativity in the U.S. Recording Industry," *Media, Culture & Society* 20 (1998): 359–79.

51. S. Craig Watkins, *Representing: Hip Hop Culture and the Production of Black Cinema* (Chicago: University of Chicago Press, 1998), 241.

52. David Sanjek, "One Size Does Not Fit All," *American Music*, winter 1997, 555.

53. Peter Knight and Alasdair Spark, "Plots All Over the Landscape," *Times Higher Education Supplement*, 25 December 1998, 22.

54. "Tupac Shakur," *Alt.culture*, 20 March 1999, <http://www.altculture.com/.index/aentries/t/txshakur.html>.

55. For details of what happened, and a detective-thriller approach to the manifold conspiracies surrounding his death (both in terms of "dead or alive?" and "who murdered Tupac?"), see Scott, *The Killing of Tupac Shakur*.

THE ENDS OF CONSPIRACY

9

The X-Files and Conspiracy

A Diagnostic Critique

Douglas Kellner

ARE WE IN AN Age of Conspiracy and Paranoia? In the United States, books about aliens and extraterrestrial abductions have become best-sellers and TV documentaries proliferate on these topics. Right-wing paramilitary groups allege a myriad of political conspiracies and strike out at government targets. Internet conspiracy sites and chat rooms abound and talk radio prospers on political rumors and controversy. Popular TV series and films feature government, corporate, and extra-terrestrial conspiracies galore while American politics, media culture, and everyday life seem to be saturated with fears and fascination with conspiracy, generating a paranoid sense that individuals have lost control of their institutions and even the ability to map and understand the machinations of a complex global society and culture.

Although conspiracy thinking and what Richard Hofstadter has called "the paranoid style of American politics" have long been charac-teristic of the American experience, there seems to be an explosion of populist paranoia and conspiracy thinking in the contemporary mo-ment, of which *The X-Files* is a significant and symptomatic part. In this study, I carry out a diagnostic critique that uses *The X-Files* to provide a critical analysis of contemporary U.S. society and culture. Distinguish-ing between a populist paranoia that demonizes irrationally dominant institutions and often projects evil onto occult and supernatural figures, and a critical paranoia that is rationally suspicious of hegemonic insti-tutions like the state, the military, or corporations, I argue that *The X-Files* combines rational social critique and mistrust with occultist pro-jection onto the supernatural that deflects attention from the real sources of social oppression.[1]

My analysis will suggest a growing crisis of confidence in the institutions of U.S. society and an openness to criticize its structures and ideology on the part of network television, previously a rather conservative ideology machine. However, the critical discourse of *The X-Files* is itself ideological and is undercut by its occultism, its imbrication of a conservative yuppie ideology, and the traditional tropes of romantic individualism. Nonetheless, *The X-Files* raises questions about the working of contemporary society, puts in question oppositions between science and reason and their other, and subverts the conventions of traditional commercial television to an unparalleled extent, providing challenging texts through which we can engage via diagnostic critique the fundamental sociopolitical and cultural issues of our time.

CONSPIRACY, POSTMODERN AESTHETICS, AND PARANOIA IN *THE X-FILES*

In the 1960s and 1970s a popular discourse concerning widespread and virulent conspiracies within American society and politics flourished. After the assassinations of John and Robert Kennedy and black political leaders like Malcolm X, Martin Luther King, and leaders of the Black Panther Party, reports of political conspiracies circulated that often indicted agencies like the FBI, the CIA, and other arms of the national security state. The seemingly endless continuation of the Vietnam War, U.S. covert and overt interventions throughout the world, and a steady stream of revelations of U.S. government-sanctioned crimes flourished. With disclosure of systematic wrongdoing by the Nixon administration in the Watergate scandals, the mainstream media began taking up conspiracy themes, and their discourses provided tools of critique of institutions that had previously been sacrosanct during the Cold War, when criticisms of the national security state were equivalent to treason.

During the same period, revelations of U.S. corporations producing unsafe cars and other products, willfully and knowingly engaging in environmental destruction, and promoting potentially catastrophic nuclear energy plants and weapons helped create a distrust of major economic organizations and practices. The widespread suspicion of dominant government and corporate forces was translated in media culture into new genres of conspiracy films. Political conspiracy films such as

Executive Action (1973), *The Parallax View* (1974), *Three Days of the Condor* (1974), *The Domino Principle* (1975), *All the President's Men* (1976), and *Twilight's Last Gleaming* (1979) are significant because they reverse the polarities of earlier Hollywood political thrillers, which generally affirmed U.S. institutions, by suggesting that the source of evil was those very agencies. They transcoded fear and distrust of government, a theme that would return with a vengeance in the 1990s, and nurtured a paranoid sense that political power was out of the reach of ordinary citizens and democratic political processes.[2]

The X-Files takes up the conspiracy and paranoia motifs of its Hollywood predecessors and goes even further in its critique of dominant institutions and depictions of depravity and intrigue. The series is generally acclaimed to be *the* television cult hit of the 1990s, and rarely has a popular artifact of media culture exuded so many layers of conspiracy and paranoia. Its world of shadowy government and corporate conspiracies, its excursions into the occult, paranormal, and supernatural, its anxious injunction to "trust no one," and its nihilistic presentation of the American system have touched a responsive chord during an era when belief in the fantastic, aliens, and government conspiracies is accelerating. Featuring the exploits of two FBI agents, Fox Mulder (David Duchovny) and Dana Scully (Gillian Anderson), *The X-Files* articulates a panorama of contemporary fears and fantasies, drawing on classical figures of the occult, present-day horrors, and political machinations as material. It thus uses the forms and iconic figures of media culture and references to contemporary historical individuals and events to comment on present-day issues and to represent salient disturbing aspects of the current era. In so doing, it raises questions concerning powerful U.S. institutions and practices.

The X-Files is particularly popular and successful, I believe, because of its skillful blending of science fiction, horror, occult, and fantasy genres with police and political and corporate conspiracy genres. In terms of *The X-Files'* thematics, its questioning of the epistemology of truth and erosion of binary oppositions between science and faith, the irrational and rational, and the natural and the supernatural enact a deconstructive postmodern epistemology. Moreover, its themes of aliens and the supernatural can be read as allegorical figures for a postmodern implosion of technology and the human, and its paranoid politics constitute a version of pop postmodernism that deploys paranoiac suspicion and mistrust to help map a difficult-to-represent political complexity and heterogeneity that seem to defy conceptual mapping and representation. Yet *The X-Files'* aesthetics and thematics exhibit some classical modernist features as well as novel postmodern ones; thus the series navigates the tricky and hazardous shoals between the modern and the postmodern.[3]

A founding gesture of high modernist aesthetics created a great divide between high and low culture, in which the artifacts of high culture were alleged to reside in an elevated sphere of beauty, truth, originality, and value, while the debased artifacts of mass culture were believed to be infected with commercialism, banality, ideology, and the lack of aesthetic form or value. The postmodern turn in aesthetics, however, rejected this distinction, arguing that what is now acclaimed as high culture was once popular (e.g., Greek drama, Shakespeare, Wagner, etc.), while the popular has its own aesthetic pleasures and values. A postmodern populism thus opens aesthetics to the artifacts of the popular and legitimates and sanctions aesthetic and thematic analysis of such forms as series television, pop music, and the other artifacts of media culture. In the following analysis, I will accordingly subject *The X-Files* to aesthetic and political scrutiny, taking it seriously as a symptomatic and interesting artifact of the contemporary, which reveals significant cultural shifts in both the forms of culture and societal values.

The *X-Files* pilot and the succeeding episode, "Deep Throat" (1/1 and 1/2; 1993), combine the forms of the political conspiracy and alien science fiction (hereafter SF) genres to present the characters, plot lines, and themes of the show.[4] The early episodes utilized rather conventional TV-narrative (pseudo)realism aesthetics with standard plot structures and character presentation. To play on quasi-documentary narrative realism, thought to be essential to TV credibility, the series opened—for the first and last time—with a text saying that the story was "inspired by actual documented accounts." The series opener shows Dana Scully, a new female FBI agent, trained as a medical scientist, entering a dark government chamber where she learns that she will be assigned to the X-Files, working with Fox Mulder, an Oxford-educated psychologist who is reputed to be an expert in crime profiling, but who was known in the FBI academy as "Spooky" Mulder because of his interest in the occult and supernatural. The actor Charles Cioffi, who plays the FBI bureaucrat informing Scully of her assignment, played the murderous psychopath in Alan Pakula's *Klute* and villains in other of his political conspiracy films, thus contributing to the disturbing aura of sinister government bureaucrats who surround the young agents.

Scully goes down to Mulder's basement office to meet her new partner, who is initially framed against a poster with a small flying saucer that reads, "I want to believe." This trope will identify Mulder's quest for truth and passion for knowledge. He ironically introduces himself as "the FBI's least wanted" and correctly assesses that Scully was "sent to spy on me," highlighting his (justified) paranoia. Yet Mulder also indicates that he is impressed with her scientific credentials, which include knowledge of her senior thesis on "Einstein's Twin Paradox: A New Interpretation," which Mulder assures her he has read. But, he explains, "It's just that in most of my work, the laws of physics rarely seem to apply."

Their initial assignment in the 1993 pilot episode involves exploring the murder of young teenagers whom Mulder suspects were victims of alien abduction and experimentation. Scully, of course, is skeptical, setting up an opposition contrasting the scientific rationalist with the paranormal supernaturalist, Mulder, who wants to believe. This common delineation between reason and faith, science and the paranormal, functions critically in The X-Files since the usual gender associations are reversed. Moreover, as the series proceeds, it deconstructs the oppositions, with Mulder often becoming more critical and skeptical, and Scully becoming more open to extrascientific explanations, faith, and what are referred to as "extreme possibilities."

Although most mainstream U.S. television classically followed a very simplistic representational strategy, The X-Files questions, undermines, and subverts traditional television codes, providing its own set of aesthetic pleasures. While American TV followed codes of simplicity, familiarity, and predictability, The X-Files, by contrast, revels in complexity and ambiguity. Whereas most network television uses a banal realism and neither strives for nor is interested in aesthetic values, The X-Files employs production teams who pursue high creative values and produce some of the most aesthetically pleasing, stylized, and intellectually challenging television yet to appear. The series thus has affiliations with classical modernism and its ideal of the complex and open text, which invites multiple readings and requires an active audience.

There are other distinctly modernist aspects of the series as well. Scully and Mulder are first and foremost truth seekers. The series has adopted as its motto, which concludes the opening title sequence,

"The Truth Is Out There," thus projecting a strong concept of truth. In addition, the series exhibits something like a modernist auteurial vision, strongly defined by the series creator, Chris Carter, who wrote many of the episodes, directed several, and played an extremely strong supervisory role over every detail of production. The show thus projects a personal vision, style, and aesthetic characteristic of the auteurs of modernism.

Indeed, *The X-Files* excels in the production of aesthetic pleasures, including the visual delight of seeing the unknown, of gaining ocular access to the supernatural and paranormal. The opening sequence unfolds with Mark Snow's mysterious music and the show title positioned against a black background. The image jumps to what appears to be a computer-generated montage of an unidentified flying object and then to what appear to be alien hieroglyphics and a strange technology that mutates into a fearful face, itself morphing into an abstract image of terror with background graphics stating "Paranormal Activity" appearing. The montage then cuts to an FBI office and Agent Mulder's badge and face, punctuated by a dimly flickering title, "Government denies knowledge," pointing to the conspiracy motif of the series. Next, Agent Scully's face and badge appear, followed by images of Mulder and Scully entering a doorway into a dangerous site, succeeded by what looks like an X-ray of a hand with a glimmering red finger and then a strange body.

Near the end of the opening title sequence, there is a morph to an image of a giant eye, which then cuts to a dramatically cloudy sky, usually emblazoned with the motto "The Truth Is Out There." The opening sequence thus signals to the viewer that she or he is about to enter unknown and mysterious spaces and to see something different, perhaps frightening and shocking. The show deals with the pleasures of seeing and knowing as the Federal Bureau of Investigation agents, Scully and Mulder, discover and perceive novelties, bizarre and paranormal phenomena, and the secret and villainous machinations of government.

Most interpretations of *The X-Files* perceive it as one-sidedly modern or postmodern, failing to see how it negotiates the boundaries between them, participating in both sides of the Great Divide. In an otherwise illuminating and interesting article, Jimmie Reeves, Mark Rodgers, and Michael Epstein write, "Although the generic sampling and episodic/serial straddle of *The X-Files* could be interpreted as boundary blurring, other aspects of the program are explicitly anti-postmodern."[5] According to these authors, *The X-Files* is "post-postmodern" because of the committed and sustained quest for truth on behalf of its protagonists, its seriousness, and its lack of the sort of postmodern cynicism, irony, and play with generic codes characteristic of such popular programs as *Beavis and Butt-Head* or *Mystery Science Theater 3000*. I claim by contrast that the show does embody postmodern aesthetic strategies, themes, and vision, despite the fact that its characters often exhibit arguably modern characteristics that do inform some of the plots and vision of the series (questing for truth, a yuppie work ethic and professionalism, belief in scientific rationality, and so on).

My argument is that the series on the whole undermines the modern paradigm of truth, representation, and subjectivity, while presenting new postmodern paradigms. Moreover, from the perspective of aesthetic strategy, *The X-Files* systematically uses postmodern pastiche that combines classical cinematic and literary genres, traditional folklore, and references to contemporary urban lore and political events, which it brings together in an implosive mixing of classical generic codes, material from a diverse realm of media culture, and journalistic contemporaneity, resulting in a postmodern blend of the traditional and contemporary. The specific postmodern aesthetic at play in the series is that proposed by Linda Hutcheon, who advances a model of postmodern appropriation and hybridity as a way of commenting on traditional generic forms and material, and of making critical comments in regard to history and contemporary social forces and events. This notion is opposed to Fredric Jameson's more ludic notion of postmodernism that sees it as a play with codes more interested in surface form than social commentary or critique.[6]

For Hutcheon, a critical postmodernism inscribes *and* contests previous forms of culture, which it sets out to undermine, and thus has a "contradictory dependence on and independence from that which temporally preceded it and which literally made it possible."[7] Hutcheon agrees with Jameson, Huyssen, and others on the point that postmodern culture is inherently quotational, reiterative, and parasitic on previous cultural forms, but she claims that the postmodern mode of quotation is intertextual parody rather than mere pastiche, as Jameson holds. For example, whereas Jameson presents Doctorow and *Ragtime* as illustrating a postmodern reduction of history to stereotypes and quotations, Hutcheon reads Doctorow as exemplary of a postmodern interrogation of the boundaries between fiction and history that opens up history to critical examination.[8] Moreover, she argues that Doctorow breaks with the perspective of the historical novel as the voice of ruling elites, decenters unifying historical narratives, and brings out voices of opposition.

In his 1991 revision of his earlier 1984 essay on postmodernism, Jameson retorts that in a postmodern context audiences for the most part cannot interpret the narrative historically and that the mixing of historical figures with fictional ones reduces the text to dehistoricized "fantasy signifiers from a variety of ideologemes in a kind of hologram."[9] In general, Hutcheon's model of postmodernism is preferable to interpret some types of postmodern texts that interrogate and engage history and politics, while other types of texts (many nostalgia films and forms of media culture, much contemporary painting, and some forms of writing) are better described by Jameson's paradigm. My argument here is that Hutcheon's notion of a critical postmodernism provides a better take on *The X-Files* than Jameson's ludic conception, though his model also illuminates some of its features.

The X-Files' postmodern aesthetic can be characterized by its aggressive use of pastiche and quotation. *The X-Files* borrows from a large number of classical TV and Hollywood film genres—science fiction, horror, fantasy, the occult, political conspiracy, melodrama, the crime drama, the medical drama, and other genres. The series mines the hoary figures of the werewolf, vampire, and alien for contemporary relevance and significance, reappropriating these figures to comment on contemporary problems and issues. It features police and medical authorities, typical social types, and more specific figures drawn from the domains of political culture, urban legend, and contemporary news and tabloid sensation. But whereas the classical forms of these genres often reproduced conservative ideological problematics, *The X-Files* problematizes dominant ideologies and classical generic codes.

The X-Files most obviously draws on 1950s science fiction movies, 1970s political conspiracy films, and the representational and semiotic codes of these genres. The alien and flying saucer motifs were popularized in a series of 1950s Hollywood SF films that featured alien invasions that were either friendly and benevolent (e.g., *The Day the Earth Stood Still*) or hostile and malevolent (e.g., *The War of the Worlds*). It also borrows from popular television series such as *The Twilight Zone*, *The Outer Limits*, *Star Trek*, and *Kolchak: The Night Stalker*. As of the sixth season, however, it was indeterminate what sorts of aliens *The X-Files* was presenting, or whether the mythos of the alien was a government conspiracy to cover over military misdeeds, a theme that exemplifies a postmodern indeterminacy and undecidability that characterizes the series as a whole.

Moreover, no previous television series had presented such critical visions of the U.S. government as *The X-Files*. The series creator and chief creative force, Chris Carter, has said that the Watergate trials were his formative political experience, and in some ways Scully and Mulder resemble Woodward and Bernstein in their tireless efforts to get at the truth, to unravel the conspiracies, to find out who did what, to lay their hands on the "smoking gun," and thus to provide irrefutable evidence of the conspiracies they seek to expose. There are countless references to other 1970s conspiracy motifs of media culture: the motto "Trust no one" echoes Don Corleone's advice to his son ("Keep your friends close, but keep your enemies closer"). And as Allison Graham summarizes,

> Mulder quotes Dirty Harry and, like Harry Caul in *The Conversation*, tears up his apartment looking for surveillance devices; bodies are suspended in *Coma*-like tanks; the government attempts to assassinate Mulder the way it did the CIA worker played by Robert Redford in *Three Days of the Condor*; people are possessed in *Exorcist*-like fashion (a film which producer Carter certainly remembers was set in post-Watergate Washington). The "lone gunman" theory of political assassinations so mocked in *The Parallax View* is given short shrift here as well through Mulder's friendship with "conspiracy nuts" who publish a bulletin called *The Lone Gunmen*. In case anyone thinks this all merely random pastiche, the boss who sets the whole scenario in motion in the first episode—and who brings Scully and Mulder together—is played by Charles Cioffi, the Nixon-clone murderer in *Klute* (Nixon's visage even appears in cartoon form on one of the Lone Gunmen's screensavers, complete with the bulled caption, "I am not a crook").[10]

Specific episodes of the series draw on popular generic texts in the mode of postmodern appropriation and pastiche, deploying familiar horror and SF stories in various episodes. For example, an early thriller, "Ice" (1/8; 1993), pastiches the situation of the popular 1950s SF movie *The Thing*, with a group of scientists isolated in the Arctic, terrorized by a strange alien creature that is inhabiting various characters and setting them off against each other in paranoid fear; the episode "Eve" (1/11;

1993) exploits the evil demon child horror genre and cloning of child monsters à la *The Boys from Brazil*; "Wet Wired" (3/23; 1996) appropriates the themes of David Cronenberg's film *Videodrome*; "Tathia Cumi" (3/24; 1996) replays the section featuring the Grand Inquisitor of Dostoyevsky's *Brothers Karamazov*; "Herrenfolk" (4/1; 1996) deploys iconography of *Children of the Damned*; and a 1997 episode, "The Post-Modern Prometheus" (5/6), broadcast in black and white, drew on figures and iconography of *Frankenstein*. Other episodes model their villains on well-known mass murderers like Jeffrey Dahmer and Henry Lee Lucas, and there are copious intertextual references to political events, figures, and artifacts of media culture, including a plethora of in-group references to the series itself, its producers, and a variety of contemporary issues.

Thus, *The X-Files* appropriates many genres, artifacts, and specific texts of media culture, utilizing postmodern strategies of pastiche and quotation. The Scully character is modeled to some extent on the ascetic and dedicated female FBI detective Clarice Starling in *Silence of the Lambs*. In one episode, "2Shy," Scully and Mulder pursue a vampire-like killer who consumes the fat of lonely, overweight women, whom he contacts through an Internet chat room, "Big and Beautiful." A conservative police officer questions whether a woman like Scully should be doing autopsies of the murdered women and whether a woman detective can retain her objectivity in such cases where the victims are women. Scully, of course, maintains her objectivity and in a final scene, drawing on the confrontation of the woman FBI agent in *Silence of the Lambs* with the murderous but intellectual killer Hannibal Lecter, effectively confronts the murderer (this iconography of the woman officer alone in a cell with a vicious criminal is replicated in the episode "The List").[11]

In addition to the problematics and forms of the horror and SF genres already cited, the series draws on formats of the crime drama, the coming-of-age drama, and the medical drama formulas. Scully and Mulder are FBI agents, and each program presents a crime or mystery that needs to be investigated. As the agents gain experience and knowledge, they mature, overcoming previous one-sidedness and naïveté, thus presenting models of growth and development. The fact that Scully is a medical doctor ensures numerous medical scenes and problems, drawing on the codes of the medical genre. The series itself is thus a postmodern TV hybrid, mixing the codes of a variety of genres, while providing meta-commentary on standard television forms and mythologies.

The X-Files exhibits a level of narrative ambiguity rarely encountered in mainstream media culture. In many episodes it is not clear whether the rationalist or supernaturalist explanation is more salient, many mysteries are not unraveled, the resolving of some problems often creates many new ones, and it is often not clear what actually happened. Moreover, the series as a whole exhibits significant postmodern ambiguity and undecidability concerning its villains, the source of its evils, and its own beliefs and values.

SERIES TELEVISION AS SOCIAL CRITIQUE: "TRUST NO ONE"

The X-Files shares some of the thematic and stylistic frames of film noir. Its plots are saturated with ambiguity and mystery, while a quest to unravel the machinations of unscrupulous individuals and institutions drives the narrative. Like noir, *The X-Files* has voice-overs, flashbacks, convoluted plots, expressionist visual styles, dark shadows and night shots, and often ambiguous resolutions—or even failure to attain closure. For the noir detective confronting threatening femme fatales, who trusts no one but himself, *The X-Files* substitutes the partnership of Scully and Mulder, who do come to trust each other. Yet like detectives in noir, the *X-Files* protagonists face an incomprehensible and overpowering universe that they find difficult, if not impossible, to understand and control.

Just as film noir emerged at the end of World War II during an era marked by fear of nuclear annihilation, political repression, and economic change, so does *The X-Files* emerge in a period of proliferating new technologies with dramatic and perhaps unanticipated effects, political fragmentation and conflict on both local and global levels, and a dramatic restructuring of global capitalism, resulting in corporate downsizing, loss of jobs and economic security, and a general unease during an era of seeming prosperity. Hence, our diagnostic critique reveals that *The X-Files* taps into salient fears and uncertainties of the present, which it articulates in its often disturbing narratives, and like film noir it uses stylized forms of media culture to allegorically critique aspects of contemporary society and culture.

The X-Files oscillates between episodes featuring aliens and government conspiracies and more classic figures of the horror and fantasy genres such as the werewolf, vampire, and mutant monsters. Demonic figures of the occult often project society's most prevalent fears and anxieties, which are soothed when the evil is destroyed. Such conservative horror/occult texts usually legitimate dominant societal forces, like the military or police, as protection against evil and threats to normality. *The X-Files*, however, is more ambivalent in its use of classical horror figures.

While the reactionary occult genre shows its monsters as inexplicable, as forces of nature, as if nature itself was evil, threatening, and in need of control and domination, *The X-Files* often shows monstrosity to be a creation of social forces, of societal evils, and not incomprehensible forces of nature. For instance, illegal strip-mining of old trees unleashed dormant insect larvae in "Darkness Falls" (1/20; 1994); the "Flukeman" mutant in the popular episode "The Host" (2/2; 1994) is a product of nuclear wastes from the accident in Chernobyl, born "in a primordial soup of radioactive sewage" that produced mutants and monstrosities. "Sleepless" (2/4; 1994) depicts Vietnam veterans who are victims of a sleep-elimination program that would make them superkillers and are subsequently driven mad by the U.S. government military program. One, the Preacher, becomes an avenging angel, who kills the soldiers who had been involved in war crimes against the Vietnamese. In "The Walk" (3/7; 1995), another Vietnam vet who had his limbs amputated develops murderous telekinetic powers to compensate for the loss of his limbs, producing another monster created by the U.S. military. And "Unrequited" (4/16; 1997) tells the story of a Vietnam POW who is left behind in Vietnam, is rescued by a U.S. right-wing paramilitary group, and returns to the United States to assassinate the generals responsible for the decision to cover up the existence of U.S. POWs still captive in Vietnam. The Vietnam War is obviously an unhealed wound for Chris Carter's generation that keeps festering and generating tales to capture its hideousness and horrors.

Thus, many *X-Files* monsters are shown to be products of human meddling with nature or evil government or corporate policies, rather than inexplicable forces of nature. Yet some demonic figures are associated with Native Americans or developing world countries; these episodes utilize reactionary stereotypes that equate native peoples with the primitive and the monstrous. "Shapes" (1/18; 1994) associates werewolf-like creatures with Native Americans; "Fresh Bones" (2/15; 1995) associates diabolic events with Haitian voodoo rituals; "Teso Dos Biches" (3/18; 1996) portrays evil unleashed when artifacts are moved from a sacred South American burial ground; and "Teliko" (4/4; 1996) portrays an African skin-eating immigrant. *The X-Files'* use of images of the occult and its monster figures are thus politically ambiguous, sometimes used to criticize dominant U.S. government or business policies and practices, and sometimes to demonize native peoples and cultures.

Yet often the evils portrayed are products of contemporary U.S. society. The character who intones in an iconic gesture, "Trust no one" is code-named "Deep Throat," inevitably evoking resonances of the Watergate scandal. *The X-Files* plays on fears of a government out of control and dangerous state and corporate conspiracies, as well as fears of the occult and aliens. Combining these motifs intensifies the atmosphere of paranoia, generating images of a universe haunted by mysterious and evil forces, which are extremely difficult to comprehend, let alone conquer. This is hardly the typical TV universe with its clear-cut distinctions between good and evil, customary morality tales, sharply drawn generic codes, and usual resolution of the mysteries or problems portrayed. Instead, *The X-Files* explores new ground, drawing on the audience's propensity to believe the worst of its government, to fear what it cannot understand, and to be open to ambiguity and "extreme possibilities."

Generally speaking, there are two sorts of plot episodes in the series, often overlapping. There is a continuing story line concerning aliens and government (or corporate) conspiracies to work with aliens on sinister projects and to cover over their presence, alternating with standard occult horror and supernatural tales. In interviews the series creator, Chris Carter, notes that he always pitched the series as one that "would scare the pants off the audience," that would provide a "roller coaster ride of thrills," that would be traditionally entertaining. But there has never been anything quite like the evolving narrative of the alien conspiracy "mythology" of *The X-Files*, as Carter christened the continuing plot line. Each season between five and seven episodes directly highlight the ongoing narrative, with many other episodes contributing small pieces. As the series evolved, the plot thickened, the conspiracies became more convoluted, and the viewer has been forced to work with a vast amount of complex narrative material concerning whether aliens do or do not exist and what sort of government conspiracy is involved in the phenomena. This complexity calls into question modern conceptions of truth, evidence, and even the nature of human beings and of human and individual identity.

It is especially in the "mythology" episodes that *The X-Files* deploys a mode of critical paranoia to subvert received attitudes, beliefs, and ways of seeing common to popular television. On the whole, television has taught its viewers to look at established institutions, authorities, and practices positively and threats to established law and order negatively. Thus, television has instilled an attitude of trust toward the existing social system, and fear of those threatening forces outside it. *The X-Files* reverses this way of seeing by instilling distrust toward established authority by representing government and the established order as exorbitantly flawed, even complicit in the worst crimes and evil imaginable. *The X-Files* feeds on and intensifies populist paranoia that government is bad, that the CIA, the FBI, the military, and other agencies of government are filled with individuals who carry out villainous actions and constitute a threat to traditional humanistic moral values and human life itself.

The series uses expressionistic lighting and camera angles, Mark Snow's moody and often disturbing music and sound effects, and oblique narratives to add to the air of mystery. Such devices disorient and perturb the audience, creating an atmosphere of fear and paranoia. Moreover, the continual use of medical technology and procedures, with Scully frequently performing autopsies or medical examinations and with both main characters shown in hospitals in life-threatening situations themselves, plays on fears of disease, doctors, and medical incarceration. *The X-Files* also exploits anxieties over U.S. government conspiracies by depicting experiments to control its citizens or to develop supersoldier weapons (e.g., "Sleepless"). In "Wet Wire," it appears that a government experiment to control individuals through television signals produces psychotic behavior (a pastiche of Cronenberg's *Videodrome*).

THE POSTMODERN SUBLIME, PARODY, AND AMBIGUITY, OR "IS THE TRUTH OUT THERE?"

By presenting shadowy government figures, covert agents, and even the agents' bosses and Mulder's father as complicit in heinous crimes, *The X-Files* makes its audiences suspicious of established government and ways of seeing. Critical paranoia thus provides a mode of representing the unrepresentable, of articulating the horrors of the present, by evoking anxieties over evil forces that are controlling the existing social system and carrying out abominable actions. This is not to affirm the sort of clinical paranoia in which the paranoid person can easily become dysfunctional if paranoia eclipses rational and critical knowledge. Critical paranoia, by contrast, can help, within proper boundaries, to map the forces that structure the world and turn the subject against oppressive forces. Although clinical paranoia projects itself beyond the world of actual social relationships into a fantasy world of imaginary entities and thereby loses all contact with reality, critical paranoia focuses one on oppressive forces within the world. Although critical paranoia assumes conspiracies and plots, presumes there are hidden and malevolent forces behind political, social, and personal events, it maintains a judicious and rational outlook on these in order to confirm or disconfirm the paranoid hypothesis. Critical paranoia thus does not disassociate itself from a reality principle, nor does it retreat into a solipsistic world of persecution fantasies. As we will see in our reading, *The X-Files* combines critical paranoia that focuses attention on oppressive institutions with supernaturalism that deflects attention from these forces to focus on the occult.

The aesthetic and ethos of *The X-Files* also embody Lyotard's notion of a postmodern sublime, which utilizes allegory, hyperbolic exaggeration, and otherness to represent the unrepresentable, to convey a sense of the complexity and horrors of the present.[12] Traditionally, in Burke, Kant, and others, the category of the sublime denominated that which defied naturalistic representation, which transcended all representation, such as the divine or the grandeur of nature. Lyotard provides the concept of the sublime with a postmodern inflection, claiming that it is the key concept for a contemporary aesthetic. He suggests that in an increasingly complex contemporary world with a blurring or destruction of previous boundaries and categories, the sublime attempts to represent the unconventional and unrepresentable, to articulate the new, and to capture the novelties and heterogeneities of the present. Building on this conception, Jameson talks of a "technological sublime," which replaces the previous aesthetic conception of the sublime that referred to attempts to represent the majesty, grandeur, and awe of nature. Today, however, natural environments are being replaced by technological environments, which take on the awesome and difficult-to-represent features of nature.

Such a use of postmodern sublime, allegory, and paranoia can help make audiences question dominant values and practices and develop critical consciousness. Distrust in the face of science, technology, government, and orthodox attitudes forces an individual to penetrate beneath the lies and illusions, to attempt to grasp the complex and inexplicable, to pursue the truth. Thus, while seeking and articulating the truth are modern ideals, *The X-Files* suggests that modern methods (science, rationality, and documentary evidence) may not be adequate to the job, that one must dig deeper, that new modes of representation and inquiry are necessary.

A highly complex political allegory is employed as the mode of representation in the mythology episodes of the series, which depict government and alien conspiracies. The pilot introduces the elements that would come to characterize the *X-Files* "mythology." The agents interview several characters who exhibit features of alien abduction, speaking of "lost time," nosebleeds, and mysterious illnesses. They discover a corpse that appears to be a strange mutant, but it disappears. They recover what may be alien tissue samples and a metal nasal implant, which in turn is destroyed in a mysterious fire. Scully and Mulder even experience a blinding flash while driving in the countryside and undergo lost time, as they investigate their case. The conclusion of the episode shows the sinister "Cigarette-Smoking Man" storing the only piece of evidence remaining, a small implant removed from one of the murdered teens, in a massive Defense Department storage room, thus evoking the possibility of a U.S. government conspiracy and cover-up.

The succeeding episodes of the government-alien conspiracies unravel an incredibly complex plot that suggests government cover-up of alien presence, experiments on humans with alien DNA, attempts to create new breeds of human/alien mutant clones with superhuman powers, and struggles between various groups and government agencies to control the conspiracies. Yet in a startling development, episodes in season five (1997–98) imply that the whole alien mythology is a government ploy to cover over the really evil things that the government and the military have been doing over the past decades since the end of World War II, that all the evidence of aliens has been a fraudulent creation of political and military agencies, and that "aliens" are a diversion from greater government evil during the Cold War.[13] "Redux" and "Redux II" (5/2 and 5/3; 1997) show Mulder coming to question his belief in aliens, beginning to think that he himself was manipulated to promote belief in aliens as part of a government conspiracy, and is becoming increasingly skeptical. The episodes also suggest that the Cigarette-Smoking Man isn't in charge, that greater forces are controlling the conspiracy, and that he is himself a tool of even more mysterious and powerful forces, who are portrayed as representatives of some global cartel. Later in the season, however, and in the summer 1998 X-Files movie, Mulder is again provided with evidence of the existence of extraterrestrials and as the sixth season unfolds appears to be reverting to the investigator of the supernatural who wants to believe.

For the most part, the series promotes belief in aliens, alien abductions, and cover-up conspiracies by actually depicting the phenomena in question. However, in one distinctively postmodern episode, "José Chung's From Outer Space" (3/20; 1996), written by Darin Morgan, the whole mythology is undermined and a highly postmodern take on truth and representation is presented.[14] The episode "José Chung" opens with a postmodern verbal pun and trick as portentous music dramatizes an extreme long shot of the night sky, the camera zooms onto what appears to be a massive spaceship, while the soundtrack is saturated with a mechanical whirring. Suddenly, however, a jump cut jolts the viewer to see men working in a metal basket on power lines and we hear workmen discussing a power failure. The images draw on Close Encounters of the Third Kind, which features a power line repairman eventually undergoing an alien encounter. But the opening sequence warns you not to trust your eyes, that one can be easily fooled, and that the show itself is engaging in possible trickery. This motif is extended and the camera pans on a "Klass County, Washington" sign, evoking the figure of Philip Klass, a noted UFO debunker and critic.[15]

After setting up the narrative in the mode of postmodern irony, appropriation, and pastiche, the scene cuts to two teenagers in a car, on their first date, engaging in clichéd language, with their car clunking to a stop as a white light fills the screen and awe-inspiring choral music suffuses the scene with drama, a direct quotation of the spaceship scene in Close Encounters. What seem to be grey aliens appear, and the couple is frightened by the lights and what appears to be a red-eyed alien. But as they express their fear and uncertainty, the camera pans on young boys dressed up as aliens, who are terrorizing the teen couple.

In a sense, this episode replays and parodies, in the mode of postmodern irony, the pilot episode, which featured teen alien abductions, but whereas the pilot utilized a deadly serious melodramatic SF mode and traditional editing and narrative framing, "José Chung" under-mines all standard television narrative forms, is highly ironic and satir-ical, and even makes fun of the program's frames and themes. The episode features a writer, José Chung, who appears to be neither His-panic nor Asian, researching a "nonfiction science fiction" novel based on the teen abduction episode. The rest of the program flashes back to the abduction, told from a variety of points of view, all of which are dra-matically disparate. Pastiching Kurosawa's *Rashomon*, it suggests a postmodern perspectivism, where there is no unitary truth, but rather each individual has their own interpretation. Thus, in this vision, whereas the truth "may be out there," it is difficult to access, multiple, and subject to a diversity of interpretations.

A diagnostic critique thus stresses how *The X-Files* questions the modern concept of truth as accessible to proper methods that guarantee secure and indubitable results. Truth in the postmodern register, by contrast, is multiple, constructed, and perspectival, and not subject to an indubitable perception, absolute grounding, or certainty.[16] The show thus undercuts the series' modernist quest for truth by suggesting that perhaps "the truth is out there," but it is hidden under multiple, dra-matically conflicting interpretations and perspectives. The "José Chung" episode suggests that sight and experience themselves cannot be trusted, that all evidence is a construct subject to multiple readings, and that even documentation does not constitute absolute knowledge or foundation for truth.

In this episode, Mulder produces a photograph with great excite-ment that seems to be of an extraterrestrial object, but later analysis re-veals it to be a fraud, thus showing again that visual evidence is not to be trusted. Hence, key tensions run through the series between truth and lies, and between the realism and rationalism of the crime drama and the occultist fantasy of the supernatural genre. Indeed, it is uncommon for a U.S. network television series to exploit generic tension between real-ism and suprarealism, naturalism and supernaturalism, and the expli-cable and inexplicable as in *The X-Files*. Indeed, it is often undecidable whether the bizarre phenomena depicted are subject to a rationalist and naturalist or supernatural explanation. While some episodes favor one mode and others the opposite, many are undecidable, and rarely has a TV series so consistently exploited such ambiguity and complexity.[17]

It is precisely this epistemological boundary blurring, this narrative indeterminacy of plot and epistemology, this questioning of standard modes of explanation that render *The X-Files* a postmodern undoing and questioning of the boundaries and distinctions characteristic of modern culture and rationality. The series' opening image in the title sequence of a misty, hazy object that looks like a flying saucer illustrates this indeterminacy. On one level, the image signifies "flying saucer" and the alien theme of the show. But it is so hazy and blurry that it could be an illusion, a military experimental object, or who knows what? Other images in the opening sequence show strange hieroglyphics and objects that might be alien writing and technology—or human concoctions. Strange figures shown mutating might be aliens—or hallucinations and fantasies. An eyeball looks out at a bright blue sky with clouds dramatically appearing—and may or may not be able to see what is out there.

It is therefore undecidable as to whether *The X-Files* promotes the supernatural or a critical scientific naturalism, and whether it ultimately upholds the deepest values and ideologies of the existing society or puts them into question. In some episodes, the occult or supernatural explanation is explicitly privileged, as viewers are often shown aliens, supernatural beings and events, and traditional and novel forms of the occult. In other episodes, however, what appears to be supernatural and occult is presented as either the machinations of human agencies and individuals or a natural phenomenon that just appears supernatural. In many episodes, and perhaps in the series as a whole, the line is blurred and it is not clear whether the phenomena under display are natural or supernatural, the product of government conspiracy or an alien presence that explodes existing categories of life and being.

Indeed, one can see these opposed readings on display in Internet discussion groups of the series, with some individuals always defending a naturalist reading, or criticizing the show when it does not conform to realist narrative frames, while others delight in the occult and supernatural elements of the show. A Web site titled "The Netpickers' Guide to *The X-Files*" lists all departures from realist narrative and scientific rationality, and many fans try to provide rational explanations for the mysterious events, while a book collects "bloopers, inconsistencies, screwed-up plots, technical glitches, and baffling references."[18] Several UFO and occultist sites celebrate the series for its daring subversion of scientific rationality and many fans are obviously drawn to its supernaturalism. Internet discussion lists and zines argue endlessly about the meaning of specific episodes and the series as a whole. That it is able to play to different audiences and generate such passionate debate helps to account for the popularity of the series.

POSTMODERN DECONSTRUCTION: "I WANT TO BELIEVE" BUT . . .

The X-Files' method is to contrast two opposing epistemological binaries and then to put into question these radical binary oppositions, somewhat in the mode and spirit of Derrida's deconstruction. The first and chief dichotomy of Western reason that the series explores is the conflict between science and religion, reason and faith, and the rational and irrational. Consider the poster shown in Mulder's office in the first episode, which becomes an icon of the series, showing a small flying saucer against a deep blue sky with the motto "I want to believe." Indeed, Mulder is driven by an obsession to experience the existence of aliens and supernatural forms of life, to have experiential confirmation of their existence, and to concretely interact with aliens and the occult.

Moreover, Mulder desperately wants to *prove* that aliens exist, that the supernatural and aliens are part of the natural order, that the occult is as real as genes and microbes. Scully is assigned to the X-Files precisely because she is a skeptic, because she does not believe in the occult or supernatural, but in scientific rationality. The series thus initially equates the woman agent Scully with science, reason, and skepticism, and the male Mulder with belief, the irrational, and occultism, thus inverting the standard gender equations (i.e., women as irrational, intuitive, and believing contrasted to men as scientific and rational).

However, it is the epistemological task of the series to subvert this dichotomy, to deconstruct the fixed oppositions and to create a more complementary epistemological vision that encompasses both poles of the opposition. As the series proceeds, Scully comes to believe, at least, in government conspiracy, evil, and the inexplicable, and opens herself to "extreme possibilities." Mulder, by contrast, comes to question whether natural or supernatural explanations can account for the bizarre occurrences that they encounter in every episode, and even if the aliens that he is so diligently pursuing actually do exist. Indeed, although Mulder is initially presented as the representative of belief and openness to the occult, he also constantly deploys scientific rationality and often presents naturalistic explanations of occult phenomena. Moreover, although he wants to believe literally in the existence of alien forms of life, he comes to question this belief, and several episodes in the fifth season show him coming to believe that the alien conspiracy is a government hoax and cover-up.

In the terms of the modern paradigm, then, the truth is out there, it is the goal of scientific research and police work, but in *The X-Files* it is often inaccessible, always challenged, and is thus a highly elusive Holy Grail. Scully and Mulder are presented as modern truth seekers, but their inability to discover the essential truths for which they are searching suggests in a postmodern register that truth is highly elusive, exists on multiple levels, and is perhaps even impossible to ascertain in a confusing and convoluted contemporary world. While the motto "The truth is out there" signifies a modern drive toward truth, the difficulty in accessing it signifies a postmodern indeterminacy and undecidability, the mark of postmodern epistemology, which on the whole is characteristic of the epistemic vision of *The X-Files*. From this perspective, "belief," not "truth," is all one can reasonably assert. In almost every episode, it is uncertain whether the phenomena observed are natural or supernatural, can be explained rationally or not, and the plot resolution is often saturated with ambiguity. Frequently, the crime is not solved or the villain is not apprehended, and often there is no clear explanation for what transpired. This marks a distinctive break with the forms of most TV crime dramas, and also questions the efficacy of the FBI and other law enforcement agencies.

The world of *The X-Files* is thus qualitatively different from this previous world of the crime drama, reflecting a postmodern distrust of existing institutions in the wake of Watergate and the revelation of copious crimes of the system, the October Surprise, Iran-Contra, and the other malfeasances of the Reagan-Bush-Clinton administrations, and FBI wrongdoing in Waco, Ruby Ridge, and elsewhere. While on one level, *The X-Files* is a rehabilitation of an image of the good FBI agent, on another level the organization as a whole is sometimes put into question, as in the U.S. government itself. Thus, *The X-Files* might be seen as an example of what Hal Foster calls "critical" or "resistance" postmodernism, which contests existing cultural forms and social organization.[19] As in Hutcheon's concept of postmodernism, it uses the strategies of postmodernism to contest dominant ideologies, ways of seeing, and modes of explanation, and to provide critical social commentary and insight.

Yet, as noted, it is ultimately undecidable who the villains are, what sorts of conspiracies are afoot, and whether the phenomena displayed can or cannot be explained by "normal" science. The politics of the series is also ambiguous. While the show often criticizes the FBI and government, it stretches credibility to believe that government agencies would allow the extent of dissent and insubordination exhibited in the young agents (during the sixth season, when once again the X-Files are closed, Mulder and Scully continue to pursue occult events, despite orders not to). Moreover, although *The X-Files* assaults patriarchical authority and conservative forces, it celebrates the all-American virtues of work, yuppie professionalism, and individualism, as well as honor, loyalty, commitment, family, religion, and other core values betrayed by the older generation during the Cold War. It is as if the Fathers betrayed the authentic American traditional values and the sons and daughters have to redeem them.

From this perspective, *The X-Files* can be read as a document of generational war, of a younger, more liberal yuppie generation, which is more professional, humane, and dedicated to higher moral values than the previous generation. Like the films *A Few Good Men*, *The Firm*, *Courage under Fire*, *The Chamber*, and many other post-1980s corporate and political conspiracy films, *The X-Files* shows the older generation tremendously compromised and arguably corrupt, especially those in military, political, and corporate bureaucracies. These texts are the revenge of yuppie professionals and the younger generation against the older conservative establishment.

Still, it is undecidable if *The X-Files* ultimately undermines, subverts, and contests dominant societal forces, ideologies, and authorities or upholds them. To some extent, it works with the traditional culture's Manichean dichotomies of good and evil, though it arguably complicates these categories. Moreover, the use of the occult and paranormal may promote irrationalism and deflect critical attention from the actual events, structures, and personalities of history, substituting populist paranoia and conspiracy for the real crimes carried out by ruling elites and reducing history to the production of conspiratorial cartoon-like figures. This is particularly egregious in "Musings of a Cigarette Smoking Man" (4/7; 1996), which places one individual at the center of a variety of conspiracies, from the Kennedy assassination to the rigging of Super Bowl games. Such tongue-in-cheek satire deflects attention from actual crimes and conspiracies, as does the figure of the occult, perhaps promoting societal irrationalism and paranoia.

Nonetheless, more than any program in TV history, *The X-Files* at least alludes to government crimes and conspiracies and puts in question the institutions and morality of the national security state with its covert apparatuses and shadowy operations. But ultimately, the politics of the series is ambiguous and indeterminate, failing to promote any positive solutions. Its pop postmodernism reproduces the failings of populism, promoting suspicion against the existing social system without specifying how one can actually solve the problems depicted. The evil depicted is so vast, the conspiracies are so complex, and the politics are so ambiguous as to promote cynicism, nihilism, and a sense of hopelessness. Yet the series has obviously touched a responsive chord and articulates fear and distrust of dominant authorities that point to cracks and fissures in a system that obviously needs to be radically changed. Moreover, Mulder and Scully continue to struggle, against all odds, to uncover the conspiracies and provide models of active and intelligent subjects struggling against oppressive forces and institutions.

Postmodern theory, then, is an attempt to depict the novel and complex dynamics of the present era, and postmodern culture provides new representational strategies to characterize the contemporary moment. *The X-Files* shows a society in transition, with its institutions, values, and identities in crisis. *The X-Files* thus, in a postmodern register, uses the generic forms and figures of media culture to comment on some of the most frightening aspects of contemporary society, including government out of control, science and technology out of control, and threats to the body and individual integrity during an era of rampant disease and novel societal and technological forces truly creating new species.

A major subtext of *The X-Files* is, in fact, the implosion between humans and technology, with experiments mixing human and alien DNA (or with science and technology creating monstrous "alien" forms of life). To some extent, the alien is us as technology invades mind and body, as we absorb technology into our bodies and minds, as we conform and adapt to a technological universe with its own specific ways of seeing, knowing, and acting. In a sense, then, the figures of aliens and alien abduction can be read as allegorical figures that represent new hybrids and implosions of humans and technology, showing a new species emerging out of genetic and military experimentation, out of cloning and technological implosion of the born and the made, creating a new species of the technohuman. From this perspective, contemporary human beings are alien, exhibiting an implosion of the human and technology, embodying an emergent technospecies adapting to a brave new technoworld.

The alien, thus, can be read as a figure for what humans have become in an era in which individuals no longer feel that they control their own destiny, in which their own bodies mutate out of control, and their minds and bodies are invaded with new societal, technological, and political forces. In exploring this new and disturbing space, *The X-Files* inhabits a liminal space between mind and body, truth and untruth, fantasy and reality, science and belief. Providing a modern mythology for our time, *The X-Files* probes our deepest fears, most disturbing fantasies, and most dramatic transformations. Whether an artifact of media culture can adequately illuminate the crevices and novel spaces of the present is questionable, though *The X-Files* gains its power and effect precisely through attempting to do so.

CONCLUDING REMARKS: REPRESENTING
THE UNREPRESENTABLE

And so, ultimately, *The X-Files* is concerned with problems of representing the unrepresentable, finding images for that which resists depiction, articulating phenomena that cannot be readily grasped with traditional discourses and modes of representation. Typically, the problem of portraying horror and the occult is a problem of finding figures for precisely those fears, fantasies, and experiences that transcend the normal and the everyday, that reside in a space outside normality, that demand unconventional representations for extreme experiences and possibilities. *The X-Files* regularly attempts to depict and explain the occult and the paranormal, but more interestingly uses these figures and phenomena to comment on contemporary fears and problems and to articulate anxieties and horrors of the present age that cannot readily fit into standard discourses and conceptual schemes.

Fredric Jameson has often written of the difficulty in figuring new postmodern space (i.e., architecture, cities, cyberspace, and the global system of transnational capitalism) and suggests that popular media culture artifacts like conspiracy films attempt to map these new spaces in an allegorical mode.[20] From this perspective, *The X-Files* is an interesting attempt in the contemporary era to represent the unrepresentable, to put on display our deepest fears and fantasies, and to utilize some of the strategies of postmodern aesthetics to probe into the dynamics of the impact of technology on human beings, the practices of the state, and the fate of the body and individual identity in the present age. *The X-Files* thus, in a postmodern register, uses the generic forms and figures of media culture to comment on some of the most frightening aspects of contemporary society, including government out of control, science and technology out of control, and threats to the body and individual integrity during an era of dramatic changes, which the term "postmodern" has been used to describe. The series thus represents an example of a pop postmodernism attempting to come to terms with some of the most disturbing features of the present age.

   The X-Files is a particularly popular and successful show because it skillfully navigates some of the defining contradictions of contemporary high-tech societies and taps into current mindsets. While it capitalizes on popular discourses of paranoia and conspiracy, articulates negative views of government, and attracts an audience critical of existing institutions, it ultimately upholds belief in authority, justice, hard work, and other dominant societal values, thus appealing to both antiauthoritarian and establishment audiences.[21] The series navigates the conflicts between reason and anti-reason, science and faith, attracting adherents of both views, while mediating oppositions between modern science and more postmodern variants.[22] It also combines a modern seriousness and pursuit of truth with postmodern irony, combining modernist aesthetic innovation with postmodern pastiche of traditional forms and styles. Thus *The X-Files* serves as a fitting icon for an age between the modern and postmodern that is attempting to resolve turbulent conflicts over values, culture, institutions, and the organization of society.

NOTES

Adapted by permission of Blackwell Publishers Journals from *Journals of Aesthetics and Art Criticism* 57 (1999): 161–75. © 1999 by American Society for Aesthetics.

   1. On diagnostic critique, see Douglas Kellner and Michael Ryan, *Camera Politica: The Politics and Ideologies of Contemporary Hollywood Film* (Bloomington:

Indiana University Press, 1988); and Douglas Kellner, *Media Culture* (London: Routledge, 1995). On the distinction between critical and clinical paranoia, a distinction used to read the novels of Thomas Pynchon, see Mark Siegel, *Pynchon: Creative Paranoia in "Gravity's Rainbow"* (Port Washington: Kennikat Press, 1978); Steven Best, "Creative Paranoia: A Postmodern Aesthetic of Cognitive Mapping in *Gravity's Rainbow*," *Centennial Review* 36 (1992): 59–87; and Steven Best and Douglas Kellner, *The Postmodern Adventure* (New York: Guilford, forthcoming). These authors distinguish between "creative paranoia" and clinical paranoia, with the former imaginatively making connections between phenomena, seeing the hidden forces behind appearances, and ingeniously mapping a complex terrain, as does Pynchon's *Gravity's Rainbow* and other writings. I am adding the adjective "critical" for a rational distrust of institutions and individuals who may be engaged in conspiracies or oppressive activities. As my study will reveal, this is a hard distinction to make in practice as phenomena like *The X-Files* combine critical with projective paranoia.

2. See the discussion in Kellner and Ryan, *Camera Politica*.

3. On my take on the postmodern debates and claim that our current moment is in a borderland between the modern and the postmodern, see Steven Best and Douglas Kellner, *Postmodern Theory: Critical Interrogations* (London: Macmillan; New York: Guilford, 1991); Steven Best and Douglas Kellner, *The Postmodern Turn* (New York: Guilford, 1997); Best and Kellner, *Postmodern Adventure*; and Kellner, *Media Culture*.

4. In labeling the key episodes cited, I will indicate the title, the year, the season, and episode number to guide readers to the appropriate programs. Such a listing for the first three seasons is found in David Lavery, Angela Hague, and Marla Cartwright, eds., *"Deny All Knowledge": Reading The X-Files* (Syracuse: Syracuse University Press, 1996), 207–10; and a listing for the first five seasons is found in *"The X-Files" Yearbook*, vol. 4, no. 6: 52–78. Several Internet sites list subsequent episode information, including the official Fox Network *X-Files* site (www.xfiles.com) and <http://www.pluggage.com/forums/xfiles> which has plot summaries and archived fan discussion of many episodes.

5. Jimmie L. Reeves, Mark C. Rodgers, and Michael Epstein, "Rewriting Popularity," in Lavery et al., eds., *"Deny All Knowledge,"* 34.

6. On postmodern aesthetics, see Fredric Jameson, *Postmodernism, or, The Cultural Logic of Late Capitalism* (Durham: Duke University Press, 1991); and Linda Hutcheon, *A Poetics of Postmodernism* (New York: Routledge, 1988), and *The Politics of Postmodernism* (New York: Routledge, 1989); and Best and Kellner, *The Postmodern Turn*. As I will show, *The X-Files* exhibits characteristic features of the postmodern aesthetic as presented in such opposing conceptions as Hutcheon and Jameson, though on the whole the series is illuminated more by Hutcheon's conception than Jameson's.

7. Hutcheon, *Poetics*, xiii, 3, 18.

8. See Jameson, *Postmodernism*, 21 ff.; and Hutcheon, *Poetics*, 61–62.

9. Jameson, *Postmodernism*, 22–23.

10. Allison Graham, "'Are You Now or Have You Ever Been?': Conspiracy Theory and *The X-Files*," in Lavery et al., eds., *"Deny All Knowledge,"* 59.

11. Although the similarities between Scully and *Silence of the Lambs* FBI agent Clarice Starling are often noted (see, for example, Reeves et al., "Rewriting Popularity," 32; Rhonda Wilcox and J. P. Williams, "'What Do You Think?'" in Lavery et al., eds., *"Deny All Knowledge,"* 102 ff.; and Linda Badley, "The Rebirth of the Clinic," in Lavery et al., eds., *"Deny All Knowledge,"* 163), the differences are also quite striking. Scully is better educated, more sophisticated, and more intellectual than Starling, who is shown in her FBI training sessions generally engaged in physical activity, and the scenario of the film also privileges her action sequences, whereas *The X-Files* more frequently shows Scully engaged in various forms of scientific and intellectual labor, thus she is also portrayed as an active and competent subject.

12. See Jean-François Lyotard, *The Postmodern Condition: A Report on Knowledge*, trans. Geoff Bennington and Brian Massumi (Manchester: Manchester University Press, 1984); and Jean-François Lyotard, *The Differend: Phrases in Dispute*, trans. Georges van Den Abbeele (Manchester: Manchester University Press, 1988).

13. A piece of history from memories of the Cold War: my first introduction to theories of aliens and flying saucers came from a book borrowed from a neighbor in Falls Church, Virginia, sometime in the early 1950s. Three doors down from me on Executive Avenue lived my friend John Goeser, whose father was a liaison between the Pentagon and CIA, or in some mode of military intelligence. I recall that the Goesers had a book that circulated through the neighborhood, *Flying Saucers Have Landed*, by George Adamski, with pictures of extraterrestrial spacecrafts, aliens, and the like that eventually became a bible of alien lore. So if indeed the government was spreading flying saucer rumors to promote a conspiracy theory that would cover over its worse crimes, Mr. G. was part of the conspiracy—or maybe he just believed . . .

14. As the series evolved, more individuals began playing a creative role in the series, and one can now distinguish between the more classically occultist episodes written by Glen Morgan and James Wong (who left the series during the second season to develop and produce *Space: Above and Beyond*), the "mythology" episodes that pursue the political conspiracy theme, often written by Carter and/or Frank Spotnitz, and the more satirical pomo episodes written by Darin Morgan. Morgan wrote "Humbug" during the second season and such episodes during the third season as "War of the Coprophages," "Clyde Bruckman's Final Repose," and "José Chung's *From Outer Space*." Such episodes are more humorous and highly satirical, and they self-consciously exhibit

postmodern pastiche, irony, and lack of resolution in more fragmentary narratives, exhibiting what appear to be overtly postmodern aesthetic strategies.

15. For an extended reading of this episode as a postmodern play with the series' codes and conventions, see Eileen R. Meehan, "Not Your Parents' FBI: *The X-Files* and 'José Chung's *From Outer Space*,'" in Arthur Asa Berger, ed., *The Postmodern Presence: Readings on Postmodernism in American Culture and Society* (Walnut Creek, CA: Alta Mira Press, 1998).

16. On postmodernism and truth, see Best and Kellner, *The Postmodern Turn*, chap. 5.

17. *The X-Files'* competitor in the ambiguity and genre boundary-busting TV sweepstakes is, of course, David Lynch's series *Twin Peaks*, which also exploited a high degree of postmodern generic implosion and boundary crossing, including David Duchovny playing an FBI agent who dressed as a woman. Yet *Twin Peaks* did not carry out the ongoing social critique of *The X-Files*, or its use of postmodern quotation and pastiche, and never became a mass pop phenomenon as did the latter, as an example of the global popular that continues to fascinate audiences throughout the world.

18. Phil Farrand, *The Nitpicker's Guide for X-Philes* (New York: Dell, 1997).

19. On the rehabilitation of the good FBI agent, see Michele Malach, "'I Want to Believe . . . in the FBI,'" in Lavery et al., eds., *"Deny All Knowledge,"* 63–76. For a discussion of "critical" or "resistance" postmodernism, see Hal Foster, "Postmodernism: A Preface," in *The Anti-Aesthetic: Essays on Postmodern Culture*, ed. Hal Foster (Seattle: Bay Press, 1983), vii–xiv.

20. See Jameson, *Postmodernism*, and *The Geopolitical Aesthetic: Cinema and Space in the World System* (Bloomington: Indiana University Press; and London: BFI, 1992).

21. Series creator Chris Carter reports that "individuals within the FBI have contacted us to say how much they enjoy the show. David, Gillian and I were given a red-carpet tour of both FBI headquarters in Washington, DC and their training academy in Quantico, Virginia. We learned a lot about proper FBI protocol and procedure." Shifting ideological gears, Carter then acknowledges that many Americans nowadays believe that "Government is not working in the best interests of the U.S. public," and wryly notes that the show's freedom to criticize the FBI has less to do with the United States' current anti-statist mood than with the demise of J. Edgar Hoover: "In his day, if you criticized the FBI, you used to do it at your own risk. You would be declared Public Enemy Number One." Cited in *Daily Telegraph* (London), 28 August 1995.

22. Thus, books have appeared describing and extolling both the supernaturalism of *The X-Files* (Jane Goldman, *The X-Files Book of the Unexplained* [New York: HarperPrism, 1995]) and its science (Jeanne Cavelos, *The Science of The X-Files* [New York: Berkeley Books, 1998]).

10

The Commodification of Conspiracy Theory

Clare Birchall

I think I tried to get at the slickness connected to the word paranoia. It was becoming a kind of commodity. It used to mean one thing and after a while it began to mean everything. It became something you bought into, like Club Med.[1]

IN THIS QUOTATION, DeLillo succinctly captures the generalization of paranoia and its escalating play as a signifier. Conspiracy theory, connected to but not synonymous with paranoia, has undergone a similar process of commodification in the last decade or so. We only need to think of the exemplary conspiracy product, *The X-Files*, to see how both conspiracy narratives and a certain epistemology have become common currency for a wider audience.

How should we approach the commodification of conspiracy theory? As with most narratives of incorporation, such an entry into the mainstream could be narrated in terms of what *appears* to have been lost along the way. *The X-Files* can certainly be read in this vein: audiences can identify with conspiracism without committing to a "belief" or facing the risks such a position usually entails. Yet this reading will prove to be a provisional "beginning" or trajectory, as the distinction between the commodified discourse of conspiracy theory and the so-called academic discourse invoked to critique commodification is obscured by the way conspiracy theory exacerbates the semiological mechanisms to be found in all discourses of knowledge production. I will consider the way commodified conspiracy theory allows a depleted investment from a newly expanded audience without dismissing the content of such products. Rather than lament where a disinvestment leaves us politically, as many commentators do, I will consider the thematic tensions of *The X-Files* in order to point toward what such critiques obfuscate: namely, the arrogation of power in certain "legitimate" discourses and an inherent anxiety over interpretation. This is not to "redeem" the commodified text in a populist, celebratory manner, but to ask what epistemological and cultural tensions it exemplifies, and what these might tell us about the very way we can approach its popular content. Given the structural or semiotic conditions of proliferation inherent in conspiracist logic—how one theory is never an end in itself but the prompt for further speculation—the kind of commodification conspiracy theory has undergone might seem inevitable: we could say it is structurally determined. Mark Fenster writes how "conspiracy theories begin to approximate an unlimited semiosis not unlike a perpetual motion machine, a regime that constantly processes signs for interpretation, producing more theories and more signs in the process."[2] Proliferation of an idea is one criterion of popularity and, within the logic of capital, ways will be found of turning any popular idea into a commercially viable product.[3] But this configuration risks positing commodification as merely a form of proliferation—presenting commodification as having subsumed proliferative drives—whereas it is important to recognize the ways proliferative practices (such as rumor and urban legend) often appear to challenge not the system as such, but certainly a particular configuration of the logic of capital.[4] In addition, if posited as an extension of proliferation, commodification is dislodged from its ideological underpinnings as a capitalist process. Commodification as a logical extension of proliferation obscures the way the determining force behind commodification is capital rather than social practices or semiotic drives (although these become bound up in the signification of commodification). In this case, commodification not only becomes a factor in the process of fetishization, but is itself fetishized—divorced from its conditions of production. Yet we cannot be indifferent to what is at stake in the commodification of conspiracy theory because an aestheticized practice allows a certain type of relationship between conspiracy theory and theorist to become the dominant paradigm.

COMMODIFIED INVESTMENT

I have detailed elsewhere the functioning of conspiracy theory as a signifier under which a range of enterprises and merchandise are marketed, some more successfully and profitably than others.[5] Of note is the way the film *Conspiracy Theory* (1997) enlists the signifier, assuming that audiences can be attracted through generic appeal. "Conspiracy theory" thus starts to signify a marketable category rather than a subterranean activity. What does the commodification of conspiracy mean for the consumer of conspiracism? The reconfigured conspiracy product (exemplified, I will argue, by *The X-Files*) allows for a greater gap between the producer and consumer of conspiracy theory. That is to say that, as a subcultural concern, conspiracy theory expressed in zines or on the Internet, for example, would have been produced for a conspiracy community who might very well be involved in some kind of production themselves.[6] In contrast, the success of *The X-Files* depends on its ability to appeal to a cross-section of the viewing audience, "active" conspiracy theorists constituting only a marginal proportion of this. Those who watch *The X-Files* might contribute to online discussion boards or be active conspiracy theorists, but the mass appeal of *The X-Files* reduces the probability of such an affiliation.

Even the most cursory glance at the range of narratives that have been labeled conspiracy theory (from Noam Chomsky's texts to the ideas expressed on Internet conspiracy boards) indicates that a continuum of both conspiracy theory and theorists needs to be identified. Only then would we be able to account for the many different stances that are adopted in relation to conspiracy theory's various guises. However, as Mark Fenster argues, a particular relationship between conspiracy theorists and theory has come to dominate the contemporary scene: "Without accepting conspiracy theory as a necessarily correct interpretation of politics, this set of cultural forms and practices identifies and attempts to replicate the productive aspects of pursuing conspiracy as an aesthetic experience."[7] Fenster further describes this aestheticized configuration of conspiracy theory:

> This is not conspiracy theory as, say, the John Birch Society or Kennedy assassination researchers conceive it, in which some past historical moment has been tragically lost because of the machinations of

a secret, evil group and must be regained; instead, this is conspiracy as a transhistorical structure infusing all of human experience, past, present, and future, and as a positively enervating experience, approaching the manically depressive pessimism of conspiracy theory with an ironic, cynical detachment from its dystopian implications.[8]

Fenster depicts a type of conspiracy theorist who distances him/herself from the logical implications of what it means to believe in a conspiracy theory: how agency is asserted but simultaneously rendered impotent by belief in an all-embracing conspiracy. He suggests that an ironic relation to conspiracy theory is a way of mediating this inherent paradox. The commodification of conspiracy theory is inextricably linked to this detachment because it facilitates the marketing of conspiracy theory to a much larger consumer group or audience than a core group of "believers."[9]

Taking "belief" out of the equation means that conspiracy theory can be marketed to, and parodically adopted by, those concerned with a generalized, rather than specific, conspiracy or injustice. On a potentially positive note, conspiracy theory can come to signify cynicism toward official accounts without requiring conspiracy theorists to invest in each conspiracy narrative. Because of the way power is organized, this parodic configuration suggests, these stories might as well be true, or it might serve us well to act *as if* they are. This logic recalls a remark by one of Don DeLillo's characters in *Underworld*: "Believe everything. Everything is true"; or another's: "[a conspiracy theory is] easy to believe. We'd be stupid not to believe it. Knowing what we know."[10] Why shouldn't we believe in the most outlandish conspiracies against the public, the argument goes, since the most incredible of all—which has ensured our enslavement to nuclear energy and weapons—has already been committed? According to this rationale, the redundancy of belief has not eradicated belief but led to its generalization. If we believe everything it will be because certain covert acts of aggression that have subsequently come to light (like those conducted under the notorious Counterintelligence Program, for example) will have meant that the possibility of conspiracy has been irrevocably posited. The remarks of DeLillo's characters indicate that information is neutralized without the investments of stock grand narratives. That is not to say that information was once either "true" or "false," but that the representational attributions "true" and "false" are exposed as unstable once metanarratives are questioned. Douglas Kellner writes that "distrust in the face of science, technology, government, and conventional attitudes forces an individual to penetrate beneath the lies and illusions, to seek the truth."[11] He thinks that this quest might take the form of a search for new modes of representation and inquiry. A pragmatic cynicism toward official narratives might result from a commercially mediated conspiracy theory, and this could prompt a deeper questioning of epistemological apparatuses, but such optimism is usually quelled in the face of assumptions about conspiracy theory's lack of political resonance.[12]

There is the risk that the aestheticization of conspiracy theory only serves to depoliticize any challenging or radical potential it might have had.[13] A commodified version of conspiracy theory highlights the way conspiracy theory provides us with no line of action, or renders its disruptive potential impotent. Such criticisms have been lodged against conspiracy theory as a whole, whether apparently marginal or mainstream, by Fenster. While he recognizes that "conspiracy as play may at its best represent a productive and challenging cultural and political practice," Fenster feels that it is more often "a cynical abandonment of profound political realities that merely reaffirms the dominant political order" and "substitutes fears of all-powerful conspiratorial groups for political activism and hope."[14]

The X-Files itself has prompted many of the same arguments. Stephen Duncombe writes, "Yes, conspiratorial forces do undermine our democracy, but knowing about it is simply 'cool . . . cool like us' as the Fox billboard campaign for the show goes. Because this variety of political culture is something that people just watch, their natural role is that of audience to a spectacle."[15] We might want to question Duncombe's classic Frankfurt School pessimism toward audiences. Developments in cultural studies have taught us to be wary, for example, of ignoring the ways audience readings can exceed the dominant or prescribed reading. While capital can be said to be indifferent to its products (the aim of Fox Network, that is to say, is not to generate conspiracy theories and present a challenge to epistemological paradigms, but to sell advertising space and secure profits), and while conspiracy theory could be characterized as just the latest "fashion," we must also see that as consumers and audiences, we are not indifferent to content *in the same way*. Indeed, conspiratorial themes might resonate in ways that exceed the code of consumption that circulates them for those who emotionally, rather than just financially, invest in them. Yet what

Duncombe's comment highlights is how *The X-Files*, as a product of Fox Network, provides a space for a dispassionate engagement with the radical implications of its content. *The X-Files* exemplifies conspiracy theory in its domestic form because the narrative sets up a thematic tension between rational, scientific knowledge and irrational, extrascientific knowledge that allows the audience to root for the side of "irrationality" in a way that eradicates the risks this might involve in everyday situations. While as viewers of *The X-Files* we can support alternative knowledge, in extra-televisual situations this support could invoke the label of paranoia and the very real implications of this: being marginalized, discounted, and positioned outside the hegemonic order. While there is guilt by association (some negative attitudes toward fans of *The X-Files*, or X-Philes, in the popular press hint at this marginalization), *The X-Files* generally allows for a safe position from which to side with the radical: it provides a nonradical investment in the radical.

In light of this depleted investment, the poster in Mulder's office resonates ironically; it reads, "I want to believe," referring to the existence of extraterrestrials. The way desire to believe displaces belief as the object of the sentence indicates the ever-receding or deferred position of belief if we are to think of it as an unobtainable desired object (or stance from which a subject might speak). The audience, in fact, is being asked to suspend its disbelief, rather than to believe. Our investment in the narrative is always negatively defined. Like the scientifically rooted Dana Scully, we do not have to wholly relinquish our dominant discourse in order to align ourselves with Mulder.

It is the displaced investment that is allowed or invited by *The X-Files* that provides the focus for many critiques. In an otherwise positive account of the resources to be found in *The X-Files*, Kellner writes that "ultimately the politics of the series is ambiguous and indeterminate, failing to promote any positive solutions. Its pop postmodernism reproduces the failings of populism, promoting suspicion against the existing social system without specifying how one can actually solve the problems depicted."[16] I would argue that to mark *The X-Files* by its failure to promote definite political action might only be the other side of the coin of populist celebrations. Both approaches, that is, assess *The X-Files* or conspiracy theory in general positively or negatively against a narrowly defined pragmatism.

If Kellner is frustrated with the unfocused suspicion *The X-Files* promotes, the questions that the show raises with regard to interpretative paradigms do not necessarily have to suffer such shortcomings. The concern over the lack of political responsibility to be found in the conspiracy culture that has produced *The X-Files* is partly a concern over what resources should be found within cultural texts by those who study them. The idea that academic study should guide and promote is implicitly advocated over the idea that it should analyze existing cultural phenomena. Rather than critique popular configurations of conspiracy theory such as *The X-Files* for emptying out the force of this accusatory narrative, I will now look to the epistemic struggle in *The X-Files* to find a resource"—not for political resistance, but for questioning discursive strategies of legitimization and academic attempts to translate conspiracy theory through a paradigm of reason, for questioning the power that is bequeathed by and invested in only certain discourses. We can consider *The X-Files* not just as a product that exemplifies the commodification of conspiracy theory and the way this commercialization relies on a certain kind of disinvestment from its audience, but as a resourceful text that presents thematic tensions that problematize the status of "official knowledge" and uses of its name as a form of delegitimization (note the refrain, "It's like something out of *The X-Files*").

I will outline the thematic tension in *The X-Files* in order to preface a consideration of the ways it gets played out in academic discourses. I will suggest that it is the close rather than distant relationship conspiracy theory has with these discourses that will stage a critique of the limits of interpretation. Ultimately, the various discursive tactics employed to distance conspiracy theory from other discourses display an anxiety over interpretation in general. The convergence between conspiracy theory and other discourses will prove to be conspiracy theory's most informative and yet most consistently denied characteristic.

THE X-FILES: EPISTEMIC CHALLENGE

At this juncture, it is necessary to "begin" this essay again: to consider what *The X-Files* does put on display, rather than meditate on the implications of what it cannot. According to Chris Carter, the creator of *The X-Files*, his inspiration was Professor John Mack, a Pulitzer Prize–winning Harvard researcher into alien abduction narratives.[17] The contrast between the academic context Mack was working within and the unorthodox nature of his subject matter must have appealed to Carter's sense of drama. In *The X-Files* it is the FBI rather than the university that becomes the site of contention, but both institutions traditionally have investments in endorsing a paradigm of "reason." Mack's research has prompted concerned colleagues to complain, nervous, perhaps, about the challenge his research presents to the implied workable "reality" much academic work is based on.[18] Indeed, Mack believes this to be the case: "When you do something that breaks with the reality of your culture . . . you are going to draw some flack. [Alien abduction] is difficult for the Western worldview, because it says several things. Not only that we're not the top of the intelligence pyramid, but that we don't have control of our fates."[19]

In Carter's television show, the FBI's potentially problematic cases are marginalized to the X-Files—they are gathered under the public erasure of the *X*, indicating the uncategorizable nature of the cases investigated under this signifier. Whereas Mack's research holds a problematic status within the academy due to questions of validity, the fictional X-Files are created precisely because the upper ranks of the FBI know there is something worth suppressing. The fictionalized FBI, or rather the "shadow government" that secretly controls major institutions including the FBI, allows a specialized inquiry (one they can always present as being invalid) to avoid a general inquiry (which they may not be able to discredit or suppress as easily).

The wide range of beliefs (such as superstition) and experiences (such as *déjà vu* or even coincidence) dismissed by scientific rationalism are nevertheless inseparable from scientific modes of thought. According to John Fiske's model, scientific rationalism must at once recognize and reject that which it cannot explain.[20] These phenomena are left for other epistemologies to decipher. Chris Carter's fictional FBI investigates extracurricular phenomena "officially" to dismiss them, but also "unofficially" to understand their significance and utility. The existence of this covert project within the wider system invests the dominant discourse (government investigation and scientific rationalism) with a will to dissimulate. Exacerbating John Fiske's reading of scientific rationalism's dismissal of other epistemologies as an ideological "effect" of discursive mechanisms, *The X-Files* explicitly presents this as the act of a conspiring agency. *The X-Files'* FBI presents certain knowledges as "not worth knowing" only because it does not want the public to know. The model here is one of containment. The problem with containment—as

The X-Files' sinister and powerful government insider and orchestrator of covert operations, "Cancer Man," knows only too well—is the tenacious possibility that the maverick allowed the luxury of conjecture and investigation may not report back. This excess (the attempts by Mulder and Scully to expose government cover-ups) is the result of attempting to keep investigations within one organization or discourse. We might also want to consider this excess in light of how certain thematic tensions in *The X-Files* can exceed the domesticated identity we have suggested it embodies.[21]

Mulder and Scully most clearly represent extrascientific, counter-hegemonic beliefs and scientific, hegemonic beliefs respectively in the pilot episode and the first season in general. With a background in medicine, Scully is assigned to the X-Files to lend a scientific viewpoint to the investigations, but also, as Mulder realizes, to investigate him. On first meeting Scully, Mulder indicates that her credentials might not be appropriate for the task at hand: he tells her he has read her thesis—"Einstein's Twin Paradox: A New Interpretation"—but warns her that, in most of his work, "the laws of physics rarely seem to apply."[22]

Mulder's theories are often initially received with skepticism by Scully, who invariably offers an explanation of the same phenomenon by scientific means. The first episode clearly displays this epistemological countering. Mulder shows Scully some mysterious marks on the body of a victim that he suspects are from an alien encounter. On seeing this "evidence," Scully suggests that they are "needle punctures, an animal bite, electrocution of some kind." Later, when the body of what appears to be a "grey" (the alien form favored by popular culture) is exhumed from a grave, Scully suggests that it is "from the chimpanzee family."

In this first episode (and this is a process repeated throughout *The X-Files*) Scully protests against extrascientific explanations—"time can't just disappear. It's a universal invariant"—and is clearly disturbed by them. When Scully does have to concede some of the epistemological ground to Mulder by suggesting an extrascientific theory of the case, she responds by laughing hysterically at herself, admitting "it's crazy" even while positing it. When Mulder asks if she realizes the consequences of her theory, she says, "You said it yourself." To which he replies, "But *you* have to write it in your report," preempting the institutional and epistemological bind Scully will find herself in when translating the case into an "acceptable" form. In the closing scene,

Scully attempts to evade such problems by stating that her "reports are personal and subjective." She adds that she does not "think [she has] gone so far as to draw any conclusions about what [she has] seen." In other words, she renounces the ideals of her scientific discourse (to make objective conclusions) in order to file a report.

In spite of Scully's increasing contact with paranormal and extraterrestrial phenomena, she repeatedly greets Mulder's logic and theories with skepticism. In some ways, Scully's opposition and the epistemic struggle in general are necessary to sustain the narrative tension. Yet it also becomes an acknowledged convention, one that is so ingrained in *The X-Files'* logic that it can be parodically referred to in later episodes.[23] While the initial opposition (in each episode, and in the series as a whole) posited by the figures of Mulder and Scully operates as a central trope, *The X-Files* does not foreclose this binarism in any simple way. The terms of the opposition are constantly being revised, negotiated, and shown to be interrelated. Reeves, Rodgers, and Epstein suggest that the opposition between Mulder and Scully can be described as one between a "hermeneutics of faith" and a "hermeneutics of suspicion."[24] Yet what is clear even after a cursory glance at these terms is that they can interchangeably be aligned with each of the characters. While Mulder has faith in the paranormal and his extrascientific convictions, he is also suspicious of official government lines and scientific metanarratives—his skepticism even periodically turns against his skepticism, as he questions his role in the conspiracy he is determined to expose. Likewise, Scully may express suspicion toward Mulder's unorthodox hypotheses, yet she has a strong religious and, somewhat paradoxically, scientific faith. The opposition between scientific rationalism and extrascientific knowledge is only provisional. Scully's knowledge often aids Mulder's investigations, while Mulder delivers his extrascientific theories in an authoritative, hyper-rational tone. There is nothing static about the poles Mulder and Scully occupy.

Indeed, the ever-widening hermeneutic circle that the duo experience propels any identity into a constant state of flux. Provisionally assigned roles, therefore, are constantly being revised according to context. The implications of this for the seemingly antagonistic relationship between scientific rationalism and extrascientific beliefs are manifold: what serves us as knowledge in one context is rendered impotent in another; as our viewpoint changes, we begin to see not necessarily new things, but things anew.

The two-part episode "Tunguska/Terma" begins with Scully being sworn in before the Senate Subcommittee on Intelligence and Terrorism. As she begins to read a prepared statement, claiming that there is a "culture of lawlessness that prevents [her] from doing [her] work," the senators insist that she disclose Agent Mulder's location. Scully maintains that she cannot reveal this information because it would compromise Mulder's investigation, which she believes to be at odds with the nefarious aims of the committee before which she is speaking. It is clear that Scully is in a double bind: the court that might hold her in contempt is the court she is trying to expose for being ruled by a "culture of lawlessness." She feels as if the court is deliberately ignoring her protestations by asking her what she cannot say rather than what she can. As she later points out, the senators are lawyers, and "lawyers always ask the wrong questions when they don't want the right answer." In the wider context of the conspiracy, the details of which Scully and Mulder are not yet acquainted with, we can see that any attempt by Scully to use the institutionalized structures of appeal are redundant because of the investment representatives of those institutions have in the conspiracy. Scully realizes that she is playing a new game by old rules.

Scully's statements before the committee carefully expose the difficulties presented by her investigations. She says, for example, "We intend to file a full report when we fully understand what it is we are investigating"—an ironic statement given the show's reliance on an indefinitely postponed resolution. The traditional detective hermeneutic is upset as the clues themselves have to be categorized before they can point to any "final" revelation. Knowledge in this case cannot begin with the evidence: she must find other clues in order to explain what the evidence is in a decentering logic of abreaction. Her method of scientific inquiry, inextricably bound to the rationalistic Enlightenment ideals behind the American Constitution, fails because the contradictions in those ideals are being exposed (science can be used to enslave as well as emancipate) and apparently democratically assigned power abused.

Scully understands that she must alter her approach according to context. She decides to turn against her belief in the governmental system when confronted with the corrupt subcommittee: "It is my natural inclination to believe that they are acting in the best interests of the truth. But I am not inclined to follow my own judgment in this case." Scully rejects her primary knowledge and employs a logic of skepticism. Her comment acknowledges the naturalized status of democratic ideals and accepts that it might not always be appropriate to follow the "democratic" government when democracy is not being properly exercised. She passes over her own judgment in favor of what she anticipates Mulder's would be. Scully fashions her turn as one against reason: she says, "I am not inclined to follow my own judgment" and yet it *is* her judgment not to follow her own judgment. This paradoxical statement suggests that reason and unreason, or rationality and irrationality, are not mutually exclusive. Sometimes it is reasonable to turn against reason, and irrational to make a rational decision, rendering these terms anything but simply defined or opposed.

While Scully has to suspend her primary belief and epistemological system (what she calls "natural") according to the information she is presented with, it is fashioned as an excessively rational move. It might serve us to recall the musical context of "suspension." To suspend in musical terms is to sustain one chord into another, producing discord. Scully's rational move to turn against her rationally founded democratic ideals—"I am not inclined to follow my own judgment in this case"—highlights the hyper-rational character of Mulder's thought. By sustaining the rational chord into the apparently irrational realm of conspiracy theory, Scully produces discord within the staging of epistemological paradigms. Traversing these two apparently opposed positions in one logic, Scully's move puts on display a characteristic of conspiracy theory that problematizes dismissive gestures. We will return to this maneuver to see what it reveals about the relationship between "official" and "unofficial" discourses.

At the final hearing, the committee repeatedly asks for Mulder and Scully's by now irretrievable evidence. In an ostensive judicial culture, a case without evidence is merely an unsubstantiated theory, a conspiracy theory, perhaps. Mulder challenges the inability of the committee members to take on board what he considers to be a reasonable change in what can be thought of as "reality," not knowing, of course, that part of their public reluctance to recognize this change is the fact that they already know of and are working to maintain the conspiracy. Mulder embarks on a monologue:

> Why is [the existence of alien life] so hard to believe? When the accepted discovery of life off this planet is on the front page of every newspaper around the world? When even the most conservative scientists and science journals are calling for the exploration of Mars and

Jupiter? With every reason to believe that life and the persistence of it is thriving outside our own terrestrial sphere? If you cannot get past this, then I suggest that this whole committee be held in contempt, for ignoring evidence that cannot be refuted.

Like Scully's appeal to the court that "there is a culture of lawlessness that prevents [her] from doing [her] work," Mulder faces the Lyotardian "differend":

> a differend would be a case of conflict between (at least) two parties, that cannot be equitably resolved for lack of a rule of judgement applicable to both arguments. One side's legitimacy does not imply the other's lack of legitimacy. However, applying a single rule of judgement to both in order to settle their differend as though it were a mere litigation would wrong (at least) one of them (and both if neither side admits this rule).[25]

Mulder is attempting to change the terms of what can and cannot be held up as evidence in a court that requires traditional evidence (witnesses deemed "credible" by the court, or ostensive evidence) in order for it to consider such a change. Mulder's request that the senators be held in contempt only highlights the way self-reflexive gestures are not written into the judicial structure. One of the councilors calls for a recess: the jury is necessarily and metaphorically "out" on this one.

In the next section, I will consider how attempts to counter conspiracy theories become locked into a polemic with them. I will also consider what happens when conspiracy theory is translated or subsumed by another discourse. Distancing tactics such as these—either attempting to discredit conspiracy theories point by point, or trying to explain them away by the very logic that founds the position from which one speaks—are fueled by an anxiety over contamination. Yet conspiracy theory is always already a structuring component of what can be thought of as legitimate interpretation or rationality. *The X-Files* puts this economy on display. The relation between conspiracy theory and other discourses that have been legitimated is in some ways incommensurable (one cannot "explain" the other), but there are certain common features that render problematic any dismissive or distancing gestures.

HYPER-DISCOURSE

On first impressions, it might seem that Elaine Showalter does justice to the idea of conspiracy theories and other alternative narratives in *Hystories: Hysterical Epidemics and Modern Media*. She claims, for example, that "Modern forms of individual and mass hysteria have much to tell us about the anxieties and fantasies of western culture."[26] Indeed, Showalter takes on board the complaints and struggles within the narratives, and even acknowledges the sometimes ambiguous position these discourses of complaint assume in relation to scientific, political, and medical discourses. However, Showalter does not entertain the possibility that to ask these narratives to prove themselves "legitimate" by the very criteria that root her discourse rather than theirs might be a reductive and disingenuous notion of an academic's role. Showalter postulates that classical hysteria can be seen collectively reemerging as recent phenomena like Gulf War Syndrome, Chronic Fatigue Syndrome, or alien abduction narratives, which she calls "psychogenic syndromes."[27] Far from using this to delegitimize the symptoms such "epidemics" produce, Showalter is rightly commenting on how psychological problems are denigrated and denied in modern culture. The resistance of sufferers, support groups, and some therapists to acknowledge the neurological origin of such complaints results from the negative connotations hysteria has been ascribed, especially, she suggests, because of its association with the feminine. From within the discourse of psychoanalysis, Showalter asks us to explore what narratives such as conspiracy theory can tell us about the "real" psychosocial demands of the turn of the century.

Showalter feels that the limit of the human imagination and the recycling of plot lines in the media mean that "Inevitably, we all live out the social stories of our time."[28] Yet, rather than focusing on this complex interrelation between the media, myth, discourse, and identity, Showalter appeals to her readers to "interrupt or halt these epidemics."[29] Of course Showalter knows that part of her project is to ask her readers to "understand" these "epidemics"—she writes, "New Hysterians and other scholars can place hysteria in its fullest sexual, historical and cultural contexts"—yet this understanding is to be only a step toward a strategic erasure of the object of understanding. We must combat these "epidemics," she suggests, with the very media—television and the press—that have helped create them: "We can . . . use the media to fight rumors as well as to spread them."[30]

In their *Times Higher Education Supplement* book review, Peter Knight and Alasdair Spark describe how the authors of a recent spate of studies concerned with conspiracy and conspiracy theory, including Showalter, present their sense of duty as alarmism about popular paranoia.[31] The authors cited by Knight and Spark perhaps unsurprisingly "identify paranoia as pseudo-scholarship," but, more significantly, they "feel they have to correct [paranoia's] inaccuracies."[32] Knight and Spark explain the general tone of these works: "It is not enough to examine and interpret conspiracy theories, these writers seem to suggest. Responsible writers must also take a stand, push back the tide of increasing gullibility by presenting What Is Really Going On in simplified form; in short, they must correct and instruct."[33] In this vein, Showalter claims that

> the hysterical epidemics of the 1990s have already gone on too long, and they continue to do damage: in distracting us from the real problems and crises of modern society, in undermining a respect for evidence and truth, and in helping to support an atmosphere of conspiracy and suspicion. They prevent us from claiming our full humanity as free and responsible beings.[34]

While Showalter's rhetoric clearly reflects the demands of her assumed role as public intellectual, the similarities to Mulder's monologue quoted above reveal a polemical gridlock. All her concerns could equally be expressed by conspiracy theorists as a reaction against governmental and bureaucratic secrecy. We could ask why Showalter does not consider the lack of trust in democratically appointed government that is expressed in fictional and documentary television programs to constitute a "real [problem] and [crisis] in modern society." In Showalter's text, social conditions are obfuscated in favor of psychological explanations. Or rather, social narratives and practices are only valuable for what they can tell us about how hysteria manifests itself, rather than as objects of study that might be able to illuminate interpretative practices or transcendental gestures of this sort. Paranoia is being drawn back into the specific, if you like, in reaction to its generalized appearance. Paranoid discourses or conspiracy theory become a symptom of hysteria. That Showalter wants to legitimize hysteria and ensure that sufferers receive appropriate treatment in private, rather than be granted testimonial space in public, is an attempt to reassert an Enlightenment ideal of reason. This becomes clear when she claims that without the encumbrance presented by challenges to reason, we will be able to "[claim] our full humanity as free and responsible beings."[35]

At a recent conference concerned with conspiracy cultures, Showalter ridiculed the discourse of Gulf War Syndrome and its associated fears of government conspiracy, supporting her refutation with the "masses of evidence [she has] *at home.*"[36] In this challenge to conspiracy theory, Showalter claims the same privileged access to irrefutable (but in the circumstances unverifiable) evidence for which she criticizes conspiracy theorists. Showalter thus fuels a polemic based on evidence and counterevidence, an epistemological stalemate comparing quantitative detail and qualitative analysis. Showalter's subsequent appeal to fellow academics to be "guardians of reason"[37] prompts a question that must serve as a spectral presence to this essay as a whole: we must ask what it is about reason (or a paradigm of interpretation) that makes it vulnerable to the challenge of conspiracy theory. Indeed, the vulnerability of a particular configuration of reason or interpretation to the challenge of conspiracy theory should not be considered an aberration. I would suggest that it is more productive for cultural theorists to question why reason needs to be guarded than to guard it themselves. Showalter might argue that she is reclaiming a legitimate space for hysteria and neurological problems in general (a project I have great sympathy with), yet, with this "call to arms," she grounds her work in the assumption that academics share a notion of "reason" never questioned in her study. Her thesis implies that not only should academics "know better," as Knight and Spark point out, but that they should guard the interpretative methodologies and available referents that can be used to ascertain this "better knowledge." By translating the experiences described in her study into a knowable and apparently comprehensive scientific discourse, and in claiming this to be the work of academics, she fails to consider what the experiences she wants to explain away can tell us about the very academic discourses she wants to do this explaining away.

The distancing tactics employed by critics such as Showalter are prompted by a logic of recognition; this is where *The X-Files*, its epistemological struggle in general, and the discordant slippage of Scully's epistemology in particular can aid us. To study the mechanisms of conspiracy theory is to recognize that it operates and proliferates in a similar fashion to other discourses. Indeed, conspiracy theory's singularity seems to reside in the way it exacerbates the operation of other, "legitimate" discourses: it is, perhaps, a "hyperreal" discourse. Following Baudrillard's formulation that hyperreal images become "more real than real," we could say that conspiracy theory is "more discourse than discourse."[38]

Baudrillard describes how "cinema plagiarizes and copies itself, remakes its classics, retroactivates its original myths, remakes silent films more perfect than the originals, etc."[39] In the postmodern cinematic, which finds cinema to be more cinema than cinema, obsessed with producing the perfect replica of itself, we can find a helpful model for the way conspiracy theory can only be differentiated from other discourses by how it exacerbates their narrative concerns and puts on display their structural conditions. This hyperreal operation, like all simulation, is subversive in its implicit suggestion that all discourses "might be nothing more than simulation."[40] In other words, the relationship between a sign and its referent, or any general truth claims, might be seen to be problematic in all discourses as well as conspiracy theory. Baudrillard's formulation illustrates how remakes copy and exaggerate what is already there in the "original." This is helpful only if we interpret the hyperreal as putting on display the workings of the real: a reading that complicates the apparent and problematic privileged status that the "real" is given in Baudrillard's thought. In order to avoid an undue nostalgia, we must see the "real" as having retained the possibility of the hyperreal within its realm. Rather than resulting in a lack of meaning as Baudrillard suggests, the hyperreal can expose a condition of the "real"—that it must be iterable—that allows for its exacerbated "other."

Herein lies the tension: conspiracy theory puts on display a possibility of reading, the invisibility of which (through processes of nonrecognition or delegitimization of conspiracy theory) other discourses rely on. The conditions that enable discourses to function can also be used to question their very foundations; and the close proximity between academic discourses and conspiracy theory places this risk in a public context.

While I do not wish to deny conspiracy theory's oppositional tone or singular characteristics, its mode of interpretation often mirrors and exaggerates those of more "rational" discourses. The excessive attention conspiracy theorists pay to narrative coherence—the way conspiracy narratives often contort plot and causality in order to make all events fit into one overarching scheme—provides a good example. But more general observations can be made: like psychoanalysis, conspiracy theory seeks to find a cause (however complex) for an effect; like historical analysis, it narrates and identifies patterns in a series of events; like anthropology it can qualitatively assess data and facts. While any one of these approaches would probably consider the conclusions of a conspiracy theorist to be illogical, we must acknowledge that in generating its own signified meanings, interpreting events and rhetoric, and attempting to ascribe meaning to phenomena and experience, conspiracy theory operates in similar ways to them. Indeed, Knight and Spark claim that the academic distaste for conspiracy theory indicates "that the real dispute is not so much between academic disciplines as between scholarship and pseudoscholarship. They all make clear that paranoid thinking is so dangerously attractive because it has all the trappings of proper academic work, but with none of the rigor or integrity."[41] While it is not uncommon for discourses to be mutually hostile since a metanarrative claim is threatened by others, we must consider the specific exclusion of the discourse of conspiracy theory by more traditional, established, and "rational" discourses. Academic exclusions of conspiracy theory assume an unproblematic distinction between fact and rumor, academic and nonacademic, and the logical and illogical. Equally, unreflexive academic attempts to contain conspiracy theory, whether within a populist narrative such as John Fiske's or a project like Showalter's, which reads conspiracy theory through the discourse of psychoanalysis, fail to see how their object of inquiry problematizes the discourses from which they write.[42]

Concerns like Showalter's highlight an anxiety over epistemology and the public sphere. How can we appeal to people who are processing their information through a different epistemological model? Showalter's study suggests that public narratives obstruct the "real" truths—truths that, if given precedence, would reconfigure the mass as a series of individuals. The influx of conspiracy theory–related Internet sites, television drama serials such as *The X-Files*, and chat shows, as well as talk radio, have made concerns like Showalter's into a concern over the way epistemologies become circulated and established outside, or on the margins of, the traditional site for knowledge production, the academy. The commodification of conspiracy theory makes the way academics and the press deal with conspiracy theory a more pressing issue to those concerned with how popular cultural objects come to be configured. Yet what we can find in one of the most popular and wide-reaching conspiracy texts—*The X-Files*—is a commodity that presents not an easily discernible polemic of the kind that Showalter gets locked into, but an epistemic challenge that complicates any attempts to demarcate where "legitimate" interpretative practices end and conspiracy theory begins. "Official" discourses need to acknowledge the challenge "objects" of study such as conspiracy theory present to the interpretative paradigms on which these discourses implicitly rely.

NOTES

I would like to thank Professor Paul Smith, Dr. Chris Greenwood, and Paul Myerscough for their helpful comments and criticisms.

1. Don DeLillo, interview with Adam Begley, "The Art of Fiction CXXXV," *Paris Review* 128 (1993): 287.

2. Mark Fenster, *Conspiracy Theories: Secrecy and Power in American Culture* (Minneapolis: University of Minnesota Press, 1999), 98.

3. Paradoxically, the generative drive of conspiracy theory could also signal waning desire for its commercial manifestations, saturation of the market also being inevitable. It is difficult, that is, to sustain interest in an unresolvable plot in the way that *The X-Files* has to, and the show's declining popularity surely reflects this narrative pressure.

4. For example, Rosemary J. Coombe writes how Proctor and Gamble had to remove its trademark after a rumor that it signified the devil circulated and profits began to drop. She writes, "the biggest threat to the company's benign, if somewhat empty, public image, came not from organized social groups with expressed political agendas, but from the anonymous recodings of mysterious agents whose interests and motivations remain inscrutable." "Postmodernity and the Rumor: Late Capitalism and the Fetishism of the Commodity Sign," in *Jean Baudrillard: The Disappearance of Art and Politics*, ed. William Stearns and William Chaloupke (London: Macmillan, 1992), 102.

5. See Clare Birchall, "Conspiracy Theory as a Hyperreal Discourse" (D.Phil. diss., University of Sussex, UK, 2000), chap. 1.

6. We should note that it is problematic to use the term "community" in relation to conspiracy theorists due to their often distrustful and competitive rhetoric. See Fenster, *Conspiracy Theories*, 181.

7. Ibid., xxi.

8. Ibid., 216.

9. In my use of the terms "belief" and "believers" it should be clear that I am thinking along the lines of a simulacrum of belief, rather than an idea of belief that has some inherent and fixed original scene or narrative.

10. Don DeLillo, *Underworld* (New York: Scribner, 1997), 801, 289.

11. Douglas Kellner, "The *X-Files* and the Aesthetics and Politics of Postmodern Pop," *Journal of Aesthetics and Art Criticism* 57 (1999): 170; see also Kellner, "*The X-Files* and Conspiracy: A Diagnostic Critique," this volume.

12. Interestingly, Kellner expresses both views in his article.

13. We could, however, think that lack of political resonance is a good thing in relation to right-wing militia groups.

14. Fenster, *Conspiracy Theories*, 219.

15. Stephen Duncombe, *Notes from the Underground: Zines and the Politics of Alternative Culture* (London: Verso, 1997), 127.

16. Kellner, "*The X-Files*," this volume.

17. See Paula Vitaris, "*The X-Files*," *Cinefantastique* (October 1995), <http://www.cfq.com>.

18. Elaine Showalter writes, "In May 1995, a Harvard faculty committee convened by Dean Daniel Tosteson submitted a report sharply critical of Mack's research." *Hystories: Hysterical Epidemics and Modern Media* (New York: Columbia University Press, 1997), 199.

19. Ibid.

20. John Fiske, *Power Plays/Power Works* (London: Verso, 1993).

21. I do not want to replicate textual details that appear elsewhere in this volume. I therefore refer those unfamiliar with *The X-Files* mythology to Kellner's article, but I may have to repeat certain details where necessary.

22. The pilot episode, written by Chris Carter, directed by Robert Mandel, *The X-Files*, series 1, episode 1.

23. See "X-Cops," written by Chris Carter, *The X-Files*, series 7, episode 12. This episode is produced in the style of the American series *Cops*, in which handheld cameras show the working lives of Los Angeles policemen. In this genre-hybrid episode, Mulder and Scully are investigating a case that the camera crew of *Cops* is following. When Scully realizes that the case will be shown on national television, she tells Mulder to be careful of what he says. Scully explains, "I may not agree with you but at least I won't hold it against you." Mulder and Scully's oppositional relationship and the way verification evades their quest are satirically referred to by Mulder when he tells the camera, "these cases are notoriously hard to quantify . . . and . . . validate in a scientific quantitative fashion as Agent Scully will tell you."

24. These terms are used by Jimmie L. Reeves, Mark C. Rodgers, and Michael Epstein, "Rewriting Popularity," in David Lavery, Angela Hague, and Marla Cartwright, eds., *"Deny All Knowledge": Reading The X-Files* (London: Faber and Faber, 1996), 35.

25. Jean-François Lyotard, *The Differend: Phrases in Dispute*, trans. Georges van Den Abbeele (Manchester: Manchester University Press, 1988), xi.

26. Showalter, *Hystories*, 12.

27. Ibid.

28. Ibid., 6.

29. Ibid., 12.

30. Ibid.

31. Peter Knight and Alasdair Spark, "Plots All Over the Landscape," *Times Higher Education Supplement*, 25 December 1998, 22.

32. Ibid.

33. Ibid.

34. Showalter, *Hystories*, 206.

35. Ibid.

36. Elaine Showalter, "Slaying the Hydra" (paper presented at "Conspiracy Cultures Conference," King Alfred's College, Winchester, UK, 18 July 1998).

37. Showalter, *Hystories*, 206.

38. I am citing Baudrillard's term in an isolated sense, without wishing to enlist Baudrillard's whole theory of the image. The notion of the hyperreal, as I interpret it, can point toward a self-referential relationship between texts (and, for my study, anything that can be equated with the position of the real in this formulation is always already textual). Baudrillard's theory of the sign is best viewed on a representational level: certain socioeconomic and aesthetic contexts, that is, may make it *seem* as if the symbol is "emancipated" from its "referential obligation," yet it is a "freedom" that was "always already" there, enabling it to function as a symbol.

39. Jean Baudrillard, *The Evil Demon of Images* (Sydney: Power Institute of Fine Arts, 1987), 28.

40. Jean Baudrillard, *Simulations*, trans. Paul Foss, Paul Patton, and Philip Beitchman (New York: Semiotext(e), 1983), 38.

41. Knight and Spark, "Plots," 22.

42. See Fiske's configuration of "popular knowledges" in *Power Plays*.

11

Forget Conspiracy

Pynchon, DeLillo, and the Conventional
Counterconspiracy Narrative

John A. McClure

CONTEMPORARY AMERICAN LITERATURE, cinema, and television, popular and elite, fictional and factual, are replete with stories of conspiracy. Most of these stories rely on and rehearse a particular set of assumptions, arguments, and narrative formulas. Conspiracies—malevolent clandestine formations—exist, both within the official world and in extra-official zones. They are a threat to democratic culture and the common good. Resisting them is the risky business of a few heroic individuals, often affiliated with institutions of public order, who possess extraordinary powers, moral as well as intellectual. By the application of these powers, and in the face of tremendous odds, these individuals are able to penetrate and map the conspiratorial formations they encounter and then to unmask the conspirators and thwart their ambitions.

This ultimately reassuring story proclaims, then, that conspiracies exist, that they threaten to destroy our democratic capitalist way of life, and that this very way (heroically individualistic, brilliantly analytic, technologically sophisticated, and deeply principled) is always throwing up heroes capable of defending it against its conspiratorial others. It tells us, in addition, that the price of our collective "freedom" and perhaps even our survival is perpetual vigilance and fiercely focused resistance. We must never "forget conspiracy,"' and we must be ready to focus full attention on exposing and eradicating conspiracies when they arise. This is, one might argue, the common sense of conservatives, liberals, and radicals alike in our culture, even though each group tends to define the conspiracies that challenge it differently.

But it is not the sense one gets when one turns to the work of two extraordinary postmodern novelists of conspiracy, Thomas Pynchon and Don DeLillo. It is not that these writers deny the existence of conspiracies. Their fiction, like that of the most popular purveyors of masculinist adventure—Clancy, Ludlum, Grisham—is saturated with conspiracy. The plot of *Gravity's Rainbow*, Pynchon's masterpiece, is driven by the protagonist's attempt to uncover a corporate conspiracy that has shaped his life. This conspiracy against his person seems, in turn, to be part of the structural conspiracy of a capitalist order, which, the novel argues, has sponsored World War II as a means of profit enhancement, corporate consolidation, and globalization. Conspiracies abound in Pynchon's other work as well: the mysterious Tristero of *The Crying of Lot 49*, the shadowy "V" conspiracy of *V.*, and the state conspiracies of *Vineland*.[1] DeLillo's work is similarly focused on conspiracy. *Libra*, a fictional study of the Kennedy assassination, links that event to rogue elements of the CIA. *Players* focuses on a terrorist group committed to blowing up the Stock Exchange, and *Mao II* on an obscure Maoist group operating in Europe and the Middle East. In *The Names*, DeLillo suggests parallels between the work of a conspiracy of freelance assassins and the larger state-funded conspiracies of the CIA. "This is the age of conspiracy," declares a figure in *Running Dog*, "the age of connections, links, secret relationships" (111).[2]

Pynchon's and DeLillo's novels tend to rehearse and confirm many of the aspects of the "official narrative" of conspiracy. But they also sharply interrogate this narrative, suggesting that conspiracies are constitutive of rather than epiphenomenal to contemporary civilization, that the recommended strategies of counterconspiracy are designed to perpetuate conspiratorial power, not to eliminate it, and that, in order to resist conspiracy at all, we must learn, paradoxically, to "forget" it.

THE CRITIQUE OF COUNTERCONSPIRACY FICTION

The authorized view of conspiracy and of the methods to be used in disarming it is encoded and valorized not only in thousands of novels, and in heroic tales of clandestine struggle, investigative journalism, whistle-blowing, and citizen action that circulate in our culture, but also in currently fashionable television series such as *The X-Files* and *Millennium*. In some of these narratives, conspiracy is represented as a punctual event, a formation that can be fully mapped and eliminated. In others it is represented as something larger, more stubbornly and structurally embedded in the real, and hence less susceptible to full disclosure and elimination. But in either case, the heroic response to the threat of conspiracy is the same: a relentless commitment to systematic investigation, exposure, and elimination. *The X-Files'* Scully and Mulder and *Millennium's* Frank Black model this response every bit as much as more traditional figures, the flamboyant "secret agents" of the Bond cycle, or the morally compromised spies of Greene's and LeCarré's novels. Like the fastidiously neat and regimented FBI agents of popular fiction, they are scrupulously trained, relentlessly driven, implacable. Scully, a forensic pathologist, is the very figure of heroic counterconspiracy: a woman, she has suppressed those aspects of the self conventionally identified with the feminine in order to become a wizard of forensic pathology. Her power, both over herself and over those she tracks, lies in her ability to probe with cool detachment the viscera of monstrous and mutilated bodies. But Scully, Mulder, and Black also project, through their perpetual pallor and exhaustion (think "Scully" as "skull"), their obvious lack of any nourishing sexual or indeed personal life. These marks of sacrifice set them and the shows in which they appear apart from more flamboyant fantasies of heroic agency, and make it possible for a whole generation of stressed-out professional-managerial–class Americans to identify with them. But they also invite us to interrogate the very ethic of obsessive engagement the shows celebrate, to wonder, finally, whether, given the ubiquity of conspiracy in the world of the series, the limits of our agents' analytical powers, and the high price they pay for their vocational commitments, it might be better to resign from the agency, "forget conspiracy," and get a life.

The critique of the conventional counterconspiracy formula that flickers across episodes of *The X-Files* and *Millennium* finds full articulation in the conspiracy novels of Pynchon and DeLillo. Turning on the fascinations that fuel them and the conventions from which they are constructed, these novels challenge the representation of conspiracy as an epiphenomenal aspect of contemporary civilization and question the conventional counterconspiracy hero's relentless preoccupation with investigation, unmasking, and elimination. (Oedipa Maas, the heroine of Pynchon's *The Crying of Lot 49*, mocks herself, late in the novel, for having "come on so like the private eye in any long-ago radio drama, believing all you needed was grit, resourcefulness, exemption from the hidebound cops' rules, to solve any great mystery" [*CL*, 124].) In the decisively postmodern worlds they map, democracy seems for the most part to be little more than a mask behind which powerful conspiratorial forces pursue their interests. The Canadian novelist Michael Ondaatje articulates this deeply disenchanted view of political possibility in *The English Patient*: "Outside of [the desert]," one character muses, "there was just trade and power, money and war. Financial and military despots shaped the world."[3] Pynchon's perspective is, for the most part, equally bleak: a laboratory worker, "gone over" to the animals kept caged for experimental purposes, speaks to his prisoners. "I would set you free," he explains,

> if I knew how. But it isn't free out here. All the animals, the plants, the minerals, even other kinds of men, are being broken and reassembled every day, to preserve an elite few, who are the loudest to theorize on freedom, but the least free of all. I can't even give you hope that it will be different someday. (*GR*, 230)

The conventional narrative of counterconspiracy is a version of those grand narratives of enlightenment and liberation whose collapse Lyotard identifies with the postmodern moment. Also announcing this collapse, Pynchon paints a bleak, Weberian picture of the world as an "iron cage" on wheels, a juggernaut careening across the planet's surface, crushing cultures and lives.

Given the grip of conspiratorial forces on virtually every aspect of the civilization, Pynchon and DeLillo suggest, efforts to expose and eliminate these forces are doomed to fail. The narrator of *Gravity's Rainbow*, reflecting on Slothrop's chances of tracing out the structure of the conspiracy that has shaped his destiny, realizes that the "data retrieval" necessary to uncover all the "*separate* connections" would have been impossible back in 1945, and that even if the computer technology had existed, the conspirators "could've bought programmers by the truckload to come in and make sure that all the information fed out was harmless" (*GR*, 582). "You can put together clues, develop a thesis, or several, about . . . why the assassins came on," a character in *The Crying of Lot 49* suggests: "You could waste your life that way and never reach the truth" (*CL*, 80). Salman Rushdie ascribes a similar vision of things to the great Colombian novelist Gabriel García Márquez: "In Márquez's experience, truth has been controlled to the point at which it has ceased to be possible to find out what it is."[4] The implication, then, is that we cannot realistically hope, in today's world, to fully expose and eliminate, even perhaps to recognize, the conspiracies that shape our lives.

If analysis is so compromised as a weapon of resistance, then a narrative of counterconspiracy that commits one to its procedures is cruelly disabling. Even to begin untangling the conspiratorial web, Pynchon repeatedly insists, one may have to embrace modes of knowledge outlawed by the conventional codes of counterconspiracy, which celebrate the power of enlightened thought, and enlightened thought alone, to penetrate the darkness of conspiracy. Astrology, telepathy, the tarot, seances, and various forms of meditative attentiveness all play their roles in elucidating (but never "solving") the awesomely complex web of clandestine forces that drive history in *Gravity's Rainbow*. Indeed, "Those like Slothrop, with the greatest interest in discovering the truth, were thrown back on dreams, psychic flashes, omens, cryptographies, drug-epistemologies, all dancing on a ground of terror, contradiction, absurdity" (*GR*, 582).

The strong implication of these texts, then, is that the directions for resistance encoded in conspiracy fiction are instruments of conspiracy itself, formulas that trap us within the world of conspiracy and make effective resistance (or separation) impossible. So in *Gravity's Rainbow* when Lyle Bland, astral voyaging from his home on Beacon Hill, becomes fascinated with an "astral IG [Farban]," a conspiracy of "coal-tar Kabbalists," his benevolent guides rebuke him. "Forget them," the guides counsel. "They are no better than the Qlippoth, the shells of the dead, you must not waste your time with them" (*GR*, 590). In *Vineland*, D. L. Chastain, contemplating her decades-long quest to track down and kill the head of a government conspiracy, wonders in retrospect if "it [had] only been, as she'd begun to fear, that many years of what the Buddha calls 'passion, enmity, folly'? Suppose that she'd been meant, all the time, to be paying attention to something else entirely?" (*V*, 380).

To focus relentlessly on conspiracies and their dismantling is, in these passages, a waste of time. But what else might one be doing, what other project might claim our attention, in a world defined by murderous conspiracies? A possible answer surfaces in *Gravity's Rainbow*: "What if They find it convenient to preach an island of life surrounded by a void," muses the narrator. "Not just the Earth in space, but your own individual life in time? What if it's *in Their interest* to have you believing that?" (*GR*, 697). In this passage the narrator is speculating on the existence of something he calls a "Soniferous Aether" (*GR*, 695), a medium that might, in conjunction with a "presence, analogous to the aether, [that] flows through time . . . bring us back a continuity, show us a kinder universe" (*GR*, 726). Elsewhere the alternatives are frankly theistic, if in a pagan mode. We are invited to attend "to all the presences we are not supposed to be seeing—wind gods, hilltop gods, sunset gods—that we train ourselves away from" (*GR*, 720). No negative theology here: Pynchon, like William James, the great pragmatist, prefers to project a pluralistic universe richer in presences than our puny positivism can imagine. The whole tradition of philosophical secularism, he repeatedly suggests, and not just the conventional conspiracy narratives that valorize its procedures, is an instrument of an "order of Analysis and Death" (*GR*, 722) that is virtually coterminous with actually existing post-Enlightenment civilization. Its delimitations of the real, its modes of understanding, its rules for verification, and its values all function to keep us confined within a fiction of the real that makes us amenable to all sorts of manipulation and deprives us of all sorts of resources for resistance.

PLOTS

It's not surprising, then, that Pynchon and DeLillo drastically rewrite the conventional counterconspiracy narrative of heroic unmasking and elimination, in which conspiracies function as the dangerous but ultimately conquerable Other to something like democracy and the freedom of ordinary life. In the rewriting favored by DeLillo, the "system" itself is an effect of conspiracy, and those who attempt to infiltrate and expose specific conspiratorial formations are instead entangled, paralyzed, and dismantled by the conspiracies themselves. The CIA historian Nicholas Branch, in DeLillo's *Libra*, winds up hopelessly imprisoned in the web he has been trying to untangle: "There are times when he thinks he can't go on. He feels disheartened, almost immobilized. . . . But he persists, he works on, he jots his notes. He knows he can't get out. The case will haunt him until the end. Of course they've known it all along" (*L*, 445).

Less fortunate even than Branch, Lyle Wynant, the protagonist of *Players*, is consumed and dismantled by the conspiracy he attempts to unmask. In the end, "shedding capabilities and traits by the second," he is "barely recognizable as male" (*P*, 212). The only sane response to conspiracy, DeLillo suggests in *The Names*, is to walk away. When James Axton discovers that he has been working for a CIA "proprietary"—a company peddling international risk insurance—he resigns his job and cooperates with the Greek officials who question him briefly:

> I told the man from the Ministry [of Public Order] everything else I knew, gave him all the names . . . all the tenuous connections. I gave him business cards, supplied approximate dates of conversations, names of restaurants, cities, airplanes. Let the investigators work up chronologies, trace routes, check the passenger manifests. Their job was public order. Let them muse on the plausibilities. (*0*, 328)

One can imagine a world-weary protagonist taking such a position at some early point in a conventional espionage thriller, and then gradually coming to accept his responsibility for "getting to the bottom of things." But DeLillo's protagonist comes to this conclusion at the end of *The Names*, and his decision to disengage is strongly if implicitly endorsed. "Public Order" has become a "job" for knaves or fools and the government a "totally entangling force . . . even more evil than we'd imagined" (*P*, 104). Where there's no significant difference between the conspirators and the government, no possibility of anything like full disclosure and redress, the wise retreat into other zones, seek privacy or the company of fellow beings equally estranged from the games of power.

In Pynchon's rewritings of the counterconspiracy narrative of entanglement, exposure, and elimination, characters also walk away from the project. Pynchon's Slothrop and D. L. Chastain, like DeLillo's Nicholas Branch and Lyle Wynant, are driven to the brink of collapse by their efforts to unmask and avenge themselves on the conspiracies that have deformed their lives. But at the moment of crisis Pynchon's protagonists abandon the quests that threaten to consume them. Their surrender is not merely strategic, not a version of that familiar problem-solving paradox that promises that if you "let go" of a problem "the answer will come to you." They give up the struggle because they are not getting anywhere, because they cannot go on, because the horizons of conspiracy have begun to seem coterminous with those of organized social life itself, and because, in spite of this fact, they have caught a glimpse of zones, within the larger "culture of conspiracy," where conspiracy, ever a presence, does not define existence. Turning aside, forgetting conspiracy, these characters discover new satisfactions and new resources for survival. These satisfactions and resources are frequently spiritually inflected. But Pynchon does not seek to loosen the grasp of one redemptive narrative—that of enlightenment—only to restore the authority of another. The openings his characters achieve do not provide them with the weapons needed to win some decisive victory over conspiracy, nor do they transport them to the impregnable heights of some supernatural refuge. The promises made, if we can speak of promises at all, are much more modest: a degree of autonomy, a period of invisibility and exemption, the chance to enjoy, fleetingly, the pleasures of caring communities, and perhaps a glimpse of something beyond the horizons set in place by "the grim rationalizing of the World" (GR, 588).

Because most engaged intellectuals share the worldview of secular rationalism, even as we attempt to "unmask" or "deconstruct" some of its expressions, this "postsecular" aspect of Pynchon's and DeLillo's counterconspiracy thinking may not register or appeal, to say the least. But the spiritually inflected strategies for resistance and survival they elaborate resonate with the work of certain impeccably secular critics of contemporary conspiracy: with Fredric Jameson's representation of the postmodern crisis of effective resistance as a crisis of distantiation, for instance, and with Foucault's call for a politics of self-care. I want to try, then, in the pages that follow, not just to rehearse Pynchon's and DeLillo's arguments for "forgetting" conspiracy, but to suggest as well that these arguments, although steeped in the language of spirituality, make a powerful kind of secular sense.

MODELS OF THE POSTMODERN CRISIS

In *Postmodernism, or, The Cultural Logic of Late Capitalism*, Fredric Jameson argues that conspiracy fiction and conspiracy theory represent a "degraded attempt . . . to think the impossible totality of the contemporary world system."[5] The inadequacy of this attempt is understandable, he suggests, because the historical triumph of this very same world order—the order of multinational capitalism—has simultaneously degraded our powers of critical reflection and presented us with an un-precedented challenge: the challenge of mapping an almost unthink-ably vast system of interrelated and radically undemocratic institu-tions. Resistance to this system has been made difficult, if not impossi-ble, Jameson continues, by its technologically sponsored eradication of distance:

> distance in general (including "critical distance") has very precisely been abolished in the new space of postmodernism. We are sub-merged in its henceforth filled and suffused volumes to the point where our now postmodern bodies are bereft of spatial coordinates and practically (let alone theoretically) incapable of distantiation; meanwhile . . . the prodigious new expansion of multinational capital ends up penetrating and colonizing those very precapitalist enclaves (Nature and the Unconscious) which offered extraterritorial and Archimedean footholds for critical effectivity.[6]

"Nature," for Jameson, seems to include not only the great stretches of forests, mountains, and plains that are its most conventional signified, but, more problematically, the premodern human communities that in-habited them. These, as he points out, have for the most part been thor-oughly penetrated by the administrative and ideological machinery of modernity. And at the same time, the development of ever more seduc-tive technologies of solicitation (image culture, with its capacity to sat-urate aural and visual zones with extraordinarily sophisticated mes-sages) has resulted in the colonization of the "unconscious," the deep-est reaches of the mind and body. This eradication of all autonomous or semiautonomous zones, "any remaining voids and empty places,"[7] has gone so far, Jameson continues, that

> we all, in one way or another, dimly feel that not only punctual and local countercultural forms of cultural resistance and guerrilla war-fare, but also even overtly political interventions . . . are all somehow secretly disarmed and reabsorbed by a system of which they them-selves might well be considered a part, since they can achieve no dis-tance from it.[8]

In other words, having lost our bearings, our bodies, and our minds, we correctly suspect our own strategies of resistance as being nothing more than expressions of that total conspiracy against which we are attempting to struggle.

Jameson's analysis, by locating the site of conspiracy's deepest work within the body and the imagination of individual subjects, would seem to require, as part of any response to conspiracy, some form of those practices of the self recommended as means of self-reclamation and resistance by Michel Foucault, William Connolly, and others.[9] But Jameson's only suggestion, in *Postmodernism*, is that we attempt to build better maps of that global capitalist order in which we are submerged. Such a program, one might counter, seems predicated on the unthreatened survival of just that kind of securely distanced subject whose demise Jameson announces: a subject situated in, and endowed with, "spaces" as yet incompletely "colonized" by global capitalism. Surely, given Jameson's analysis of the situation, any effective struggle would have to proceed on two fronts, attempting to recapture and revise both the most "private" spaces and the most "public." It might even be necessary to "forget conspiracy"—that is, to refuse its fascinations and draw energy away from its "cognitive mapping"—in order to resist it.

A second model of postmodern crisis can also be of use in illuminating the logic of the strategic forgetting advocated in Pynchon's and DeLillo's work. David Harvey argues, in *The Condition of Postmodernity*, that the astonishing "time-space compression" produced by what might be called the technologies of acceleration has produced a whole range of effects, including "sensory overload," tension, and chronic disorientation.[10] While some "bow down [in exhausted silence] before the overwhelming sense of how vast, intractable, and outside any individual or even collective control everything is," others "try and ride the tiger of time-space compression through construction of a language and an imagery that can mirror and hopefully command it."[11] That is, in the face of a speed-up that registers itself viscerally in individual temporalities, physical and mental, some seek respite in surrender, stillness, and silence, while others strive to turn the speed-up itself into a carnival dance. It could be argued that both of these responses are registered in Pynchon's and DeLillo's work, the first in their stories of surrender and forgetting, the second in their "flamboyant rhetoric."[12] But I'll want to argue that in these texts the recourse to silence and the confession of powerlessness constitute something less like an unconditional surrender to the power of things, more like an effort to break the spell of endless solicitation and perpetual speed-up: to find refuge and replenishment in another spatial and temporal zone.

TAKING A DISTANCE: THE LOGIC OF FORGETTING

Pynchon's and DeLillo's novels are notoriously diffuse and complex. To suggest that they are shaped to the logic of any single argument would be to betray both their complexity and one's own lingering commitment to the imperative of conventional counterconspiracy: expose the plot. But this does not mean that the texts are uninterested in offering us *any* suggestions whatsoever for dealing with the conspiratorial systems they depict. On the contrary, they explore a whole range of strategies for dealing with conspiracy. One of these is the work of "cognitive mapping" recommended by Jameson. Even as they are calling the adequacy of this approach into question, Pynchon and DeLillo produce extraordinarily detailed and brilliantly penetrating descriptions of various institutions of control. At the same time they effect, in the extraordinary ludic exuberance of their work, a literary model of another kind of defiance of control. And they celebrate, in passing, various forms of subversion, sabotage, and countercultural solidarity, from "monkey-wrenching," the disabling of logging and heavy construction equipment, to "a calculated withdrawal, from the life of the Republic, from its machinery" (CL, 124). But their most radical proposal, and the one on which I will focus for the remainder of this essay, has to do with a systematic dismantling of the socially constructed self, and draws heavily on Eastern traditions of spiritual formation.

Gravity's Rainbow starts off in the manner of a conventional counterconspiracy thriller. Tyrone Slothrop, our protagonist, seems to be the subject of a great deal of clandestine interest, and he grows increasingly determined to discover the source of this interest. His efforts lead to some unpleasant disclosures, and for a time he follows the usual path, dedicating himself to tracking down and exposing his adversaries. But at a certain point, baffled in his efforts, he turns aside. He's been trying to track his tormenters down in the chaotic "Zone"—Germany just after the end of World War II. But now he begins to lose direction and momentum. Joining the great "frontierless streaming" of displaced persons (GR, 549) coursing across the landscape, he now dreams only of getting home to the States. As he "drifts in and out of dozens of these quiet, hungry, scuffling migrations" (*GR*, 551), Slothrop's mind and heart also turn away from his campaign. "[W]hy was he out here," Slothrop asks himself in a passage that highlights his transformation,

> getting mixed up in other people's private feuds when he was sup-
> posed to be . . . whatever it was . . . uh . . .
>   Yeah! Yeah what happened to Imipolex G, all that Jamf a-and that
> S-Gerat, s'posed to be a hardboiled private eye here, gonna go out all
> alone and beat the odds, avenge my friend that They killed, get my ID
> back and find that piece of mystery hardware. (*GR*, 561)

The novel, far from indicting Slothrop for his forgetfulness, rewards him for it: the further he gets from the quest, the happier, kinder, and more useful he becomes. He helps some children, alerts the Zone Hereros to an imminent attack, and plays the role of the "Pig-Hero Plechazunga" in a real-life skirmish between harmless townspeople and the army of occupation.

Woven through the narrative of his adventures in this period is the suggestion that Slothrop has begun, without ever quite intending to, to recognize and free himself from the internalized enemy described by Jameson. But for Pynchon, this process of distantiation requires something more than a clearing of the mind of the media-amplified solicitations of consumer culture. Traced across the text is the suggestion that what must be dismantled, if one is to recover some element of autonomy, is nothing less than the self itself, at least in its Western, rational form.

Thus Slothrop begins to think of himself not as a heroic adversary to the conspiracy that has entangled him, but as its creature, an occupied being. At a certain point, "he starts to implicate himself in the Combination against who he" is struggling (*GR*, 624), to think of himself as a host to "fifth columnists, well inside his head" (*GR*, 624): "The Man has a branch office in each of our brains," the narrator explains, "his corporate emblem is a white albatross, each local rep has a cover known as the Ego" (*GR*, 712-13). In an effort to expel this internalized oppressor, weaken the hold of ego, Slothrop begins "plucking the albatross of self" (*GR*, 623). He stops moving so fast and begins practicing the kind of inner stilling of the engines of analysis and interpretation that is central to a number of Eastern projects of self-dismantling: there are "[s]hapes he will allow to enter but won't interpret, not any more"

(*GR*, 567). The shift makes him more generous (*GR*, 551) and empathetic, not only with people but with other living things as well: "Trees now—Slothrop's intensely alert to trees, finally. When he comes in among trees he will spend time touching them, studying them, sitting very quietly near them" (*GR*, 552–53). He becomes, in fact, a kind of mountain monk, Zen wanderer, Franciscan nature mystic, a prototypical hippie: "He's letting his hair and beard grow, wearing a dungaree shirt and trousers. . . . But he likes to spend whole days naked, ants crawling up his legs, butterflies lighting on his shoulders, watching the life on the mountain" (*GR*, 623).

Slothrop's compassionate identification with trees and pigs marks him, at this point, as someone who is in the process of taking "the fork in the road America never took" (*GR*, 556), the turn tested but not taken by his forest-clearing (*GR*, 553), pig-slaughtering (*GR*, 555) colonial ancestors. His discovery of a "route back" (*GR*, 556) is not in any dramatic way confirmed by the narrative, unless we understand his disappearance, like that of the explorers celebrated in another passage (*GR*, 589), as a cryptic sign of success. But his self-dismantling does enable him to make contact with replenishing human and spiritual forces and to elude the agents who are seeking to track him down. His self "stripped" away, he becomes, as it were, invisible: "It's doubtful if he can ever be 'found' again, in the conventional sense of 'positively identified and detained'" (*GR*, 712). (For an extraordinary treatment of this same theme of escape through self-"nihilation," see Charles Johnson's splendid novel of slavery and liberation, *The Ox-Herding Tale*.)

This story of partial liberation from a self that is the Other's makes sense of the extravagant conceit that drives the plot of *Gravity's Rainbow*, the suggestion that Slothrop was turned over as an infant to a community of corporate conspirators, who successfully conditioned him to respond erotically to war and death. Perhaps, Pynchon suggests, the very logic of self-formation in this culture, the logic of patriarchy and the Oedipal battle, renders Western men conscripts in the army of empire, an army that hurls them against other peoples and species, and occasionally, against other Western men. If this is the case, then liberation from Europe's imperial "order of Analysis and Death" (*GR*, 722) becomes, as generations of leftist psychoanalysts have suggested, a matter of self-unmaking. But for Pynchon, as for DeLillo, spiritual disciplines may be better equipped to effect this process than those of that discipline that is familiarly known, after all, as "analysis."

Certainly religious strategies of self-unmaking are privileged in Don DeLillo's *White Noise*, another novel about conspiracy's intimate grip and its undoing. For DeLillo, as for Pynchon and Jameson, the entire system of global capitalism—governments, corporations, media, schools—constitutes a kind of monumental wealth- and power-amassing conspiracy against the populace. And for DeLillo as for Pynchon and Jameson, this conspiracy has achieved an unprecedented degree of penetration into the minds of its victims. The world of *White Noise* is one in which children recite advertising slogans in their sleep, adults repeat brand names like charms to calm their anxieties, and the voice of authority—fathers, professors, newscasters, government officials—broadcasts false assurances to an increasingly threatened population twenty-four hours a day.

White Noise is not one of DeLillo's more conventional counterconspiracy novels. Its protagonist, Jack Gladney, is no would-be hero: he's a willing accomplice in the web of lies that sustains the system. DeLillo uses Jack, then, not to dramatize the futility of conventional counterconspiracy efforts, but to analyze the hold of the official conspiracy over an ordinary citizen and to trace a path that might lead such a citizen (everyman) some distance out of conspiracy's grip. DeLillo's conception of that path is even more clearly indebted than Pynchon's to those religious traditions that see the self as a function of "the world's" conspiracy against the soul, and seek by self-dismantling to achieve a kind of freedom.

Two shocks disturb the Gladney family's relation to "the world": Jack and his wife, Babette, find that the satisfactions and distractions offered by consumer society (shopping, status, drugs, the cult of family) cannot keep them from feeling terrified at and obsessed by the thought of their own mortality. And Jack finds that threat dramatically augmented when he is exposed to a toxic cloud that spreads over his town from a ruptured chemical tank car. These are significant blows precisely because, according to DeLillo's analysis, the contemporary system maintains control (at least over its more privileged members) by intervening in a fundamental ontological process, that by which individuals, terrified by impermanence and mortality, try desperately to establish a secure and satisfactory world around themselves, or to keep their anxieties at bay by means of a whole range of distractions, from public displays of invincible power, to the chatter that jams the mind's airwaves and the rituals of consumption that address the gnawing sense of emptiness and lack. This ontological dynamic enables anyone who can gain a monopoly on the trade in reassurances and distractions to harness the individual's energies and control his or her behavior. Once upon a time institutionalized religions enjoyed that monopoly; now it is held by "democratic capitalism." It is in this sense, then, that the self betrays the individual to the conspiracies that exploit him or her.

As the satisfactions of consumer culture increasingly fail to contain the Gladneys' burgeoning dread, they begin looking elsewhere for help, and find ways to begin facing mortality itself. Jack comes to the conclusion that his dread of death can only be cured by a dismantling of the self: "I'd like to lose interest in myself," he tells a friend (*WN*, 152), and another friend suggests that "if death can be seen as less strange and unreferenced, your sense of self in relation to death will diminish, and so will your fear" (*WN*, 229). Gradually, Jack and Babette are drawn by these intuitions into a strange ritual; night after night, they join a gathering at a freeway ramp outside town:

> We go to the overpass all the time. Babette, Wilder and I. We take a thermos of iced tea, park the car, watch the setting sun. . . . We find *little to say* to each other. More cars arrive, parking in a line that extends down to the residential zone. People walk up the incline and onto the overpass, carrying fruit and nuts, cool drinks, mainly the middle-aged, the elderly . . . but younger couples also. . . . Some people are scared by the sunsets, some determined to be elated, but most of us *don't know* how to feel, are ready to go either way. . . . There is anticipation in the air but it is not the expectant midsummer hum of a shirt-sleeve crowd, a sandlot game, with coherent precedents, a history of secure response. This *waiting* is introverted, uneven, almost backward and shy, tending toward *silence* . . . *we don't know* what we are watching or what it means. . . . It is not until sometime after dark has fallen, the insects screaming in the heat, that we slowly begin to disperse, shyly, politely, car after car, *restored to our separate and defensible selves.* (*WN*, 324-25; emphases added)

The congregation gathers before the very sign of transience and mortality: the setting sun. And the "postmodern sunset" (*WN*, 227) they face is both physically and symbolically supercharged with mortality, its glory amplified by residues of the toxic spill and "the everyday drift of effluents, pollutants, contaminants, and deliriants" (*WN*, 170). Facing death, they slip, like Slothrop as he drifts across a Europe devastated by war, into unfamiliar states of stillness, silence, and unknowing. The headlong rush of activity gives way to waiting, the jabbering stops, and suddenly it is possible to acknowledge one's own ignorance, to stop playing or deferring to authority. Paradoxically, this "introverted" behavior leads to experiences of selflessness and solidarity. Only at the end of the informal ceremony are the participants "restored to [their] separate and defensible selves."

The novel does not suggest that this experience works miracles of transformation on Jack and the other participants; we are back, in the next and final scene, shopping. But it does mark the moment as one of promise, if not for some sort of imminent political transformation, then at least for the opening up (the recovery) of alternative spaces, both mental and social.

In both *Gravity's Rainbow* and *White Noise*, then, central characters stumble accidentally and without significant instruction onto strategies of self-slowing and self-unmaking that enable them to recover some distance from the invasive solicitations of a conspiratorial system. Although these strategies are marked as religious, even as Buddhist (consider the numerous references to *The Tibetan Book of the Dead*, Zen koans, and Taoism, which strongly inflected Zen, in *White Noise*), the characters are not conscious of their derivation, their historical provenance. Their "spiritual poverty" (*CL*, 170), represented as a historical achievement of the current regime of knowledge, condemns their efforts at transformation, if not to complete failure, then to only ambiguous success. This situation changes, though, in Pynchon's *Vineland*, where a working-class woman, daughter of a soldier in America's imperial army and child of the 1960s, undertakes the formal study of Buddhist-inflected martial arts. Pynchon marks here the moment, after World War II, when Eastern spiritual practices became available to America's less privileged citizens, and martial arts dojos began to open up, next to Pentecostal churches, in dilapidated commercial strips across America.

D. L. Chastain, Pynchon's woman warrior, is introduced to the martial arts by her father, a military policeman. But her first real teacher is a Japanese master, Inoshiro Sensei, who provides her with "refuge from what lay breathing invisible somewhere back in the geometric sprawl of yards and fences and dumpsters of Dependents' Housing," where she lives with her parents (*V*, 125). The "life in the martial arts" that D.

L. learns from the Sensei and then from Sister Rochelle of the Kunoichi Attentives, saves her, Pynchon suggests, "from the powerlessness and the sooner or later self-poisoning hatred that had been waiting for her" (*V*, 121) as a woman and a child of the working class, not just at home but out in the culture at large. And it enables her to negotiate that culture, through some of its most turbulent years, with something like grace.

Pynchon is quite emphatic, here, in his endorsement of the path of disciplined instruction followed by D. L. She learns to fight, and this and other body-centered practices are represented as powerful instruments of self-reclamation:

> she spoke of her time with Inoshiro Sensei as returning to her self, reclaiming her body, "Which they always like to brainwash you about, like they know it better, trying to keep you as spaced away from it as they can. Maybe they think people are easier to control that way." (*V*, 128)

But she also learns to make peace with herself and those closest to her. She can "sit attentive, pressureless," as her mother preaches at her: "one more side benefit of life in the martial arts" (*V*, 121). And gradually, over the years, she learns the hardest lesson of all, to pay attention to the events unfolding within and around her. At first her capacity for such discipline is dramatically, almost fatally limited. Caught up in a plot to assassinate Brock Vond, the head of a government conspiracy, she attacks the wrong man, and is forced to surrender years of her life in an effort to save him. Sister Rochelle's bitter rebuke to the careless D. L. encapsulates, in negative form, the virtues of the tradition she has betrayed. "We've always believed in your sincerity," D. L.'s teacher begins, "but it can't get you much further— when do we ever see you concentrate, where's the attention span . . . on again off again over the years, no continuity, no persistence, no . . . fucking . . . attention" (*V*, 155; ellipses in the original). Sister Rochelle's lecture reminds us that Buddhist meditation is not designed to sponsor mental torpor. On the contrary, the goal is to discipline the mind away from what Gary Snyder calls, in "Buddhism and the Coming Revolution," "ego-driven anxieties and aggressions," so that one can act with greater clarity and responsibility.[13] Pynchon argues, in *Vineland*, that the radical movements of the sixties failed precisely because most radicals were still deeply childish in their impulses and appetites. And he suggests, through his depiction of D. L., that one way to address such obstacles is through certain forms of disciplined spiritual formation.

But in practicing such disciplines, *Vineland* suggests, one also comes to see the struggle differently, less as an inevitably frontal clash with the massed power of the state and those it serves, than as an ongoing effort to take a distance from powers whose defeat will be achieved, if it is achieved at all, only in the fullness of time. For Pynchon, the strategy of direct confrontation is suicidal, both because at this moment it will certainly fail and because the demands of the struggle shape the combatants—like Rex in *Vineland*—in the image of their opponents. D. L.'s practice teaches her, in the end, to reconsider her long campaign against Brock Vond; she dismisses it, in the passage cited earlier, as having ensnared her in "many years of what the Buddha calls 'passion, enmity, folly'" (*V*, 380).

The suggestion, here, is not that it is foolish to fight back: there are "those you must resist" (*V*, 127), Inoshiro tells D. L. It is that the way to resist effectively, over time, without "poisoning [the] spirit" (*V*, 132), is to distribute one's attention between that which one opposes and that which one cherishes. The alternative to the model of relentless, fiercely focused opposition is exemplified in the oppositional style of the Traverse-Becker clan, an extended working-class family linked by tradition to the great anarchist movements of the Northwest. We encounter them, at the end of the novel, celebrating their annual reunion in the woods of Vineland County. Televisions and radios blare, gargantuan feasts are served, people argue politics and personal history long into the night. But when Jess Traverse, the clan's hero, makes his yearly speech, the words he recites return us to familiar spiritual terrain. They are "a passage from Emerson . . . quoted in a jailhouse copy of *The Varieties of Religious Experience*, by William James." "'Secret retributions,'" Jess reads,

> are always restoring the level, when disturbed, of the divine justice. It is impossible to tilt the beam. All the tyrants and proprietors and monopolists in the world in vain set their shoulders to heave the bar. Settles forever more the ponderous equator in its line, and man and mote, and star and sun, must range to it, or be pulverized by the recoil. (*V*, 369)

There's a tradition being traced here, from the Eastern texts in which Emerson first encountered the notion of karma he's translating in the passage, through radical Transcendentalism itself, to the pragmatism of James, a tireless worker in the anti-imperial cause, and into the bloodstream of American radicalism. Emerson's passage, like the meditative practices derived from the same Eastern traditions, challenges the assumptions of secular counterconspiracy that secure conspiracy's power. For in the cosmos Emerson describes, the full burden of transformation does not fall, as it does in the conventional counterconspiracy narratives of center and Left alike, on a few individuals acting in the few moments left before all is lost. It is better, Pynchon suggests, in implicitly endorsing Emerson's view, to acknowledge one's relative powerlessness and to trust in the assistance provided, periodically, by the way of things itself.

Whether such trust is warranted in any metaphysical sense, James and (I think) Pynchon would claim, is beside the point. What the trust offers is a kind of parole from the prison yard of secular rationalism, in which it is all up to us, we are always overpowered, and there is never enough time. Better to risk forgetting conspiracy, turning away and in, even losing oneself in dreams of an ethical universe, than to condemn oneself to such a regime.

If Pynchon and DeLillo call on us to "forget conspiracy," then, the forgetting they recommend is partial and strategic, a means of recovering certain forms of distance from power and of gaining access to resources for survival and resistance systematically obscured by the dominant knowledge regime. The spiritually inflected model of sustainable resistance they trace emphasizes self-transformation rather than social revolution, the discovery of sites of refuge rather than the capture of power. It refuses the idealization of relentlessness, insisting that it is possible, and profoundly enabling, to distribute one's attention and energies in a manner that leaves room for the "care of the self" and the nurturing of all that is threatened by conspiracy. All this may simply be a reflection of the exhaustion and intellectual desperation endemic to a historical moment when the forces of global capitalism seem to hold all or most of the cards. But one could argue, instead, that Pynchon and DeLillo articulate the impulses of a generation that has been compelled by events to rethink a hyper-rationalistic, relentlessly confrontational tradition of resistance, and that is trying to imagine community, resistance, and even the cosmos differently.

NOTES

1. References to Thomas Pynchon's works are given in the text. The editions cited and their abbreviations are the following: *The Crying of Lot 49* (CL) (1966; New York: Harper and Row, 1986); *Gravity's Rainbow* (GR) (1973; New York: Penguin, 1987); *Vineland* (V) (Boston: Little, Brown, 1990).

2. References to Don DeLillo's works are given in the text. The editions cited and their abbreviations are the following: *Libra* (L) (New York: Viking, 1988); *Mao II* (M) (New York: Viking, 1991); *The Names* (N) (1982; New York: Vintage, 1989); *Players* (P) (1977; New York: Vintage, 1989); *Running Dog* (RD) (1978; New York: Vintage, 1986); *White Noise* (WN) (1985; New York: Penguin, 1986).

3. Michael Ondaatje, *The English Patient* (New York: Vintage, 1993), 250.

4. Salman Rushdie, *Imaginary Homelands* (New York: Penguin, 1991), 301.

5. Fredric Jameson, *Postmodernism, or, The Cultural Logic of Late Capitalism* (Durham: Duke University Press, 1991), 38.

6. Ibid., 48-49.

7. Ibid., 412.

8. Ibid., 49.

9. William E. Connolly, *Why I Am Not a Secularist* (Minneapolis: University of Minnesota Press, 1999).

10. David Harvey, *The Condition of Postmodernity* (Oxford: Basil Blackwell, 1990), 286.

11. Ibid., 350, 351.

12. Ibid., 351.

13. Gary Snyder, "Buddhism and the Coming Revolution," in *Big Sky Mind: Buddhism and the Beat Generation*, ed. Carole Tonkinson (New York: Riverhead Books, 1995), 179.

Contributors

CLARE BIRCHALL's doctoral thesis considers conspiracy theory as a necessary possibility of interpretation. She has several other published articles, including one in New Formations on the Internet conspiracy theories that surrounded the death of Diana. She is currently lecturing at Sussex University, UK.

JACK BRATICH is a doctoral student at the Institute of Communications Research at the University of Illinois, Urbana-Champaign. His specialization is in cultural theory and media studies. He is currently finishing up his dissertation on conspiracy theories, entitled "Grassy Knoll-edges: Paranoia, Politics, and Popular Culture."

BRIDGET BROWN is a doctoral candidate in the American studies program at New York University. She is currently completing her dissertation, which is an interdisciplinary cultural study of the alien abduction phenomenon, "'What Can We Do to Help You Stop Screaming?': The History and Politics of Alien Abduction."

JODI DEAN is an associate professor of political science at Hobart and William Smith Colleges. She is the author of *Aliens in America: Conspiracy Cultures from Outerspace to Cyberspace.*

INGRID WALKER FIELDS is an associate professor of English at Transylvania University, where she teaches American literature and popular culture.

DOUGLAS KELLNER is George F. Kneller Philosphy of Education Chair in Social Sciences and Comparative Education at UCLA. He is the author of numerous articles and books on the media, philosophy, and postmodernism, including *Media Culture.*

PETER KNIGHT teaches American studies at the University of Manchester, UK. He is the author of *Conspiracy Culture: From the Kennedy Assassination to "The X-Files."*

FRAN MASON is a lecturer in English and American studies at King Alfred's College, Winchester, UK.

JOHN A. McCLURE teaches in the English department at Rutgers University. He is the author of *Kipling and Conrad: The Colonial Fiction* and *Late Imperial Romance*, a study of the work of Thomas Pynchon, Don DeLillo, Robert Stone, and Joan Didion. He is currently writing about the turn to religion in postmodern culture and fiction.

TIMOTHY MELLEY teaches American literature at Miami University, Ohio. He is the author of *Empire of Conspiracy: The Culture of Paranoia in Postwar America.*

EITHNE QUINN is a lecturer in American studies at the University of Central Lancashire, UK. She is currently completing a book on gangsta rap music for Columbia University Press.

SKIP WILLMAN is a Brittain Fellow at the Georgia Institute of Technology. The essay published here forms part of his current book project on conspiracy and contingency theories in postmodern culture. He has previously published essays in *Contemporary Literature* and *Modern Fiction Studies.*

Index